Frederick George Scott.

The Great War as I Saw It

The Great War as I Saw It

BY

Canon Frederick George Scott, C.M.G., D.S.O.
Late Senior Chaplain
First Canadian Division, C.E.F.

Author of "Later Canadian Poems," and "Hymn of the Empire."

Printed and bound by Antony Rowe Ltd, Eastbourne

F. D. GOODCHILD COMPANY
Publishers - - - Toronto

CONTENTS

PAGE

CHAPTER I.

How I got into the War—July to September, 1914 . . 15

CHAPTER II.

The Voyage to England—September 29th to October 18th, 1914. 25

CHAPTER III.

On Salisbury Plain—October 18th, 1914 to January 1st, 1915. 30

CHAPTER IV.

Off to France—January to March, 1915. 34

CHAPTER V.

Before the Storm—March and April, 1915. 48

CHAPTER VI.

The Second Battle of Ypres—April 22nd, 1915. . . . 55

CHAPTER VII.

Festubert and Givenchy—May and June, 1915. . . . 74

CHAPTER VIII.

A Lull in Operations—Ploegsteert, July to December, 1915. 93

CHAPTER IX.

Our First Christmas in France. 118

CHAPTER X.

Spring, 1916. 122

CHAPTER XI.

The Attack on Mount Sorrel—Summer, 1916. . . . 128

CHAPTER XII.

The Battle of the Somme—Autumn, 1916. 134

CHAPTER XIII.

Our Home at Camblain l'Abbé—November, 1916. . . 149

CHAPTER XIV.

My Search is Rewarded. 154

CHAPTER XV.

A Time of Preparation—Christmas, 1916 to April, 1917. . 159

CHAPTER XVI.

The Capture of Vimy Ridge—April 9th, 1917. . . . 167

CHAPTER XVII.

A Month on the Ridge—April and May, 1917. . . . 173

5

THE WAR AS I SAW IT

CHAPTER XVIII.   PAGE
A Well-earned Rest—May and June, 1917.   .   .   . 179

CHAPTER XIX.
Paris Leave—June, 1917. 186

CHAPTER XX.
We take Hill 70—July and August, 1917.   .   .   . 192

CHAPTER XXI.
Every day Life—August and September, 1917.   .   . 203

CHAPTER XXII.
A Tragedy of War.   210

CHAPTER XXIII.
Visits to Rome and Paschendaele—Oct. and Nov., 1917.   . 216

CHAPTER XXIV.
Our Last War Christmas. 230

CHAPTER XXV.
Victory Year Opens—January and February, 1918.   .   . 234

CHAPTER XXVI.
The German Offensive—March, 1918.   240

CHAPTER XXVII.
In Front of Arras—April, 1918.   248

CHAPTER XXVIII.
Sports and Pastimes—May and June, 1918.   .   .   . 254

CHAPTER XXIX.
The Beginning of the End.   267

CHAPTER XXX.
The Battle of Amiens—August 8th to August 16th, 1918.   . 274

CHAPTER XXXI.
We Return to Arras—August, 1918.   288

CHAPTER XXXII.
The Smashing of the Drocourt-Quéant Line—Sept. 2nd, 1918. 292

CHAPTER XXXIII.
Preparing for the Final Blow—September, 1918. .   .   . 298

CHAPTER XXXIV.
The Crossing of the Canal du Nord—September 27th, 1918. . 307

CHAPTER XXXV.
VICTORY—November 11th, 1918.   318

Index.   321

"THE UNBROKEN LINE."

We who have trod the borderlands of death,
  Where courage high walks hand in hand with fear,
Shall we not hearken what the Spirit saith,
  "All ye were brothers there, be brothers here?"

We who have struggled through the baffling night,
  Where men were men and every man divine,
While round us brave hearts perished for the right
  By chaliced shell-holes stained with life's rich wine,

Let us not lose the exalted love which came
  From comradeship with danger and the joy
Of strong souls kindled into living flame
  By one supreme desire, one high employ.

Let us draw closer in these narrower years,
  Before us still the eternal visions spread;
We who outmastered death and all its fears
  Are one great army still, living and dead.

F. G. S.

FOREWORD

IT is with great pleasure I accede to the request of Canon Scott to write a foreword to his book.

I first heard of my friend and comrade after the second battle of Ypres when he accompanied his beloved Canadians to Bethune after their glorious stand in that poisonous gap—which in my own mind he immortalised in verse:-

O England of our fathers, and England of our sons,
Above the roar of battling hosts, the thunder of the guns,
A mother's voice was calling us, we heard it oversea,
The blood which thou didst give us, is the blood we spill for thee.

Little did I think when I first saw him that he could possibly, at his time of life, bear the rough and tumble of the heaviest fighting in history, and come through with buoyancy of spirit younger men envied and older men recognized as the sign and fruit of self-forgetfulness and the inspiration and cheering of others.

Always in the thick of the fighting, bearing almost a charmed life, ignoring any suggestion that he should be posted to a softer job "further back," he held on to the very end.

The last time I saw him was in a hospital at Etaples badly wounded, yet cheery as ever—having done his duty nobly.

All the Canadians in France knew him, and his devotion and fearlessness were known all along the line, and his poems will, I am bold to prophesy, last longer in the ages to come than most of the histories of the war.

I feel sure that his book—if anything like himself—will interest and inspire all who read it.

LLEWELLYN H. GWYNNE.

Bishop of Khartoum,
Deputy Chaplain General
to the C. of E. Chaplains
in France.

PREFACE

IT is with a feeling of great hesitation that I send out this account of my personal experiences in the Great War. As I read it over, I am dismayed at finding how feebly it suggests the bitterness and the greatness of the sacrifice of our men. As the book is written from an entirely personal point of view, the use of the first personal pronoun is of course inevitable, but I trust that the narration of my experience has been used only as a lens through which the great and glorious deeds of our men may be seen by others. I have refrained, as far as possible, except where circumstances seemed to demand it, from mentioning the names of officers or the numbers of battalions.

I cannot let the book go out without thanking, for many acts of kindness, Lieut.-General Sir Edwin Alderson, K.C.B., Lieut.-General Sir Arthur Currie, G.C.M.G., K.C.B., and Major-General Sir Archibald Macdonell, K.C.B., C.M.G., D.S.O., who were each in turn Commanders of the First Canadian Division. In all the efforts the chaplains made for the welfare of the Division, they always had the backing of these true Christian Knights. Their kindness and consideration at all times were unbounded, and the degree of liberty which they allowed me was a privilege for which I cannot be too thankful, and which I trust I did not abuse.

If, by these faulty and inadequate reminiscences, dug out of memories which have blended together in emotions too deep and indefinable to be expressed in words, I have reproduced something of the atmosphere in which our glorious men played their part in the deliverance of the world, I shall consider my task not in vain.

May the ears of Canada never grow deaf to the plea of widows and orphans and our crippled men for care and support. May the eyes of Canada never be blind to that glorious light which shines upon our young national life from the deeds of those "Who counted not their lives dear unto themselves," and may the lips of Canada never be dumb to tell to future generations the tales of heroism which will kindle the imagination and fire the patriotism of children that are yet unborn.

The Great War as I Saw It

CHAPTER I.

How I Got Into The War.

July to September, 1914.

IT happened on this wise. It was on the evening of the 31st of July, 1914, that I went down to a newspaper office in Quebec to stand amid the crowd and watch the bulletins which were posted up every now and then, and to hear the news of the war. One after another the reports were given, and at last there flashed upon the board the words, "General Hughes offers a force of twenty thousand men to England in case war is declared against Germany." I turned to a friend and said, "That means that I have got to go to the war." Cold shivers went up and down my spine as I thought of it, and my friend replied, "Of course it does not mean that you should go. You have a parish and duties at home." I said, "No. I am a Chaplain of the 8th Royal Rifles. I must volunteer, and if I am accepted, I will go." It was a queer sensation, because I had never been to war before and I did not know how I should be able to stand the shell fire. I had read in books of people whose minds were keen and brave, but whose hind legs persisted in running away under the sound of guns. Now I knew that an ordinary officer on running away under fire would get the sympathy of a large number of people, who would say, "The poor fellow has got shell shock," and they would make allowance for him. But if a chaplain ran away, about six hundred men would say at once, "We have no more use for religion." So it was with very mingled feelings that I contemplated an expedition to the battle-fields of France, and I trusted that the difficulties of Europe would be settled without our intervention.

However, preparations for war went on. On Sunday, August 2nd, in the afternoon, I telephoned to Militia Headquarters and gave in my name as a volunteer for the Great War. When I went to church that evening and told the wardens that I was off to France, they were much surprised and disconcerted. When I was preaching at the service and looked down at the congregation, I had a queer feeling that some mysterious power was dragging me into a whirlpool, and the ordinary life around me and the things that were so dear to me had already begun to fade away.

15

THE WAR AS I SAW IT

On Tuesday, August the Fourth, war was declared, and the Expeditionary Force began to be mobilized in earnest. It is like recalling a horrible dream when I look back to those days of apprehension and dread. The world seemed suddenly to have gone mad. All civilization appeared to be tottering. The Japanese Prime Minister, on the night war was declared, said, "This is the end of Europe." In a sense his words were true. Already we see power shifted from nations in Europe to that great Empire which is in its youth, whose home is in Europe, but whose dominions are scattered over the wide world, and also to that new Empire of America, which came in to the war at the end with such determination and high resolve. The destinies of mankind are now in the hands of the English-speaking nations and France.

In those hot August days, a camp at Valcartier was prepared in a lovely valley surrounded by the old granite hills of the Laurentians, the oldest range of mountains in the world. The Canadian units began to collect, and the lines of white tents were laid out. On Saturday, August 22nd, at seven in the morning, the detachment of volunteers from Quebec marched off from the drill-shed to entrain for Valcartier. Our friends came to see us off and the band played "The Girl I Left Behind Me," in the traditional manner. On our arrival at Valcartier we marched over to the ground assigned to us, and the men set to work to put up the tents. I hope I am casting no slur upon the 8th Royal Rifles of Quebec, when I say that I think we were all pretty green in the matter of field experience. The South African veterans amongst us, both officers and men, saved the situation. But I know that the cooking arrangements rather "fell down", and I think a little bread and cheese, very late at night, was all we had to eat. We were lucky to get that. Little did we know then of the field kitchens, with their pipes smoking and dinners cooking, which later on used to follow up the battalions as they moved.

The camp at Valcartier was really a wonderful place. Rapidly the roads were laid out, the tents were run up, and from west and east and north and south men poured in. There was activity everywhere. Water was laid on, and the men got the privilege of taking shower-baths, beside the dusty roads. Bands played; pipers retired to the woods and practised unearthly music calculated to fire the breast of the Scotsman with a lust for blood. We had rifle practice on the marvellous ranges. We had sham battles in which the men engaged so intensely that on one occasion, when the enemy met, one over-eager soldier belaboured his opponent with the butt end of his rifle as though he were a real German, and the poor victim, who had not been taught to say "Kamarad", suffered grievous wounds and had to be taken away in an ambulance. Though many gales and tempests had blown round those ancient mountains, nothing had ever equalled the latent power in the hearts of the stalwart young Canadians who had come so swiftly and eagerly at the call of the Empire. It is astonishing how the war spirit grips one. In Valcartier began that splendid comradeship which spread out to all the divisions of the Canadian Corps, and which binds those who went to the great adventure in a brotherhood stronger than has ever been known before.

Valcartier was to me a weird experience. The tents were cold. The ground was very hard. I got it into my mind that a chaplain should live the same life as the private soldier, and should avoid all luxuries. So I tried to sleep at night under my blanket, making a little hole in the ground for my thigh bone to rest in. After lying awake for some nights under these conditions, I found that the privates, especially the old soldiers, had learnt the art of making themselves comfortable and were hunting for straw for beds. I saw the wisdom of this and got a Wolesley sleeping bag, which I afterwards lost when my billet was shelled at Ypres. Under this new arrangement I was able to get a little rest. A kind friend in Quebec provided fifty oil stoves for the use of the Quebec contingent and so we became quite comfortable.

The dominating spirit of the camp was General Hughes, who rode about with his aides-de-camp in great splendour like Napoleon. To me it seemed that his personality and his despotic rule hung like a dark shadow over the camp. He was especially interesting and terrible to us chaplains, because rumour had it that he did not believe in chaplains, and no one could find out whether he was going to take us or not. The chaplains in consequence were very polite when inadvertently they found themselves in his august presence. I was clad in a private's uniform, which was handed to me out of a box in the drill-shed the night before the 8th Royal Rifles left Quebec, and I was most punctilious in the matter of saluting General Hughes whenever we chanced to meet.

The day after we arrived at the camp was a Sunday. The weather looked dark and showery, but we were to hold our first church parade, and, as I was the senior chaplain in rank, I was ordered to take it over. We assembled about three thousand strong, on a little rise in the ground, and here the men were formed in a hollow square. Rain was threatening, but perhaps might have held off had it not been for the action of one of the members of my congregation, who in the rear ranks was overheard by my son to utter the prayer—"O Lord, have mercy in this hour, and send us now a gentle shower." The prayer of the young saint was answered immediately, the rain came down in torrents, the church parade was called off, and I went back to my tent to get dry.

Day after day passed and more men poured in. They were a splendid lot, full of life, energy and keen delight in the great enterprise. Visitors from the city thronged the camp in the afternoons and evenings. A cinema was opened, but was brought to a fiery end by the men, who said that the old man in charge of it never changed his films.

One of the most gruesome experiences I had was taking the funeral of a young fellow who had committed suicide. I shall never forget the dismal service which was held, for some reason or other, at ten o'clock at night. Rain was falling, and we marched off into the woods by the light of two smoky lanterns to the place selected as a military cemetery. To add to the weirdness of the scene two pipers played a dirge. In the dim light of the lanterns, with the dropping rain over head and the dripping trees around us, we laid the poor boy to rest. The whole scene made a lasting impression on those who were present.

Meanwhile the camp extended and improvements were made, and many changes occurred in the disposition of the units. At one time the Quebec men were joined with a Montreal unit, then they were taken and joined with a New Brunswick detachment and formed into a battalion. Of course we grew more military, and I had assigned to me a batman whom I shall call Stephenson. I selected him because of his piety—he was a theological student from Ontario. I found afterwards that it is unwise to select batmen for their piety. Stephenson was a failure as a batman. When some duty had been neglected by him and I was on the point of giving vent to that spirit of turbulent anger, which I soon found was one of the natural and necessary equipments of an officer, he would say, "Would you like me to recite Browning's 'Prospice' "? What could the enraged Saul do on such occasions but forgive, throw down the javelin and listen to the music of the harping David? Stephenson was with me till I left Salisbury Plain for France. He nearly exterminated me once by setting a stone water-bottle to heat on my stove without unscrewing the stopper. I arrived in my tent quite late and seeing the thing on the stove quickly unscrewed it. The steam blew out with terrific force and filled the tent. A moment or two more and the bottle would have burst with disastrous consequences. When I told Stephenson of the enormity of his offence and that he might have been the cause of my death, and would have sent me to the grave covered with dishonour for having been killed by the bursting of a hot water-bottle—an unworthy end for one about to enter the greatest war the world has ever known—he only smiled faintly and asked me if I should like to hear him recite a poem.

News from overseas continued to be bad. Day after day brought us tidings of the German advance. The martial spirits amongst us were always afraid to hear that the war would be over before we got to England. I, but did not tell the people so, was afraid it wouldn't. I must confess I did not see in those days how a British force composed of men from farms, factories, offices and universities could get together in time to meet and overthrow the trained legions of Germany. It was certainly a period of anxious thought and deep foreboding, but I felt that I belonged to a race that has never been conquered. Above all, right and, therefore, God was on our side.

The scenery around Valcartier is very beautiful. It was a joy now and then to get a horse and ride away from the camp to where the Jacques Cartier river comes down from the mountains, and to dream of the old days when the world was at peace and we could enjoy the lovely prospects of nature, without the anxious care that now gnawed at our hearts. The place had been a favorite haunt of mine in the days gone by, when I used to take a book of poems and spend the whole day beside the river, reading and dozing and listening to the myriad small voices of the woods.

Still, the centre of interest now was the camp, with its turmoil and bustle and indefinite longing to be up and doing. The officer commanding my battalion had brought his own chaplain with him, and it was plainly evident that I was not wanted. This made it, I must confess, somewhat embarassing. My tent, which was at the corner of the front line, was furnished only with my bed-roll and a box or two, and was not a particularly cheerful home. I used to feel rather lonely at times. Now and then I would go to Quebec for the day. On one occasion, when I had been feeling particularly seedy, I returned to camp at eleven o'clock at night. It was cold and rainy. I made my way from the station to my tent. In doing so I had to pass a Highland Battalion from Vancouver. When I came to their lines, to my dismay I was halted by a sentry with a fixed bayonet, who shouted in the darkness, "Who goes there?" I gave the answer, but instead of being satisfied with my reply, the wretched youth stood unmoved, with his bayonet about six inches from my body, causing me a most unpleasant sensation. He said I should have to come to the guard-room and be identified. In the meantime, another sentry appeared, also with a fixed bayonet, and said that I had to be identified. Little did I think that the whole thing was a game of the young rascals, and that they were beguiling the tedious moments of the sentry-go by pulling a chaplain's leg. They confessed it to me months afterwards in France. However, I was unsuspecting and had come submissive into the great war. I said that if they would remove their bayonets from propinquity to my person—because the sight of them was causing me a fresh attack of the pains that had racked me all day— I would go with them to the guard-room. At this they said, "Well, Sir, we'll let you pass. We'll take your word and say no more about it." So off I went to my dripping canvas home, hoping that the war would be brought to a speedy termination.

Every night I used to do what I called "parish visiting." I would go round among the tents, and sitting on the ground have a talk with the men. Very interesting and charming these talks were. I was much impressed with the miscellaneous interests and life histories of the men who had been so quickly drawn together. All were fast being shaken down into their places, and I think the great lessons of unselfishness and the duty of pulling together were being stamped upon the lives that had hitherto been more or less at loose ends. I used to sit in the tents talking long after lights were out, not wishing to break the discussion of some interesting life problem. This frequently entailed upon me great difficuly in finding my way back to my tent, for the evenings were closing in rapidly and it was hard to thread one's way among the various ropes and pegs which kept the tents in position. On one occasion when going down the lines, I tripped over a rope. Up to that moment the tent had been in perfect silence, but, as though I had fired a magazine of high explosives, a torrent of profanity burst forth from the inhabitants at my misadventure. Of course the men inside did not know to whom they were talking, but I stood there with my blood curdling, wondering how far I was personally responsible for the language poured forth, and terrified lest anyone should look and find out who had disturbed their slumbers. I stole off into the darkness as quickly as I could, more than ever longing for a speedy termination of the great war, and resolving to be more careful in future about tripping over tent ropes.

We had church parades regularly now on Sundays and early celebrations of the Holy Communion for the various units. Several weeks had gone by and as yet we had no definite information from General Hughes as to which or how many chaplains would be accepted. It was very annoying. Some of us could not make satisfactory arrangements for our parishes, until there was a certainty in the matter. The question came to me as to whether I ought to go, now that the Quebec men had been merged into a battalion of which I was not to be the chaplain. One evening as I was going to town, I put the matter before my friend Colonel, now General, Turner. It was a lovely night. The moon was shining, and stretching far off into the valley were the rows of white tents with the dark mountains enclosing them around. We stood outside the farm-house used as headquarters, which overlooked the camp. When I asked the Colonel whether, now that I was separated from my men, I ought to leave my parish and go, he said to me, "Look at those lines of tents and think of the men in them. How many of those men will ever come back? The best expert opinion reckons that this war will last at least two years. The wastage of human life in war is tremendous. The battalions have to be filled and refilled again and again. Don't decide in a hurry, but think over what I have told you." On the next evening when I returned from Quebec, I went to the Colonel and said, "I have thought the matter over and I am going."

The time was now drawing near for our departure and at last word was sent round that General Hughes wished to meet all the chaplains on the verandah of his bungalow. The time set was the cheerful hour of five a.m. I lay awake all night with a loud ticking alarm clock beside me, till about half an hour before the wretched thing was to go off. With great expedition I rose and shaved and making myself as smart as possible in the private's uniform, hurried off to the General's camp home. There the other chaplains

21

were assembled, about twenty-five or thirty in all. We all felt very
sleepy and very chilly as we waited with expectancy the utterance
which was going to seal our fate. The General soon appeared in all
the magnificence and power of his position. We rose and saluted.
When he metaphorically told us to "stand easy", we all sat down. I
do not know what the feelings of the others were, but I had an
impression that we were rather an awkward squad, neither fish, flesh,
nor fowl. The General gave us a heart to heart talk. He told us he
was going to send us with "the boys." From his manner I inferred
that he looked upon us a kind of auxiliary and quite dispensable sani-
tary section. I gathered that he did not want us to be very exact-
ing as to the performance of religious duties by the men. Rather
we were to go in and out amongst them, make friends of them
and cheer them on their way. Above all we were to remember
that because a man said "Damn", it did not mean necessarily that
he was going to hell. At the conclusion of the address, we were
allowed to ask questions, and one of our number unadvisedly
asked if he would be allowed to carry a revolver. "No," said Sam
with great firmness, ''take a bottle of castor oil." We didn't dare
to be amused at the incident in the presence of the Chief, but we
had a good laugh over it when we got back to our tents.

Two Sundays before we left, the most remarkable church parade in the history of the division was held, at which fully fifteen
thousand men were present. The Senior Chaplain asked me to
preach. A large platform had been erected, on which the chaplains
stood, and on the platform also were two signallers, whose duty
it was to signal to the battalions and bands the numbers of the
hymns. On the chairs in front of the platform were seated the Duke
and Duchess of Connaught, the Princess Patricia, Sir Robert
Borden, and other notables. Beyond them were gathered the men
in battalions. At one side were the massed bands. It was a wonderful sight. The sun was shining. Autumn tints coloured the maple
trees on the sides of the ancient mountains. Here was Canada
quickening into national life and girding on the sword to take her
place among the independent nations of the world. It had been my
privilege, fifteen years before, to preach at the farewell service
in Quebec Cathedral for the Canadian Contingent going to the
South African war. It seemed to me then that never again should I
have such an experience. Yet on that occasion there were only a
thousand men present, and here were fifteen times that number.

HOW I GOT INTO THE WAR

At that time the war was with a small and half-civilized nation in Africa, now the war was with the foremost nations of Europe. On that occasion I used the second personal pronoun "you", now I was privileged to use the first personal pronoun "we". Almost to the last I did not know what text to choose and trusted to the inspiration of the moment what to say. My mind was confused with the vastness of the outlook. At last the words came to me which are the very foundation stone of human endeavour and human progress, "He that loseth his life for My sake shall find it." I do not know exactly what I said, and I do not suppose it mattered much, for it was hard to make oneself heard. I was content if the words of the text alone were audible. We sang that great hymn, "O God our help in ages past," which came into such prominence as an imperial anthem during the war. As we sang the words—

"Before the hills in order stood,
Or earth received her frame"—

I looked at the everlasting mountains around us, where the sound of our worship died away, and thought how they had watched and waited for this day to come, and how, in the ages that were to dawn upon Canadian life and expansion, they would stand as monuments of the consecration of Canada to the service of mankind.

Things began to move rapidly now. People from town told us that already a fleet of liners was waiting in the harbour, ready to carry overseas the thirty-three thousand men of the Canadian contingent.

At last the eventful day of our departure arrived. On September 28th, with several other units, the 14th Battalion, to which I had been attached, marched off to the entraining point. I took one last look at the great camp which had now become a place of such absorbing interest and I wondered if I should ever see again that huge amphitheatre with its encompassing mountain witnesses. The men were in high spirits and good humour prevailed.

We saw the three companies of Engineers moving off, each followed by those mysterious pontoons which followed them wherever they went and suggested the bridging of the Rhine and our advance to Berlin. Someone called out, "What are those boats?" and a voice replied, "That's the Canadian Navy." We had a pleasant trip in the train to Quebec, enlivened by jokes and songs. On our arrival at the docks, we were taken to the custom-house wharf and marched on board the fine Cunard liner "Andania", which now rests, her troubles over, at the bottom of the Irish Sea. On the vessel, besides half of the 14th Battalion, there was the 16th (Canadian Scottish) Battalion, chiefly from Vancouver, and the Signal Company. Thus we had a ship full to overflowing of some of the noblest young fellows to whom the world has given birth. So ended our war experience in Valcartier Camp.

Nearly five years passed before I saw that sacred spot again. It was in August 1919. The war was ended, peace had been signed, and the great force of brother knights had been dispersed. Little crosses by the highways and byways of France and Belgium now marked the resting-place of thousands of those whose eager hearts took flame among these autumn hills. As I motored past the deserted camp after sunset, my heart thrilled with strange memories and the sense of an abiding presence of something weird and ghostly. Here were the old roads, there were the vacant hutments. Here were the worn paths across the fields where the men had gone. The evening breeze whispered fitfully across the untrodden grass and one by one the strong mountains, as though fixing themselves more firmly in iron resolve, cast off the radiant hues of evening and stood out black and grim against the starlit sky.

CHAPTER II

THE VOYAGE TO ENGLAND

September 29th to October 18th, 1914

THE "Andania" moved out to mid-stream and anchored off Cape Diamond. The harbour was full of liners, crowded with men in khaki. It was a great sensation to feel oneself at last merged into the great army life and no longer free to come and go. I looked at the City and saw the familar outline of the Terrace and Chateau Frontenac and, over all, the Citadel, one of my favourite haunts in times past. A great gulf separated us now from the life we had known. We began to realize that the individual was submerged in the great flood of corporate life, and the words of the text came to me, "He that loseth his life for My sake shall find it."

The evening was spent in settling down to our new quarters in what was, especially after the camp at Valcartier, a luxurious home. Dinner at night became the regimental mess, and the saloon with its sumptuous furnishings made a fine setting for the nightly gathering of officers. We lay stationary all that night and on the next evening, Sept. the 29th, at six o'clock we weighed anchor and went at slow speed down the stream. Several other vessels had preceded us, the orders to move being sent by wireless. We passed the Terrace where cheer after cheer went up from the black line of spectators crowded against the railing. Our men climbed up into the rigging and their cheers went forth to the land that they were leaving. It was a glorious evening. The sun had set and the great golden light, fast deepening into crimson, burnt behind the northern hills and lit up the windows of the houses on the cliffs of Levis opposite. We moved down past the Custom House. We saw the St. Charles Valley and the Beauport shore, but ever our eyes turned to the grim outline of Cape Diamond and the city set upon the hill. Beside me on the upper deck stood a young officer. We were talking together and wondering if we should ever see that rock again. He never did. He and his only brother were killed in the war. We reached the end of the Island of Orleans, and looking back saw a deeper crimson flood the sky, till the purple mists of evening hid Quebec from our view.

25

THE WAR AS I SAW IT

We had a lovely sail down the St. Lawrence in superb weather and three days later entered the great harbour of Gaspé Basin. Here the green arms of the hills encompassed us, as though Canada were reluctant to let us go. Gaspé Basin has historical memories for Canada, for it was there that Wolfe assembled his fleet on his voyage to the capture of Quebec. We lay at anchor all day, and at night the moon came up and flooded the great water with light, against which stood out the black outline of thirty ships, so full of eager and vigorous life. About midnight I went on deck to contemplate the scene. The night was calm and still. The vessels lay dark and silent with all lights screened. The effect was one of lonely grandeur. What was it going to mean to us? What did fate hold in store? Among those hills, the outline of which I could now but faintly see, were the lakes and salmon rivers in the heart of the great forests which make our Canadian wild life so fascinating. We were being torn from that life and sent headlong into the seething militarism of a decadent European feudalism. I was leaning on the rail looking at the track of moonlight, when a young lad came up to me and said, "Excuse me, Sir, but may I talk to you for a while? It is such a weird sight that it has got on my nerves." He was a young boy of seventeen who had come from Vancouver. Many times afterwards I met him in France and Belgium, when big things were being done in the war, and we talked together over that night in Gaspé Basin and the strange thoughts that crowded upon us then. He was not the only one in that great fleet of transports who felt the significance of the enterprise.

On Saturday afternoon we resumed our journey and steamed out of the narrows. Outside the bay the ships formed into a column of three abreast, making a line nine miles in length. Several cruisers, and later a battleship and battle cruiser, mounted guard over the expedition. Off Cape Race, the steamship "Florizel" joined us, bringing the Newfoundland troops. Our family party was now complete.

It was indeed a family party. On every ship we had friends. It seemed as if Canada herself were steaming across the ocean. Day after day, in perfect weather, keeping our relative positions in absolute order, we sped over the deep. There was none of the usual sense of loneliness which characterizes the ocean voyage. We looked at the line of vessels and we felt that one spirit and one determination quickened the whole fleet into individual life.

THE VOYAGE TO ENGLAND

On board the "Andania" the spirit of the men was excellent. There was physical drill daily to keep them fit. There was the gymnasium for the officers. We had boxing matches for all, and sword dances also for the Highlanders. In the early morning at five-thirty, the pipers used to play réveille down the passages. Not being a Scotsman, the music always woke me up. At such moments I considered it my duty to try to understand the music of the pipes. But in the early hours of the morning I made what I thought were discoveries. First I found out that all pipe melodies have the same bass. Secondly I found out that all pipe melodies have the same treble. On one occasion the pipers left the security of the Highlanders' quarters and invaded the precincts of the 14th Battalion, who retaliated by turning the hose on them. A genuine battle between the contending factions was only averted by the diplomacy of the O.C.

I had made friends with the wireless operators on board the ship, and every night I used to go up to their cabin on the upper deck and they would give me reports of the news which had been flashed out to the leading cruiser. They told me of the continued German successes and of the fall of Antwerp. The news was not calculated to act as a soothing nightcap before going to bed. I was sworn to secrecy and so I did not let the men know what was happening at the front. I used to look round at the bright faces of the young officers in the saloon and think of all that those young fellows might have to endure before the world was saved. It gave everyone on board a special sacredness in my eyes, and one felt strangely inadequate and unworthy to be with them.

The men lived below decks and some of them were packed in pretty tightly. Had the weather been rough there would have been a good deal of suffering. During the voyage our supply of flour gave out, but as we had a lot of wheat on board, the men were set to grind it in a coffee mill. More than fifty per cent of the men, I found, were members of the Church of England, and so I determined to have a celebration of Holy Communion, for all who cared to attend, at five o'clock every morning. I always had a certain number present, and very delightful were these services at that early hour. Outside on deck we could hear the tramp and orders of those engaged in physical drill, and inside the saloon where I had arranged the altar there knelt a small gathering of young fellows from various parts of Canada, who were pleased to find that the old

Church was going with them on their strange pilgrimage.
The well-known hymn—

"Eternal Father strong to save,
Whose arm hath bound the restless wave"

had never appealed to me much in the past, but it took on a new
meaning at our Sunday church parade, for we all felt that we
were a rather vulnerable body in any determined attack that might
be made upon us by the German navy. Now and then vessels would
be sighted on the horizon and there was always much excitement
and speculation as to what they might be. We could see the cruisers
making off in the direction of the strangers and taking a survey of
the ocean at long range.

One day a man on the "Royal George" fell overboard, and a
boat was instantly lowered to pick him up. The whole fleet came
to a stand-still and all our glasses were turned towards the scene
of rescue. Often in our battles when we saw the hideous slaughter
of human beings, I have thought of the care for the individual
life which stopped that great fleet in order to save one man.

Our destination, of course, was not known to us. Some thought
we might go directly to France, others that we should land in England. When at last, skirting the south coast of Ireland, we got into
the English Channel, we felt more than ever the reality of our adventure. I believe we were destined for Southampton; but rumour
had it that a German submarine was waiting for us in the Channel,
so we turned into the harbour of Plymouth. It was night when we
arrived. A low cloud and mist hung over the dark choppy waves
of the Channel. From the forts at Plymouth and from vessels in
the harbour, long searchlights moved like the fingers of a great
ghostly hand that longed to clutch at something. We saw the small
patrol boats darting about in all directions and we felt with a secret
thrill that we had got into that part of the world which was at war.
We arrived at Plymouth on the evening of October 14th, our voyage having lasted more than a fortnight. Surely no expedition,
ancient or modern, save that perhaps which Columbus led towards
the undiscovered continent of his dreams, was ever fraught with
greater significance to the world at large. We are still too close to
the event to be able to measure its true import. Its real meaning
was that the American continent with all its huge resources, its
potential value in the ages to come, had entered upon the sphere
of world politics, and ultimately would hold in its hands the sceptre

of world dominion. Even the British thought that we had come merely to assist the Mother Country in her difficulties. Those who were at the helm in Canada, however, knew that we were not fighting for the security of the Mother Country only, but for the security of Canadian nationalism itself. Whatever the ages hold in store for us in this great and rich Dominion which stretches from sea to sea and from the river unto the world's end, depended upon our coming out victors in the great European struggle.

CHAPTER III

ON SALISBURY PLAIN.

October 18th, 1914, to January 1st, 1915.

ON Sunday the 18th, our men entrained and travelled to Patney, and from thence marched to Westdown South, Salisbury Plain. There tents had been prepared and we settled down to life in our new English home. At first the situation was very pleasant. Around us on all sides spread the lines of tents. The weather was delightful. A ride over the mysterious plain was something never to be forgotten. The little villages around were lovely and quaint. The old town of Salisbury, with its wonderful Cathedral and memories of old England, threw the glamour of romance and chivalry over the new soldiers in the new crusade. But winter drew on, and such a winter it was. The rains descended, the floods came and the storms beat upon our tents, and the tents which were old and thin allowed a fine sprinkling of moisture to fall upon our faces. The green sward was soon trampled into deep and clinging mud. There was nothing for the men to do. Ammunition was short, there was little rifle practice. The weather was so bad that a route march meant a lot of wet soldiers with nowhere to dry their clothes upon their return. In some places the mud went over my long rubber boots. The gales of heaven swept over the plain unimpeded. Tents were blown down. On one particularly gloomy night, I met a chaplain friend of mine in the big Y.M.C.A. marquee. I said to him, "For goodness sake let us do something for the men. Let us have a sing-song." He agreed, and we stood in the middle of the marquee with our backs to the pole and began to sing a hymn. I do not know what it was. I started the air and was going on so beautifully that the men were beginning to be attracted and were coming around us. Suddenly my friend struck in with a high tenor note. Hardly had the sound gone forth when, like the fall of the walls of Jericho at the sound of Joshua's trumpets, a mighty gale struck the building, and with a ripping sound the whole thing collapsed. In the rain and darkness we rushed to the assistance of the attendants and extinguished the lamps, which had been upset, while the men made their way to the counters and put the cigarettes and other dainties into their pockets, lest they should get wet. On another occasion, the Paymaster's tent blew away as he was paying off the battalion. Five shilling notes flew over the plain like white birds over the sea. The men quickly chased them and gathered them up, and on finding them stained with mud thought it unnecessary to return them. On another night the huge marquee where Harrod's ran the mess for a large number of officers, blew down just as we were going to dinner, and we had to forage in the various canteens for tinned salmon and packages of biscuits.

Still, in spite of all, the spirits of our men never failed. One night when a heavy rain had turned every hollow into a lake, and every gully into a rushing cataract, I went down to some tents on a lower level than my own. I waded through water nearly a foot deep and came to a tent from which I saw a faint light emerging. I looked inside and there with their backs to the pole stood some stalwart young Canadians. On an island in the tent, was a pile of blankets, on which burnt a solitary candle. "Hello, boys, how are you getting on?" "Fine, Sir, fine," was their ready response. "Well, boys, keep that spirit up," I said, "and we'll win the war."

At first we had no "wet" canteen where beer could be procured. The inns in the villages around became sources of great attraction to the men, and the publicans did their best to make what they could out of the well-paid Canadian troops. The maintenance of discipline under such circumstances was difficult. We were a civilian army, and our men had come over to do a gigantic task. Everyone knew that, when the hour for performance came, they would be ready, but till that hour came they were intolerant of restraint.

The English people did not understand us, and many of our men certainly gave them good reason to be doubtful. Rumour had it at one time that we were going to be taken out of the mud and quartered in Exeter. Then the rumour was that the Exeter people said, "If the Canadians are sent here, we'll all leave the town." I did not mind, I told the men I would make my billet in the Bishop's Palace.

The C.O. of one of the battalions was tempted to do what David did with such disastrous results, namely number the people. He called the roll of his battalion and found that four hundred and fifty men were absent without leave. But as I have said, we all knew that when the moment for big things came, every man would be at his post and would do his bit.

Just before Christmas the 3rd Brigade were moved into huts at Lark Hill. They were certainly an improvement upon the tents, but they were draughty and leaky. From my window I could see, on the few occasions when the weather permitted it, the weird and ancient circles of Stonehenge.

The calm repose of those huge stones, which had watched unmoved the passing of human epochs, brought peace to the mind. They called to memory the lines;—

> "Our little systems have their day,
>   They have their day and cease to be:
>   They are but broken lights of Thee,
> And Thou, O Lord, art more than they."

In order to give Christmas its religious significance, I asked permission of the Rector of Amesbury to use his church for a midnight Eucharist on Christmas Eve. He gladly gave his consent and notice of the service was sent round to the units of the Brigade. In the thick fog the men gathered and marched down the road to the village, where the church windows threw a soft light into the mist that hung over the ancient burial ground. The church inside was bright and beautiful. The old arches and pillars and the little side chapels told of days gone by, when the worship of the holy nuns, who had their convent there, rose up to God day by day. The altar was vested in white and the candles shone out bright and fair. The organist had kindly consented to play the Christmas hymns, in which the men joined heartily. It was a service never to be forgotten, and as I told the men, in the short address I gave them, never before perhaps, in the history of that venerable fane, had it witnessed a more striking assembly. From a distance of nearly seven thousand miles some of them had come, and this was to be our last Christmas before we entered the life and death struggle of the nations. Row after row of men knelt to receive the Bread of Life, and it was a rare privilege to administer it to them. The fog was heavier on our return and some of us had great difficulty in finding our lines.

It seemed sometimes as if we had been forgotten by the War Office, but this was not the case. We had visits from the King, Lord Roberts and other high officials. All these were impressed with the physique and high spirits of our men.

The conditions under which we lived were certainly atrocious, and an outbreak of meningitis cast a gloom over the camp. It was met bravely and skilfully by our medical men, of whose self-sacrifice and devotion no praise is too high. The same is true of their conduct all through the war.

ON SALISBURY PLAIN

Our life on the Plain was certainly a puzzle to us. Why were we kept there? When were we going to leave? Were we not wanted in France? These were the questions we asked one another. I met an Imperial officer one day, who had just returned from the front. I asked him when we were going to train for the trenches. "Why" he said, "what better training could you have than you are getting here? If you can stand the life here, you can stand the life in France." I think he was right. That strange experience was just what we needed to inure us to hardship, and it left a stamp of resolution and efficiency on the First Division which it never lost.

CHAPTER IV

OFF TO FRANCE

January To March, 1915.

TOWARDS the end of January, rumors became more frequent that our departure was close at hand, and we could see signs of the coming movement in many quarters. The disposition of the chaplains was still a matter of uncertainty. At last we were informed that only five chaplains were to proceed with the troops to France. This was the original number which the War Office had told us to bring from Canada. The news fell like a thunderbolt upon us, and we at once determined to get the order changed. The Senior Roman Catholic Chaplain and myself, by permission of the General, made a special journey to the War Office. The Chaplain-General received us, if not coldly, at least austerely. We told him that we had come from Canada to be with the men and did not want to leave them. He replied by saying that the Canadians had been ordered by Lord Kitchener to bring only five chaplains with them, and they had brought thirty-one. He said, looking at me, "That is not military discipline; we must obey orders." I explained to him that since the Canadian Government was paying the chaplains the people thought it did not matter how many we had. Even this did not seem to convince him. "Besides", he said, "they tell me that of all the troops in England the Canadians are the most disorderly and undisciplined, and they have got thirty-one chaplains." "But", I replied, "you ought to see what they would have been like, if we had brought only five." We succeeded in our mission in so far that he promised to speak to Lord Kitchener that afternoon and see if the wild Canadians could not take more chaplains with them to France than were allotted to British Divisions. The result was that eleven of our chaplains were to be sent.

Early in February we were told that our Division was to go in a few days. In spite of the mud and discomfort we had taken root in Salisbury Plain. I remember looking with affection one night at the Cathedral bathed in moonlight, and at the quaint streets of the dear old town, over which hung the shadow of war. Could it be possible that England was about to be crushed under

34

the heel of a foreign tyrant? If such were to be her fate, death on the battlefield would be easy to bear. What Briton could endure to live under the yoke or by the permission of a vulgar German autocrat?

On entering the mess one evening I was horrified to read in the orders that Canon Scott was to report immediately for duty to No. 2 General Hospital. It was a great blow to be torn from the men of the fighting forces. I at once began to think out a plan of campaign. I went over to the G. O. C. of my brigade, and told him that I was to report to No. 2 General Hospital. I said, with perfect truth, that I did not know where No. 2 General Hospital was, but I had determined to begin the hunt for it in France. I asked him if he would take me across with the Headquarters Staff, so that I might begin my search at the front. He had a twinkle in his eye as he told me that if I could get on board the transport, he would make no objection. I was delighted with the prospect of going over with the men.

When the time came to pack up, I was overwhelmed by the number of things that I had accumulated during the winter. I disposed of a lot of useless camp furniture, such as folding tables and collapsible chairs, and my faithful friend the oil stove. With a well-filled Wolseley kit-bag and a number of haversacks bursting with their contents, I was ready for the journey. On February 11th, on a lovely afternoon, I started off with the Headquarters Staff. We arrived at Avonmouth and made our way to the docks. It was delightful to think that I was going with the men. I had no batman and no real standing with the unit with which I was travelling. However, I did not let this worry me. I got a friend to carry my kit-bag, and then covering myself with haversacks, till I looked, as the men said, like a Christmas tree, I made my way to the ship with a broad grin of satisfaction on my face. As I went up the gangway so attired and looking exceedingly pleased with myself, my appearance excited the suspicion of the officer in command of the ship, who was watching the troops come on board. Mistaking the cause of my good spirits, he called a captain to him and said, "There is an officer coming on board who is drunk; go and ask him who he is." The captain accordingly came over and greeting me pleasantly said, "How do you do, Sir?" "Very well, thank you," I replied, smiling all the more. I was afraid he had come up to send me back. Having been a teetotaler for twenty-two years, I knew nothing of the horrible suspicion under which I lay at the moment. The captain then said, "Who are you, Sir?" and I, thinking of my happy escape from army red tape, answered quite innocently, with a a still broader grin, "I'm No. 2, General Hospital." This, of course confirmed the captain's worst suspicions. He went back to the O. C. of the ship. "Who does he say he is?" said the Colonel. "He says he is No. 2 General Hospital," the Captain replied. "Let him come on board" said the Colonel. He thought I was safer on board the ship than left behind in that condition on the wharf. With great delight I found all dangers had been passed and I was actually about to sail for France.

The boat which took us and the 3rd Artillery Brigade, was a small vessel called "The City of Chester." We were horribly crowded, so my bed had to be made on the table in the saloon. A doctor lay on the sofa at the side and several young officers slept on the floor. We had not been out many hours before a terrific gale blew up from the West, and we had to point our bow towards Canada. I told the men there was some satisfaction in that. We were exceedingly uncomfortable. My bed one night slid off the table on to the sleeping doctor and nearly crushed him. I squeezed out some wonderfully religious expressions from him in his state of partial unconsciousness. I replaced myself on the table, and then slid off on to the chairs on the other side. I finally found a happy and safe haven on the floor. On some of the other transports they fared even worse. My son, with a lot of other privates, was lying on the floor of the lowest deck in his boat, when a voice shouted down the gangway, "Lookout boys, there's a horse coming down." They cleared away just in time for a horse to land safely in the hold, having performed one of those miraculous feats which horses so often do without damage to themselves.

On the 15th of February we arrived off the west coast of France and disembarked at St. Nazaire. Our life now took on fresh interest. Everything about us was new and strange. As a Quebecer I felt quite at home in a French town. A good sleep in a comfortable hotel was a great refreshment after the voyage. In the afternoon of the following day we entrained for the front. I spread out my Wolesley sleeping bag on the straw in a box car in which there were several other officers. Our progress was slow, but it was a great thing to feel that we were travelling through France, that country of romance and chivalry. Our journey took more than two days, and we arrived at Hazebrouck one week after leaving Salisbury Plain. The town has since been badly wrecked, but then it was undamaged. The Brigadier lent me a horse and I rode with his staff over to Caestre where the brigade was to be billeted. In the same town were the 15th and 16th Battalions and the 3rd Field Ambulance. I had a room that night in the Chateau, a rather rambling modern house. The next morning I went out to find a billet for myself. I called on the Mayor and Mayoress, a nice old couple who not only gave me a comfortable room in their house, but insisted upon my accepting it free of charge. They also gave me breakfast in the kitchen downstairs. I was delighted to be so well housed and was going on my way rejoicing when I met an officer who told me that the Brigade Major wanted to see me in a hurry. I went over to his office and was addressed by him in a very military manner. He wanted to know why I was there and asked what unit I was attached to. I told him No. 2 General Hospital. He said, "Where is it?" "I don't know", I replied, "I came over to France to look for it." He said, "It is at Lavington on Salisbury Plain," and added, "You will have to report to General Alderson and get some attachment till the hospital comes over." His manner was so cold and businesslike that it was quite unnerving and I began to realize more than ever that I was in the Army. Accordingly that afternoon I walked over to the General's Headquarters, at Strazeele, some five miles away, and he attached me to the Brigade until my unit should come to France. I never knew when it did come to France, for I never asked. "Sufficient unto the day is the evil thereof" was my motto. I held on to my job at the front. But the threat which the Brigadier held over me, that if I went into the trenches or anywhere out of his immediate ken I should be sent back to No. 2 General Hospital, was something which weighed upon my spirits very heavily at times, and caused me to acquire great adroitness in the art of dodging. In fact, I made up my mind that three things had to be avoided if I wished to live through the campaign—sentries, cesspools, and generals. They were all sources of special danger, as everyone who has been at the front can testify. Over and over again on my rambles in the dark, nothing has saved me from being stuck by a sentry but the white gleam of my clerical collar, which on this account I had frequently thought of painting with luminous paint. One night I stepped into a cesspool and had to sit on a chair while my batman pumped water over me almost as ill-savoured as the pool itself. On another occasion, when, against orders, I was going into the trenches in Ploegsteert, I saw the General and his staff coming down the road. Quick as thought, I cantered my horse into an orchard behind a farm house, where there was a battery of Imperials. The men were surprised, not to say alarmed, at the sudden appearance of a chaplain in their midst. When I told them, however, that I was dodging a general, they received me with the utmost kindness and sympathy. They had often done the same themselves, and offered me some light refreshments.

On the following Sunday we had our first church parade in the war zone. We were delighted during the service to hear in the distance the sound of guns and shells. As the war went on we preferred church parades when we could not hear guns and shells.

After a brief stay in Caestre the whole brigade marched off to Armentieres. Near Flêtre, the Army Commander, General Smith-Dorrien, stood by the roadside and took the salute as we passed. I went with the 15th Battalion, and, as I told the men, being a Canon, marched with the machine gun section. We went by the delightful old town of Bailleul. The fields were green. The hedges were beginning to show signs of spring life. The little villages were quaint and picturesque, but the pavé road was rough and tiring. Bailleul made a delightful break in the journey. The old Spanish town hall, with its tower, the fine old church and spire and the houses around the Grande Place, will always live in one's memory. The place is all a ruin now, but then it formed a pleasant home and meeting place for friends from many parts. We skirted the borders of Belgium and arrived at Armentieres in the afternoon. The place had been shelled and was partly deserted, but was still a populous town. I made my home with the Brigade transport in a large school. In the courtyard our horses and mules were picketed. I had never heard mules bray before and I had a good sample next morning of what they can do, for with the buildings around them the sound had an added force. The streets of Armentieres were well laid out and some of the private residences were very fine. It is astonishing how our camp life at Salisbury had made us love cities. Armentieres has since been destroyed and its church ruined. Many of us have pleasant memories of the town, and the cemetery there is the resting place of numbers of brave Canadians.

I ran across an imperial Chaplain there, whom I had met in England. He told me he had a sad duty to perform that night. It was to prepare for death three men who were to be shot at daybreak. He felt it very keenly, and I afterwards found from experience how bitter the duty was.

We were brought to Armentieres in order to be put into the trenches with some of the British units for instruction. On Wednesday evening, February the 24th, the men were marched off to the trenches for the first time and I went with a company of the 15th Battalion, who were to be attached to the Durham Light Infantry. I was warned to keep myself in the background as it was said that the chaplains were not allowed in the front line. The trenches were at Houplines to the east of Armentieres. We marched down the streets till we came to the edge of the town and there a guide met us and we went in single file across the field. We could see the German flare-lights and could hear the crack of rifles. It was intensely interesting, and the mystery of the war seemed to clear as we came nearer to the scene of action. The men went down into the narrow trench and I followed. I was welcomed by a very nice young captain whom I never heard of again till I saw the cross that marked his grave in the Salient. The trenches in those days were not what they afterwards became. Double rows of sandbags built like a wall were considered an adequate protection. I do not think there was any real parados. The dugouts were on a level with the trench and were roofed with pieces of corrugated iron covered with two layers of sandbags. They were a strange contrast to the dugouts thirty feet deep, lined with wood, which we afterwards made for our trench homes.

I was immensely pleased at having at last got into the front line. Even if I were sent out I had at least seen the trenches. The captain brought me to his tiny dugout and told me that he and I could squeeze in there together for the night. He then asked me if I should like to see the trench, and took me with him on his rounds. By this time it was dark and rainy and very muddy. As we were going along the trench a tall officer, followed by another met us and exchanged a word with the captain. They then came up to me and the first one peered at me in the darkness and said in abrupt military fashion, "Who are you?" I thought my last hour had come, or at least I was going to be sent back. I told him I was a chaplain with the Canadians. "Did you come over with the men?" "Yes", I said. "Capital", he replied, "Won't you come and have lunch with me tomorrow?" "Where do you live?" I said. The other officer came up to my rescue at this moment and said, "The General's Headquarters are in such and such a place in Armentieres," "Good Heavens", I whispered in a low tone to the officer, "Is he a general?" "Yes" he said. "I hope my deportment was all that it ought to have been in the presence of a general," I replied. "It was excellent, Padre," he said, with a laugh. So I arranged to go and have luncheon with him two days afterwards, for I was to spend forty-eight hours in the trenches. The first officer turned out to be General Congreve, V. C., a most gallant man. He told me at luncheon that if he could press a button and blow the whole German nation into the air he would do it. I felt a little bit shocked then, because I did not know the Germans as I afterwards did. I spent nearly four years at the front hunting for that button.

The captain and I had very little room to move about in in his dugout. I was very much impressed with the unostentatious way in which he said, "If you want to say your prayers, Padre, you can kneel over in that corner first, because there is only room for one at a time. I will say mine afterwards"—and he did. He was a Roman Catholic, and had lived in India, and was a very fine type of man. When I read the words two years afterwards on a cross in a cemetery near Poperinghe, "Of your charity pray for the soul of Major Harter, M.C.," I did it gladly and devoutly.

I had brought with me in a small pyx, the Blessed Sacrament, and the next morning I gave Communion to a number of the men. One young officer, a boy of eighteen, who had just left school to come to the front, asked me to have the service in his dugout. The men came in three or four at a time and knelt on the muddy floor. Every now and then we could hear the crack of a bullet overhead striking the sandbags. The officer was afterwards killed, and the great promise of his life was not fulfilled in this world.

There was a great deal of rifle fire in the trenches in those days. The captain told me the Canadians were adepts in getting rid of their ammunition and kept firing all night long. Further down the line were the "Queen's Own Westminsters." They were a splendid body of young men and received us very kindly. On my way over to them the next morning, I found in a lonely part of a trench a man who had taken off his shirt and was examining the seams of it with interest. I knew he was hunting for one of those insects which afterwards played no small part in the general discomfort of the Great War, and I thought it would be a good opportunity to learn privately what they looked like. So I took a magnifying glass out of my pocket and said, "Well, my boy, let me have a look for I too am interested in botany." He pointed to a seam in his shirt and said, "There, Sir, there is one." I was just going to examine it under the glass when, crack! a bullet hit the sandbags near-by, and he told me the trench was enfiladed. I said, "My dear boy, I think I will postpone this scientific research until we get to safer quarters, for if I am knocked out, the first question my congregation will ask will be, "What was our beloved pastor doing when he was hit?" If they hear that I was hunting in a man's shirt for one of these insects, they will not think it a worthy ending to my life." He grinned, put on his shirt, and moved down the trench.

That afternoon a good many shells passed over our heads and of course the novelty of the thing made it most interesting. After a war experience of nearly four years, one is almost ashamed to look back upon those early days which were like war in a nursery. The hideous thing was then only in its infancy. Poison gas, liquid fire, trench mortars, hand grenades, machine guns, (except a very few) and tanks were then unknown. The human mind had not then made, as it afterward did, the sole object of its energy the destruction of human life. Yet with a deepening knowledge of the instruments of death has come, I trust, a more revolting sense of the horrors and futility of war. The romance and chivalry of the profession of arms has gone forever. Let us hope that in the years to come the human mind will bend all its energies to right the wrongs and avert the contentions that result in bloodshed.

On the following Sunday, we had a church parade in the square in Armentieres. Two or three men watched the sky with field glasses lest an enemy plane should come up. We had now finished our instruction in trench warfare and were going to take over

part of the front line. We were mached off one afternoon to the
village of Bac St. Maur, where we rested for the night. I had dinner with the officers of the 15th Battalion, and went out afterwards to a big factory at the end of the straggling brick village
to see my son, whose battalion was quartered there. On returning I found the night was very dark, and every door and window in the long rows of houses was tightly closed. No lights
were allowed in the town. Once more my faculty for losing my
way asserted itself, and I could not tell which was the house where
I had dined. It was to be my billet for the night. The
whole place was silent, and I wandered up and
down the long street. I met a few soldiers and when I asked if
they could tell me where I had had dinner they naturally began
to eye me with suspicion. At the same time it was no laughing
matter. I had had a long walk in the afternoon and had the
prospect of another on the following day. I was separated from
my kit-bag and my safety razor, which always, at the front, constituted my home, and the night was beginning to get cold. Besides it was more or less damaging to one's character as a chaplain to be found wandering aimlessly about the streets at night
asking where you had dined. My habits were not as well known
to the men then as they were after a few years of war. In de-
spair I went down the road behind the village, and there to my
joy I saw a friendly light emerging from the door of a coach house.
I went up to it and entered and found to my relief the guard of
the 16th Battalion. They had a big fire in the chimney-place, and
were smoking and making tea. It was then about one o'clock,
and they were both surprised and amused at my plight, but gave
me a very glad welcome and offered me a bed and blankets on the
floor. I was just going to accept them when I asked if the blankets were "crummy". The men burst out laughing. "You bet
your life they are, Sir," they cried. "Well, boys," I said, "I think
that I prefer to spend the night walking about the village and
trying to compose a poem." Once more I made my way down
the dark street, examining closely every door and window. At
last I found a crack of light which came from one of the houses.
I knocked at the door and it was opened by an officer from Quebec, who had been engaged with some others in a quiet game of
cards. He was amused at my homeless condition and kindly
took me in and gave me a comfortable bed in his own room. On

the next morning of course I was "ragged" tremendously on my disappearance during the night.

The next day we marched off to the village of Sailly-sur-Lys, which was to become our rear headquarters during our occupation of the trenches. The little place had been damaged by shells, but every available house was occupied. Our battalion moved up the country road and was dispersed among the farm houses and barns in the neighbourhood.

I made my home with some officers in a small and dirty farm house. The novelty of the situation, however, gave it a certain charm for the time. We were crowded into two or three little rooms and lay on piles of straw. We were short of rations, but each officer contributed something from his private store. I had a few articles of tinned food with me and they proved to be of use. From that moment I determined never to be without a tin of bully beef in my haversack, and I formed the bully beef habit in the trenches which lasted till the end and always amused the men. The general cesspool and manure heap of the farm was, as usual, in the midst of the buildings, and was particularly unsavoury. A cow waded through it and the family hens fattened on it. Opposite our window in one of the buildings dwelt an enormous sow with a large litter of young ones. When any of the ladies of the family went to throw refuse on the manure heap, the old sow, driven by the pangs of hunger, would stand on her hind legs and poke her huge face out over the half door of her prison appealing in pig language for some of the discarded dainties. Often nothing would stop her squeals but a smart slap on her fat cheeks by the lady's tender hand. In the hayloft of the barn the men were quartered. Their candles made the place an exceedingly dangerous abode. There was only one small hole down which they could escape in case of fire. It is a wonder we did not have more fires in our billets than we did.

The trenches assigned to our Brigade were to the right of Fleurbaix. They were poorly constructed, but as the time went on were greatly improved by the labours of our men. The Brigadier assigned to me for my personal use a tiny mud-plastered cottage with thatched roof and a little garden in front. It was in the Rue du Bois, a road which ran parallel with the trenches about 800 yards behind them. I was very proud to have a home all to myself, and chalked on the door the word' "Chaplain". In one room two piles of straw not only gave me a bed for myself but enabled me to give hospitality to any officer who needed a billet. Another room I fitted up as a chapel. An old box covered with the silk Union Jack and white cloth and adorned with two candles and cross served as an altar. There were no chairs to be had, but the plain white walls were not unsuited to the purpose to which the room was dedicated.

In this chapel I held several services. It was a fine sight to see a group of tall and stalwart young Highlanders present. Their heads almost reached to the low ceiling, and when they sang, the little building trembled with the sound.

Every night when there were any men to be buried, I used to receive notice from the front line, and after dark I would set out preceded by my batman, Murdoch MacDonald, a proper young Highlander, carrying a rifle with fixed bayonet on his shoulder. It made one feel very proud to go off down the dark road so attended. When we got to the place of burial I would hold a short service over the open graves in which the bodies were laid to rest. Our casualties were light then, but in those days we had not become accustomed to the loss of comrades and so we felt the toll of death very bitterly.

It made a great difference to me to have a house of my own. Previously I had found it most difficult to get any place in which to lay my head. On one occasion, I had obtained permission from a kind-hearted farmer's wife to rent one corner of the kitchen in her two-roomed house. It was on a Saturday night and when the family had retired to their room I spread my sleeping bag in the corner and went to bed. I got up when the family had gone to Mass in the morning. All through the day the kitchen was crowded, and I saw that if I went to bed that night I should not have the opportunity of getting up again until the family went to Mass on the following Sunday. So I paid the woman five francs for my lodging and started out in pursuit of another. I managed to find a room in another little farmhouse, somewhat larger and cleaner. My room was a small one and had an earth floor. The ceiling was so low that I could touch the beams with my head when I stood on my toes. But in it were two enormous double beds, a table and a chair. What more could one want? A large cupboard full of straw furnished a billet for Murdoch and he was allowed to do my simple cooking on the family stove.

OFF TO FRANCE

Small as my billet was, I was able on one occasion to take in and house three officers of the Leicesters, who arrived one night in preparation for the battle of Neuve Chapelle. I also stowed away a sergeant in the cupboard with Murdoch. My three guests were very hungry and very tired and enjoyed a good sleep in the ponderous beds. I saw a photo of one of the lads afterwards in the Roll of Honour page of the "Graphic," and I remembered the delightful talk I had had with him during his visit.

At that time we were all very much interested in a large fifteen-inch howitzer, which had been placed behind a farmhouse, fast crumbling into ruins. It was distant two fields from my abode. To our simple minds, it seemed that the war would soon come to an end when the Germans heard that such weapons were being turned against them. We were informed too, that three other guns of the same make and calibre were being brought to France. The gun was the invention of a retired admiral who lived in a farmhouse nearby and who, when it was loaded, fired it off by pressing an electric button. The officer in charge of the gun was very pleasant and several times took me in his car to interesting places. I went with him to Laventie on the day of the battle of Neuve Chapelle, and saw for the first time the effects of an attack and the wounded being brought back in ambulances.

There was one large barn not far off full of beautiful yellow straw which held several hundred men. I had a service in it one night. The atmosphere was smoky and mysterious, and the hundreds of little candles propped up on mess-tins over the straw, looked like a special illumination. A large heap of straw at the end of the barn served as a platform, and in lieu of an organ I had a mandolin player to start the hymns. The service went very well, the men joining in heartily.

The night before the battle of Neuve Chapelle, I went over to see the captain in charge of the big gun, and he showed me the orders for the next day, issued by the British General. He told me that at seven o'clock it would be "Hell let loose", all down the line. Next morning I woke up before seven, and blocked up my ears so that I should not be deafened by the noise of artillery. But for some reason or other the plans had been changed and I was quite disappointed that the Germans did not get the hammering it was intended to give them. We were on the left of the British line during the battle of Neuve Chapelle, and were not really in the fight. The British suffered very heavily and did not meet with the success which they had hoped for.

My son was wounded in this engagement and was sent out with the loss of an eye. On returning from seeing him put into a hospital train at Merville, I was held up for some hours in the darkness by the British Cavalry streaming past in a long line. I was delighted to see them for I thought we had broken through. On the next day to our great disappointment we saw them going back again.

Near Canadian Headquarters at Sailly there was a large steam laundry which was used as a bath for our men. It was a godsend to them, for the scarcity of water made cleanliness difficult. The laundry during bath hours was a curious spectacle. Scores of large cauldrons of steaming water covered the floor. In each sat a man with only his head and shoulders showing, looking as if he were being boiled to death. In the mists of the heated atmosphere and in the dim light of candles, one was reminded of Doré's illustrations of Dante's Inferno. In one of them he represents a certain type of sinner as being tormented forever in boiling water.

We had now finished our time in this part of the line and the Division was ordered back for a rest. The General was troubled about my transportation as I had no horse, but I quoted my favourite text, "The Lord will provide." It made him quite angry when I quoted the text, and he told me that we were engaged in a big war and could not take things so casually. When, however, he had seen me on various occasions picked up by stray motor cars and lorries and get to our destination before he did, he began to think there was more in the text than he had imagined. I was accused of helping Providence unduly by base subterfuges such as standing in the middle of a road and compelling the motor to stop until I got in. I considered that my being able to stop the car was really a part of the providing. In fact I found that, if one only had courage to stand long enough in the middle of the road without moving, almost any car, were it that of a private or a general, would come to a standstill. It was only a natural thing, when the car had stopped, to go to the occupants and say, "I know the Lord has sent you for the purpose of giving me a lift." It was quite a natural consequence of this for me to be taken in. One day at Estaires I tried to commandeer a fine car standing in the square, but desisted when I was informed by the driver that it was the private property of the Prince of Wales. I am sure that if the Prince had been there to hear the text, he would have driven me anywhere I wanted to go.

On the present occasion, I had not gone far down the road before a car picked me up and took me on my way—an incident which I narrated to the General afterwards with intense satisfaction.

CHAPTER V

BEFORE THE STORM

March to April, 1915

OUR rest-time at Estaires at the end of March was a delightful period of good fellowship. The beautiful early spring was beginning to assert its power over nature. The grass was green. The trees and hedgerows were full of sap and the buds ready to burst into new life. As one walked down the roads in the bright sunshine, and smelt the fresh winds bearing the scent of springtime, an exquisite feeling of delight filled the soul. Birds were singing in the sky, and it was pitiful to think that any other thoughts but those of rapture at the joy of living should ever cross the mind.

A sergeant found me a comfortable billet in a house near the Church. A dear old man and his two venerable daughters were the only occupants. Like all the French people we met, their little home was to them a source of endless joy. Everything was bright and clean, and they took great pleasure in showing off its beauties. There was a large room with glass roof and sides, like a conservatory. On the wall was the fresco of a landscape, drawn by some strolling artist, which gave my hosts infinite delight. There was a river flowing out of some very green woods, with a brilliant blue sky overhead. We used to sit on chairs opposite and discuss the woodland scene, and I must say it brought back memories to me of many a Canadian brook and the charming home life of Canadian woods, from which, as it seemed then, we were likely to be cut off forever.

The Bishop of London paid a visit to our men, and addressed them from the steps of the Town Hall in the Grande Place. The officers and men were charmed with his personality.

It was a joy to me that we were to spend Easter at such a convenient place. On Good Friday afternoon we had a voluntary service in front of the Town Hall. It seemed very fitting that these men who had come in the spirit of self-sacrifice, should be invited to contemplate, for at least an hour, the great world sacrifice of Calvary. A table was brought out from an estaminet nearby and placed in front of the steps. I mounted on this and so was

48

able to address the crowd which soon assembled there. We sang some of the Good Friday hymns, "When I survey the wondrous Cross", and "Jesu, Lover of my Soul." There must have been several hundred present. I remember specially the faces of several who were themselves called upon within a few weeks to make the supreme sacrifice. Like almost all other religious services at the front, this one had to struggle with the exigencies of war. A stream of lorries at the side of the Grande Place and the noisy motor cycles of despatch riders made an accompaniment to the address which rendered both speaking and hearing difficult.

Easter Day rose bright and clear. I had a hall situated down a narrow lane, which had been used as a cinema. There was a platform at one end and facing it, rows of benches. On the platform I arranged the altar, with the silk Union Jack as a frontal and with cross and lighted candles for ornaments. It looked bright and church-like amid the sordid surroundings. We had several celebrations of the Holy Communion, the first being at six a. m. A large number of officers and men came to perform their Easter duties. A strange solemnity prevailed. It was the first Easter spent away from home; it was the last Easter that most of those gallant young souls spent on earth. The other chaplains had equally large attendances. We sang the Easter hymn at each service, and the music more than anything else carried us back to the days that were.

But our stay in Estaires was only for a time, and soon orders came that we were to move. On April 7th, a bright and lovely spring morning, the whole Division began its fateful journey to Ypres and marched off to Cassel, about thirty miles behind the Salient. The men were in good spirits, and by this time were becoming accustomed to the pavé roads. We passed through Caestre, where I saw my old friends, the Mayor and Mayoress. That afternoon I was taken by two British officers to the little hotel in Cassel for luncheon. The extensive view over the country from the windows reminded me of dear old Quebec. After luncheon my friends motored me to Ypres. The city at that time had not been heavily shelled, except the Cloth Hall and Cathedral. The shops around the square were still carrying on their business and people there were selling post-cards and other small articles. We went into the Cathedral, which had been badly damaged. The roof was more or less intact and the altar and pulpit in their

4

places. I saw what an impressive place it must have been. The Cloth Hall had been burnt, but the beautiful stone façade was still undamaged. A fire engine and horses were quartered under the central tower. There was a quiet air of light and beauty in the quaint old buildings that suggested the mediaeval prosperity of the city. Behind the better class of houses there were the usual gardens, laid out with taste, and often containing fountains and rustic bridges. The French and the Belgians delighted in striving to make a landscape garden in the small area at their command.

I shall always be thankful that I had the opportunity of paying this visit to Ypres while it still retained vestiges of its former beauty. Dark and hideous dreams of drives on ambulances in the midnight hours haunt me now when the name of Ypres is mentioned. I hear the rattle of lorries and motorcycles and the tramp of horses on the cobblestones. The grim ruins on either side of the road stand out hard and sombre in the dim light of the starry sky. There is the passing of innumerable men and the danger of the traffic-crowded streets. But Ypres, as I saw it then, was full of beauty touched with the sadness of the coming ruin.

In the afternoon, I motored back to our brigade on the outskirts of Cassel. After dinner I started off to find my new billet. As usual I lost my way. I went off down the country roads. The farms were silent and dark. There was no one to tell me where my battalion was. I must have gone a long distance in the many detours I made. The country was still a place of mystery to me, and "The little owls that hoot and call" seemed to be the voice of the night itself. The roads were winding and lonely and the air was full of the pleasant odours of the spring fields. It was getting very late and I despaired of finding a roof under which to spend the night. I determined to walk back to the nearest village. As I had marched with the men that day all the way from Estaires, a distance of about twenty miles, I was quite reasonably tired and anxious to get a bed. I got back to the main road which leads to St. Sylvestre. On approaching the little village I was halted by a British sentry who was mounting guard over a line of Army Service Corps lorries. I went on and encountered more sentries till I stood in the town itself and made my difficulty known to a soldier who was passing. I asked him if he knew where I could get a lodging for the night. He told me that some officers had their headquarters in the Curé's house, and that if I were to knock at the door, very probably I could find a room in which to stay. I went to the house which was pointed out to me and knocked. There was a light in a window upstairs so I knew that my knocking would be heard. Presently a voice called out from the hollow passage and asked me to open the door and come in. I did so, and in the dim light saw at the end of the hall a white figure which was barely distinguishable and which I took to be the individual who had spoken to me. Consequently I addressed my conversation to it. The shadowy form asked me what I wanted and I explained that I had lost my way and asked where the headquarters of my battalion were. The being replied that it did not know but invited me to come in and spend the night. At that moment somebody from the upstairs region came with an electric torch, and the light lit up the empty hall. To my surprise I found that I had been addressing my conversation to the life-sized statue of some saint which was standing on a pedestal at the foot of the stairs. I rather mystified my host by saying that I had been talking to the image in the hall. However, in spite of this, he asked me to come upstairs where he would give me a bed. By this time several of the British officers who occupied the upper flat had become interested in the arrival of the midnight visitor, and were looking over the bannisters. I can remember feeling that my only chance of receiving hospitality depended on my presenting a respectable appearance. I was on my best behaviour. It was greatly to my confusion, therefore, as I walked upstairs under the inspection of those of the upper flat, that I stumbled on the narrow steps. In order to reassure my would-be friends, I called out, "Don't be alarmed, I am a chaplain and a teetotaller". They burst out laughing and on my arrival at the top greeted me very heartily. I was taken into a long bedroom where there were five beds in a row, one of which was assigned to me. Not only was I given a bed, but one of their servants went and brought me a hot-cross bun and a glass of milk. In return for such wholehearted and magnificent hospitality, I sat on the edge of the bed and recited poems to my hosts, who at that hour of the morning were not averse to anything which might be conducive to sleep. On the next day I was made an honorary member of their mess. I should like to bear testimony here to the extraordinary cordiality and kind hospitality which was always shown to us by British officers.

Later on in the day, I found the 13th Battalion just a few miles outside Cassel at a place called Terdeghem. It was a quaint little village with an interesting church. I got a billet in a farmhouse. It was a curious building of brick and stood on the road where a little gate opened into a delightful garden, full of oldfashioned flowers. My room was reached by a flight of steps from the kitchen and was very comfortable. I disliked, however, the heavy fluffy bed. Murdoch MacDonald used to sleep in the kitchen.

There were some charming walks around Terdeghem. One which I liked to take led to a very old and picturesque chateau, surrounded by a moat. I was immensely impressed with the rows of high trees on which the rooks built their noisy cities. Sometimes a double line of these trees, like an avenue, would stretch across a field. Often, as I have walked home in the dark after parish visiting, I have stood between the long rows of trees and listened to the wind sighing through their bare branches and looked up at the stars that "were tangled in them". Then the dread mystery of war and fate and destruction would come over me. It was a relief to think how comfortable and unconcerned the rooks were in their nests with their children about them in bed. They had wings too wherewith to fly away and be at rest.

Cassel was used at that time by the French Army, so we were excluded from it unless we had a special permit. It was a delightful old town, and from its commanding position on a rock has been used as a fortress more or less since the days of Julius Ceasar. The Grand Place is delightful and quaint. From it, through various archways, one looks down upon the rich verdure of the fields that stretch far off into the distance.

We had a parade of our four battalions one day, when General Smith-Dorrien came to inspect us. The place chosen was a green slope not far from the entrance to the town. The General reviewed the men, and then gave a talk to the officers. As far as I can recollect, he was most sanguine about the speedy termination of the war. He told us that all we had to do was to keep worrying the Germans, and that the final crushing stroke would be given on the east by the Russians. He also told us that to us was assigned the place of honour on the extreme left of the British line next to the French Colonial troops. I overheard an irreverent officer near me say, "Damn the place of honour", and I thought of Sam Hughes and his warning about not objecting to swearing. The General, whom I had met before, asked me to walk with him up to his car and then said, "I have had reports about the Canadian Artillery, and I am delighted at their efficiency. I have also heard the best accounts of the Infantry, but do you think, in the event of a sudden onslaught by the Germans, that the Canadians will hold their ground? They are untried troops." I told him that I was sure that one thing the Canadians would do would be to hold on. Before a fortnight had passed, in the awful struggle near Langemarcke, the Canadians proved their ability to hold their ground.

Shortly after the General's visit we were ordered to move, and by some oversight on Murdoch MacDonald's part, my kit was not ready in time to be taken by the Brigade transport. In consequence, to my dismay, I saw the men march off from Terdeghem to parts unknown, and found myself seated on my kit by the wayside with no apparent hope of following. I administered a rebuke to Murdoch as sternly as was consistent with the position of a chaplain, and then asked him to see if he could find any sort of vehicle at all to carry my stuff off in the direction towards which the battalion had marched. I must say I felt very lonely and a "bit out of it", as I sat by the wayside wondering if I had lost the Brigade for good. In the meantime, Murdoch scoured the village for a horse and carriage. Suddenly, to my surprise, a despatch rider on a motorcycle came down the road and stopped and asked me if I knew where Canon Scott was. I said, "I'm the man", and he handed me a letter. It turned out to be one from General Smith-Dorrien, asking me to allow him to send a poem which I had written, called "On the Rue du Bois" to "The Times." It was such a kind friendly letter that at once it dispelled my sense of loneliness, and when Murdoch arrived and told me that there was not a horse in the place at my disposal, I replied that I did not mind so much now since I had the British General for a friend. I left Murdoch to guard my goods and chattels and went off myself down the road to the old Chateau and farmhouse. There I was lucky enough to obtain a cart with three wheels. It was an extremely long and heavily built vehicle and looked as if it dated from the 17th century. The horse that was put into it looked as if it had been born about the same period. The old man who held the solitary rein and sat over the third wheel under the bow looked to be of almost equal antiquity. It must have been about thirty feet from the tip of the old horse's nose to the end of the cart. However I was glad to get any means of transportation at all, so I followed the thing to the road where my kit was waiting, Murdoch MacDonald put all my worldly possessions on the equipage. They seemed to occupy very little room in the huge structure. Murdoch, shouldering his rifle, followed it, and I, rather ashamed of the grotesque appearance of my caravan, marched on as quickly as I could in front, hoping to escape the ridicule which I knew would be heaped upon me by all ranks of my beloved brigade. A man we met told us that the battalion had gone to Steenvoorde, so thither we made our way. On our arrival I was taken to the Chateau and kindly treated by the laird and his family, who allowed me to spread out my bed-roll on the dining room floor.

On the following morning an Imperial officer very kindly took me and my kit to Ypres. There at the end of Yser Canal, I found a pleasant billet in a large house belonging to a Mr. Vandervyver, who, with his mother, gave me a kind reception and a most comfortably furnished room. Later on, the units of our brigade arrived and I marched up with the 14th Battalion to the village of Wieltje. Over it, though we knew it not, hung the gloom of impending tragedy. Around it now cluster memories of the bitter price in blood and anguish which we were soon called upon to pay for the overthrow of tyranny. It was a lovely spring evening when we arrived, and the men were able to sit down on the green grass and have their supper before going into the trenches by St. Julien. I walked back down that memorable road which two years later I travelled for the last time on my return from Paschendaele. The great sunset lit the sky with beautiful colours. The rows of trees along that fateful way were ready to burst into new life. The air was fresh and invigorating. To the south, lay the hill which is known to the world as Hill 60, afterwards the scene of such bitter fighting. Before me in the distance, soft and mellow in the evening light, rose the towers and spires of Ypres— Ypres! the very name sends a strange thrill through the heart. For all time, the word will stand as a symbol for brutal assaults and ruthless destruction on the one hand and heroic resolve and dogged resistance on the other. On any grim monument raised to the Demon of War, the sole word "YPRES" would be a sufficient and fitting inscription.

CHAPTER VI.

The Second Battle of Ypres

April 22nd, 1915

Behind my house at Ypres there was an old-fashioned garden which was attended to very carefully by my landlady. A summerhouse gave a fine view of the waters of the Yser Canal, which was there quite wide. It was nice to see again a good-sized body of water, for the little streams often dignified by the name of rivers did not satisfy the Canadian ideas as to what rivers should be. A battalion was quartered in a large brick building several stories high on the east side of the canal. There was consequently much stir of life at that point, and from my summerhouse on the wall I could talk to the men passing by. My billet was filled with a lot of heavy furniture which was prized very highly by its owners. Madame told me that she had buried twelve valuable clocks in the garden in case of a German advance. She also told me that her grandfather had seen from the windows the British going to the battle of Waterloo. She had both a piano and a harmonium, and took great pleasure in playing some of the hymns in our Canadian hymn book. I was so comfortable that I hoped our residence at Ypres might be of long duration. At night, however, desultory shells fell into the city. We could hear them ripping along with a sound like a trolley on a track, and then there would be a fearful crash. One night when returning from Brigade Headquarters near Wieltje, I saw a magnificent display of fireworks to the South. I afterwards heard that it was the night the British attacked Hill 60.

On Sunday, the 18th of April, I had a service for the 15th Battalion in one of the stories of the brick building beside the canal. Something told me that big things were going to happen. I had a feeling that we were resting on the top of a volcano. At the end of the service I prepared for any sudden call to ministration on the battlefield by reserving the Blessed Sacrament.

On Monday some men had narrow escapes when a house was shelled and on the following day I went to the centre of the town with two officers to see the house which had been hit. They appeared to be in a hurry to get to the Square, so I went up one

55

of the side streets to look at the damaged house. In a cellar near by I found an old woman making lace. Her hunchback son was sitting beside her. While I was making a few purchases, we heard the ripping sound of an approaching shell. It grew louder, till at last a terrific crash told us that the monster had fallen not far off. At that moment a number of people crowded into an adjoining cellar, where they fell on their knees and began to say a litany. I stood at the door looking at them. It was a pitiful sight. There were one or two old men and some women, and some little children and a young girl who was in hysterics. They seemed so helpless, so defenceless against the rain of shells.

I went off down the street towards the Square where the last shell had fallen, and there on the corner I saw a large house absolutely crushed in. It had formerly been a club, for there were billiard tables in the upper room. The front wall had crashed down upon the pavement, and from the debris some men were digging out the body of an officer who had been standing there when the shell fell. His was the first terribly mangled body that I had ever seen. He was laid face downwards on a stretcher and borne away. At that moment a soldier came up and told me that one of the officers with whom I had entered the town about half an hour ago had been killed, and his body had been taken to a British ambulance in the city. I walked across the Square, and there I saw the stretcher-bearers carrying off some civilians who had been hit by splinters of the shell. In the hospital were many dead bodies and wounded men for there had been over one hundred casualties in the city that day. We had hardly arrived when once again we heard the ripping sound which had such a sinister meaning. Then followed a terrific explosion. The final and dreadful bombardment of Ypres had begun. At intervals of ten minutes the huge seventeen-inch shells fell, sounding the death knell of the beautiful old town.

On the next morning, the brother-in-law of the officer who had been killed called on me and asked me to go and see the Town Major and secure a piece of ground which might be used for the Canadian Cemetery. The Town Major gave us permission to mark off a plot in the new British cemetery. It was in an open field near the jail, known by the name of the Plain d'Amour, and by it was a branch canal. Our Headquarters ordered the Engineers to mark off the place, and that night we laid the body to rest.

THE SECOND BATTLE OF YPRES

The following morning was Thursday, the memorable 22nd of April. The day was bright and beautiful. After burying another man in the Canadian lot, I went off to have lunch and write some letters in my billet. In the afternoon one of the 16th Battalion came in and asked me to have a celebration of the Holy Communion on the following morning, as some of the men would like to attend. I asked him to stay to tea and amuse himself till I had finished my letters. While I was writing I heard the ripping sound of an approaching shell, quickly followed by a tremendous crash. Some building quite close by had evidently been struck. I put on my cap and went out, when the landlady followed me and said, "I hope you are not going into the town." "I am just going to see where the shell has struck", I replied, "and will come back immediately." I never saw her again. As I went up the street I saw the shell had hit a large building which had been used as a hospital. The smoke from the shell was still rolling up into the clear sky. Thinking my services might be needed in helping to remove the patients, I started off in the direction of the building. There I was joined by a stretcher-bearer and we went through the gate into the large garden where we saw the still smoking hole in the ground which the shell had made. I remember that, as I looked into it, I had the same sort of eerie feeling which I had experienced when looking down the crater of Vesuvius. There was something uncanny about the arrival of shells out of the clear sky. They seemed to be things supernatural. The holes made by the seventeen inch shells with which Ypres was assailed were monstrous in size. The engineers had measured one in a field; it was no less than thirty-nine feet across and fifteen feet deep. The stretcher-bearer who was with me said as he looked at this one, "You could put three ambulances into it." We had not contemplated the scene very long before once again there was the ripping sound and a huge explosion, and we found ourselves lying on the ground. Whether we had thrown ourselves down or had been blown down I could not make out. We got up and the man went back to his ambulance and I went into the building to see if I could help in getting out the wounded. The place I entered was a large chapel and had been used as a ward. There were rows of neat beds on each side, but not a living soul was to be seen. It seemed so ghostly and mysterious that I called out, "Is anyone here?" There was no reply. I went down to the end of the chapel and from thence into a courtyard, where a Belgian told me that a number of people were in a cellar at the other end of a glass passage. I walked down the passage to go to the cellar, when once again there was the ominous ripping sound and a shell burst and all the glass was blown about my ears. An old man in a dazed condition came from the cellar at the end of the passage and told me that all the people had gone. I was helping him across the courtyard towards a gateway when a man came in from the street and took the old fellow on his back and carried him off. By the gateway was a room used as a guardroom. There I found a sentry with three or four Imperials. One of the lads had lost his nerve and was lying under a wooden bench. I tried to cheer them by telling them it was very unlikely that any more shells would come in our direction. I remembered reading in one of Marryatt's books that an officer in the Navy declared he had saved his life by always sticking his head into the hole in the ship which a cannon ball had made, as it was a million chances to one against another cannon ball striking that particular place. Still, at regular intervals, we heard the ripping sound and the huge explosion of a shell. Later on, two members of the 14th Battalion came in, and a woman and a little boy carrying milk. We did our best to restore the lady's courage and hoped that the bombardment would soon cease.

It was about seven p. m., when all of a sudden, we heard the roar of transports and the shouting of people in the street, and I went out to see what was the matter. To my horror I saw a battery of artillery galloping into the town. Civilians were rushing down the pavements on each side of the road, and had even filled the limbers. I called out to one of the drivers and asked him what it meant. "It is a general retreat", he shouted. "The Germans are on our heels." "Where are the infantry?" I called out. "They have all gone." That was one of the most awful moments in my life. I said to myself, "Has old England lost the War after all?" My mouth became suddenly dry as though filled with ashes. A young fellow on horseback stopped and, dismounting, very gallantly said, "Here, Sir, take my horse." "No thank you," I said, but I was grateful to him all the same for his self-sacrifice. I returned to the guardroom and told the sentries what had happened. The lady and the young boy disappeared and the men and I debated as to what we should do. The words, "The Germans are on our heels", were still ringing in my ears. I did not quite know what they signified. Whether they meant in military language that the Germans were ten miles away or were really round the next corner, I did not know, but I took the precaution of looking up the street before entering the gateway. On talking the matter over, the men and I thought it might be the part of discretion to make our way down past the Railway Station to the Vlamertinghe road, as none of us wanted to be taken prisoners. We therefore went down some side streets and crossed the bridge on the road that leads to Vlamertinghe. There I found an ammunition column hurrying out of the town, and the man riding one of the horses on a limber invited me to mount the other, which was saddled. It is so long, however, since I left the circus ring that I cannot mount a galloping horse unless I put my foot into the stirrup. So after two or three ineffectual attempts at a running mount, I climbed up into the limber and asked the driver if it was a general retreat. "No", he said, "I don't think so, only the Germans are close at hand and we were ordered to put the ammunition column further off." "Well", I said, "If it isn't a general retreat, I must go back to my lines or I shall be shot for desertion." I got off the limber and out of the crowd of people, and was making my way back, when I saw a car with a staff officer in it coming up in the direction of the City. I stopped the car and asked the officer if he would give me a ride back to Ypres. When I got in, I said to him quite innocently, "Is this a general retreat?" His nerves were evidently on edge, and he turned on me fiercely, saying, "Padré, never use such a word out here. That word must never be mentioned at the front." I replied, in excuse, that I had been told it was a retreat by a battery that was coming back from the front. "Padré," he continued, "that word must never be used." I am not sure that he did not enforce his commands by some strong theological terms. "Padré, that word must never be used out here." "Well," I said, "this is the first war I have ever been at, and if I can arrange matters it is the last, but I promise you I will never use it again." Not the least flicker of a smile passed over his face. Of course, as time went on and I advanced in military knowledge, I came to know the way in which my question ought to have been phrased. Instead of saying, "Is this a general retreat?", I ought to have said, "Are we straightening the line?" or "Are we pinching the Salient?" We went on till we came to a general who was standing by the road waiting to "straighten the line". I got out of the car and asked him where I should go. He seemed to be in a great hurry and said gruffly, "You had better go back to your lines." I did not know where they were, but I determined to go in their direction. The general got into the car which turned round and made off towards Vlamertinghe, and I, after a long and envious look in his direction, continued my return to Ypres.

People were still pouring out of the City. I recrossed the bridge, and making my way towards the cemetery, met two men of one of our battalions who were going back. I handed them each a card with my address on it and asked them, in case of my being taken prisoner, to write and tell my family that I was in good health and that my kit was at Mr. Vandervyver's on the Quai. The short cut to my billet led past the quiet cemetery where our two comrades had been laid to rest. It seemed so peaceful that I could not help envying them that their race was won.

It was dark now, but a bright moon was shining and lit up the waters of the branch canal as I walked along the bank towards my home. The sound of firing at the front was continuous and showed that a great battle was raging. I went by the house where the C. O. of the 16th Battalion had had his headquarters as I passed that afternoon. It was now quite deserted and the windows in it and in the houses round the square were all shattered. Not a living thing could I see. I walked across to my billet and found the shutters of the house closed. On the table where my letters were, a smoky oil lamp was burning. Not a human being was there. I never felt so lonely in my life, and those words, "The Germans are on our heels", still kept ringing in my ears. I took the lamp and went upstairs to my room. I was determined that the Germans should not get possession of the photographs of my family. I put them in my pocket, and over my shoulder the pair of glasses which the Bishop and clergy of Quebec had given me on my departure. I also hung round my neck the pyx containing the Blessed Sacrament, then I went out on the street, not knowing what way to take. To my infinite delight, some men came marching up in the moonlight from the end of the canal. I recognized them as the 16th Battalion, Canadian Scottish, and I called out, "Where are you going, boys?" The reply came glad and cheerful. "We are going to reinforce the line, Sir, the Germans have broken through." "That's all right, boys", I said, "play the game. I will go with

THE SECOND BATTLE OF YPRES

you." Never before was I more glad to meet human beings. The splendid battalion marched up through the streets towards St. Jean. The men wore their overcoats and full kits. I passed up and down the battalion talking to officers and men. As I was marching beside them, a sergeant called out to me, "Where are we going, Sir?" "That depends upon the lives you have led." A roar of laughter went up from the men. If I had known how near the truth my words were, I probably would not have said them. When we got to St. Jean, a sergeant told me that the 14th Battalion was holding the line. The news was received gladly, and the men were eager to go forward and share the glory of their comrades. Later on, as I was marching in front of the battalion a man of the 15th met us. He was in a state of great excitement, and said, "The men are poisoned, Sir, the Germans have turned on gas and our men are dying." I said to him very sternly, "Now, my boy, not another word about that here." "But it's true, Sir,". "Well, that may be, but these men have got to go there all the same, and the gas may have gone before they arrive, so promise me not another word about the poison." He gave me his promise and when I met him a month afterwards in Bailleul he told me he had never said a word about the gas to any of the men that night.

We passed through Weiltje where all was stir and commotion, and the dressing stations were already full, and then we deployed into the fields on a rise in the ground near St. Julien. By this time, our men had become aware of the gas, because, although the German attack had been made a good many hours before, the poisonous fumes still clung about the fields and made us cough. Our men were halted along the field and sat down waiting for orders. The crack of thousands of rifles and the savage roar of artillery were incessant, and the German flare-lights round the salient appeared to encircle us. There was a hurried consultation of officers and then the orders were given to the different companies. An officer who was killed that night came down and told us that the Germans were in the wood which we could see before us at some distance in the moonlight, and that a house from which we saw gleams of light was held by German machine guns. The men were told that they had to take the wood at the point of the bayonet and were not to fire, as the 10th Battalion would be in front of them. I passed down the line and told them that they had a chance to do

61

a bigger thing for Canada that night than had ever been done before. "It's a great day for Canada, boys." I said. The words afterwards became a watchword, for the men said that whenever I told them that, it meant that half of them were going to be killed. The battalion rose and fixed bayonets and stood ready for the command to charge. It was a thrilling moment, for we were in the midst of one of the decisive battles of the war. A shrapnel burst just as the men moved off and a man dropped in the rear rank. I went over to him and found he was bleeding in the neck. I bound him up and then taking his kit, which he was loath to lose, was helping him to walk towards the dressing station when I saw what I thought were sand-bags in the moonlight. I called out, "Is anybody there?" A voice replied, "Yes, Sir, there is a dying man here." I went over and there I found two stretcher-bearers beside a young fellow called Duffy, who was unconscious. He had been struck by a piece of shrapnel in the head and his brain was protruding. Duffy was a well-known athlete and had won the Marathon race. We tried to lift him, but with his equipment on he was too heavy, so I sent off the wounded man to Wieltje with one of the stretcher-bearers who was to return with a bearer party. The other one and I watched by Duffy. It was an awful and wonderful time. Our field batteries never slackened their fire and the wood echoed back the crackling sound of the guns. The flare lights all round gave a lurid background to the scene. At the foot of the long slope, down which the brave lads had gone to the attack, I saw the black outline of the trees. Over all fell the soft light of the moon. A great storm of emotion swept through me and I prayed for our men in their awful charge, for I knew that the Angel of Death was passing down our lines that night. When the bearer party arrived, we lifted Duffy on to the stretcher, and the men handed me their rifles and we moved off. I hung the rifles on my shoulder, and I thought if one of them goes off and blows my brains out, there will be a little paragraph in the Canadian papers, "Canon Scott accidentally killed by the discharge of a rifle," and my friends will say, "What a fool he was to fuss about rifles, why didn't he stick to his own job?" However, they were Ross rifles and had probably jammed. There were many wounded being carried or making their way towards Wieltje. The road was under shell fire all the way. When we got to the dressing station which was a small red-brick estaminet, we were confronted by a horrible sight. On the pavement before it were rows and rows of stretcher cases, and inside the place, which was dimly lighted by candles and lamps, I found the doctor and his staff working away like Trojans. The operating room was a veritable shambles. The doctor had his shirt sleeves rolled up and his hands and arms were covered with blood.

The wounded were brought in from outside and laid on the table, where the doctor attended to them. Some ghastly sights were disclosed when the stretcher-bearers ripped off the blood-stained clothes and laid bare the hideous wounds. At the end of the room, an old woman, with a face like the witch of Endor, apparently quite unmoved by anything that was happening, was grinding coffee in a mill and making a black concoction which she sold to the men. It was no doubt a good thing for them to get a little stimulant. In another room the floor was covered with wounded waiting to be evacuated. There were many Turcos present. Some of them were suffering terribly from the effects of the gas. Fresh cases were being brought down the road every moment, and laid out on the cold pavement till they could be attended to.

About two in the morning a despatch rider arrived and meeting me at the door asked if I could speak French. He said, "Tell the Turcos and every one else who can walk to clear off to Ypres as soon as they can; the Germans are close at hand." Indeed it sounded so, because the rifle fire was very close. I went into the room and delivered my message, in French and English, to the wounded men. Immediately there was a general stampede of all who could possibly drag themselves towards the city. It was indeed a piteous procession which passed out of the door. Turcos with heads bandaged, or arms bound up or one leg limping, and our own men equally disabled, helped one another down that terrible road towards the City. Soon all the people who could walk had gone. But there in the room, and along the pavement outside, lay helpless men. I went to the M.O. and asked him what we were to do with the stretcher cases. "Well" he said, "I suppose we shall have to leave them because all the ambulances have gone." "How can we desert them?" I said. The Medical Officer was of course bound by orders to go back with his men but I myself felt quite free in the matter, so I said, "I will stay and be made prisoner." "Well," he said, "so will I. Possibly I shall get into trouble for it, but I cannot leave them to the enemy without any one to look after them." So we made a compact that we would both stay behind and be made prisoners. I went over to another Field Ambulance, where a former curate of mine was chaplain. They had luckily been able to evacuate their wounded and were all going off. I told him that I should probably be made a prisoner that night, but asked him to cable home and tell my family that I was in good health and that the Germans treated chaplains, when they took them prisoners, very kindly. Then I made my way back. There was a tremendous noise of guns now at the front. It was a horrible thought that our men were up there bearing the brunt of German fury and hatred. Their faces passed through my mind as individuals were recalled. The men whom I knew so well, young, strong and full of hope and life, men from whom Canada had so much to expect, men whose lives were so precious to dear ones far away, were now up in that poisoned atmosphere and under the hideous hail of bullets and shells. The thought almost drove a chaplain to madness. One felt so powerless and longed to be up and doing. Not once or twice in the Great War, have I longed to be a combatant officer with enemy scalps to my credit. Our men had been absolutely guiltless of war ambitions. It was not their fault that they were over here. That the Kaiser's insatiable, mad lust for power should be able to launch destruction upon Canadian hearts and homes was intolerable. I looked down the Ypres road, and there, to my horror, saw the lovely City lit up with flames. The smoke rolled up into the moonlit sky, and behind the dull glow of the fires I saw the Cloth Hall tower stand out in bold defiance. There was nothing for us to do then and for nearly four years more but keep our heads cool, set our teeth and deepen our resolve.

The dressing station had received more stretcher cases, and still more were coming in. The Medical Officer and his staff were working most heroically. I told him I had given instructions about cabling home should I be taken prisoner, and then I suddenly remembered that I had a scathing poem on the Kaiser in my pocket. I had written it in the quiet beauties of Beaupré, below Quebec, when the war first began. When I wrote it, I was told that if I were ever taken prisoner in Germany with that poem in my pocket, I should be shot or hanged. At that time, the German front line seemed so far off that it was like saying, "If you get to the moon the man there will eat you up." But the changes and chances of war had suddenly brought me face to face with the fact that I had resolved to be taken prisoner, and from what I heard and saw the event was not unlikely. So I said to the M.O. "I have just remembered that I have got in my pocket a printed copy of a very terrible poem which I wrote about the Kaiser. Of course you know I don't mind being shot or hanged by the Germans, but, if I am, who will write the poems of the War?" The M.O. laughed and thinking it unwise on general principles to wave a red rag in front of a mad bull, advised me to tear up my verses. I did so with great reluctance, but the precaution was unnecessary as the Germans never got through after all.

All along those terrible fields of death the battle raged. Young Canadians, new to war, but old in the inheritance of the blood of British freedom, were holding the line. The dressing station was soon full again, and, later on, a despatch rider came from the 3rd Infantry Brigade Headquarters in Shell-Trap Farm to tell us that more help was needed there. One of the M.O's assistants and a sergeant started off and I followed, We went down the road and then turned to the right up to the moated farmhouse where the Brigade was. As we went forward towards the battle front, the night air was sharp and bracing. Gun-flashes lit up the horizon, but above us the moon and stars looked quietly down. Wonderful deeds of heroism were being done by our men along those shell-ploughed fields, under that placid sky. What they endured, no living tongue can tell. Their Maker alone knows what they suffered and how they died. The eloquent tribute which history will give to their fame is that, in spite of the enemy's immense superiority in numbers, and his brutal launching of poisonous gas, he did not get through.

In a ditch by the wayside, a battalion was waiting to follow up the charge. Every man among the Canadians was "on the job" that night. We crossed the field to the farmhouse which we found filled to overflowing. Ambulances were waiting there to carry the wounded back to Ypres. I saw many friends carried in, and men were lying on the pavement outside. Bullets were cracking against the outer brick walls. One Highlander mounted guard over a wounded German prisoner. He had captured him and was filled with the hunter's pride in his game. "I got him myself, Sir, and I was just going to run him through with my bayonet when he told me he had five children. As I have five children myself, I could not kill him. So I brought him out here." I looked down at the big prostrate German who was watching us with interest largely rooted in fear. "Funf kinder?" (five children)) "Ja, ja." I wasn't going to be beaten by a German, so I told him I had seven children and his face fell. I found out afterwards that a great many Germans, when they were captured, said they had five children. The Germans I think used to be put through a sort of catechism before they went into action, in case they should be taken prisoners. For example, they always told us they were sure we were going to win the war. They always said they were glad to be taken prisoners. When they were married men, they said they had five children and so appealed to our pity. People do not realize even yet how very thorough the Germans were in everything that they thought was going to bring them the mastership of the world. When a German soldier saw the game was up, he surrendered at once and thus was preserved to fight for his country in the next war.

In the stable of the farm, I found many seriously wounded men lying on the straw, and I took down messages which they were sending to their relatives at home. On the other side of the wall, we could hear the bullets striking. As I had the Blessed Sacrament with me I was able to give communion to a number of the wounded. By this time the grey of approaching day began to silver the eastern sky. It was indeed a comfort to feel that the great clockwork of the universe went on just as if nothing was happening. Over and over again in the war the approach of dawn has put new life into one. It was such a tremendous and glorious thing to think that the world rolled on through space and turned on its axis, whatever turmoil foolish people were making upon its surface.

With the dawn came the orders to clear the wounded. The ambulances were sent off and one of the doctors told me to come with him, as the General had commanded the place to be cleared of all but the necessary military staff. It was about four in the morning when we started. There was a momentary quieting down in the firing as we crossed the bridge over the moat, but shells were still crashing in the fields, and through the air we heard every now and then the whistling of bullets. We kept our heads low and were hurrying on when we encountered a signaller with two horses, which he had to take back to the main road. One of these he offered to me. I had not been wanting to mount higher in the air, but I did not like the fellow to think I had got "cold feet." So I accepted it graciously, but annoyed him very much by insisting upon lengthening the stirrups before I mounted. He got impatient at what he considered an unnecessary delay, but I told him I would not ride with my knees up to my chin for all the Germans in the world. When I was mounted, we started off at a good gallop across the fields to the Ypres road. It was an exciting ride, and I must confess, looking back upon it, a thoroughly enjoyable one, reminding me of old stories of battles and the Indian escapes of my boyhood's novels. When we arrived at the main road, I had to deliver up my horse to its owner, and then I decided to walk to Ypres, as by so doing I could speak to the many Imperial men that were marching up to reinforce the line. I refused many kind offers of lifts on lorries and waggons. The British battalions were coming up and I was sorry for them. The young fellows looked so tired and hungry. They had been in France, I think, only twenty-four hours. At any rate, they had had a long march, and, as it turned out, were going up, most of them, to their death, I took great pleasure in hailing them cheerfully and telling them that it was all right, as the Canadians had held the line, and that the Germans were not going to get through. One sergeant said, "You put a lot of braces in my tunic when you talk like that, Sir." Nothing is more wonderful than the way in which men under tense anxiety will respond to the slightest note of cheer. This was the case all through the war. The slightest word or suggestion would often turn a man from a feeling of powerless dejection into one of defiant determination. These young Britishers whom I met that morning were a splendid type of men. Later on the machine-gun fire over the fields mowed them down in pitiful and ruthless destruction. As I journeyed towards Ypres I saw smoke rolling up from various parts of the city and down the road, in the air, I saw the flashes of bursting shrapnel. I passed St Jean and made my way to my house by the canal.

The shutters were still shut and the door was open. I entered and found in the dining room that the lamp was still burning on the table. It was now about seven o'clock and Mr. Vandervyver had returned and was upstairs arranging his toilet. I went out into the garden and called one of the sentries to tell Murdoch MacDonald to come to me. While I was talking to the sentry, an officer came by and warned me to get away from that corner because the Germans were likely to shell it as it was the only road in the neighbourhood for the passage of troops to and from the front. When Murdoch arrived, I told him I wanted to have breakfast, for I had had nothing to eat since luncheon the day before and had done a lot of walking. He looked surprised and said, "Fancy having breakfast when the town is being shelled." "Well," I said, "don't you know we always read in the papers, when a man is hanged, that before he went out to the gallows he ate a hearty breakfast? There must be some philosophy in it. At any rate, you might as well die on a full stomach as an empty one." So Murdoch began to get breakfast ready in the kitchen, where Mr Vandervyver's maid was already preparing a meal for her master. I shaved and had a good clean up and was sitting in the dining room arranging the many letters and messages which I had received from men who asked me to write to their relatives. Breakfast had just been set on the table when I heard the loudest bang I have ever heard in my life. A seventeen inch shell had fallen in the corner of the garden where the sentry had been standing. The windows of the house were blown in, the ceiling came down and soot from the chimneys was scattered over everything. I suddenly found myself, still in a sitting posture, some feet beyond the chair in which I had been resting. Mr. Vandervyver ran downstairs and out into the street with his toilet so disarranged that he looked as if he were going to take a swim. Murdoch MacDonald disappeared and I did not see him again for several days. A poor old woman in the street had been hit in the head and was being taken off by a neighbour and a man was lying in the road with a broken leg. All my papers were unfortunately lost in the debris of the ceiling. I went upstairs and got a few more of my remaining treasures and came back to the dining room. There I scraped away the dust and found two boiled eggs. I got some biscuits from the sideboard and went and filled my waterbottle with tea in the damaged kitchen. I was just starting out of the door when another shell hit the building on the opposite side of the street. It had been used as a billet by some of our men. The sentry I had been talking to had disappeared and all they could find of him were his boots with his feet in them. In the building opposite, we found a Highlander badly wounded and I got stretcher-bearers to come and carry him off to the 2nd Field Ambulance in the Square nearby. Their headquarters had been moved to Vlamertinghe and they were evacuating that morning. The civilians now had got out of the town. All sorts of carts and wheelbarrows had been called into requisition. There were still some wounded men in the dressing station and a sergeant was in charge. I managed to commandeer a motor ambulance and stow them in it. Shells were falling fast in that part of the town. It was perfectly impossible to linger any longer. A certain old inhabitant, however, would not leave. He said he would trust to the good God and stay in the cellar of his house till the war was over. Poor man, if he did not change his mind, his body must be in the cellar still, for the last time I saw the place, which henceforth was known as "Hell Fire Corner," there was not one stone left upon another. Only a little brick wall remained to show where the garden and house of my landlord had been. I collected the men of the Ambulance and started off with them to Vlamertinghe. On the way we added to our numbers men who had either lost their units or were being sent back from the line.

As we passed through the Grande Place, which now wore a very much more dilapidated appearance than it had three days before, we found a soldier on the pavement completely intoxicated. He was quite unconscious and could not walk. There was nothing to do but to make him as comfortable as possible till he should awake next day to the horrors of the real world. We carried him into a room of a house and laid him on a heap of straw. I undid the collar of his shirt so that he might have full scope for extra blood pressure and left him to his fate. I heard afterwards that the house was struck and that he was wounded and taken away to a place of safety. When we got down to the bridge on the Vlamertinghe road, an Imperial Signal Officer met me in great distress. His men had been putting up telegraph wires on the other side of the canal and a shell had fallen and killed thirteen of them. He asked our men to carry the bodies back over the bridge and lay them side by side in an outhouse. The men did so, and the row of mutilated, twisted and bleeding forms was pitiful to see. The officer was very grateful to us, but the bodies were probably never buried because that part of the city was soon a ruin. We went on down the road towards Vlamertinghe, past the big asylum, so long known as a dressing station, with its wonderful and commodious cellars. It had been hit and the upstairs part was no longer used.

The people along the road were leaving their homes as fast as they could. One little procession will always stand out in my mind. In front one small boy of about six years old was pulling a toy cart in which two younger children were packed. Behind followed the mother with a large bundle on her back. Then came the father with a still bigger one. There they were trudging along, leaving

their home behind with its happy memories, to go forth as penni-
less refugees, compelled to live on the charity of others. It was
through no fault of their own, but only through the monstrous
greed and ambition of a despot crazed with feudal dreams of a
by-gone age. As I looked at that little procession, and at many
other similar ones, the words of the Gospel kept ringing in my ears,
"Inasmuch as ye have done it unto one of the least of these my
brethren, ye have done it unto me." These words I felt sounded the
doom of the Kaiser. Many and many a time when the war from
our point of view has been going badly, and men would ask
me, "How about the war, Sir?" or, "Are we winning the war,
Sir?" I would reply, "Boys, unless the devil has got into heaven
we are going to win. If he has, the German Emperor will have a
good friend there. But he hasn't, and any nation which tramples
on the rights and liberties of humanity, glories in it, makes it a
matter of national boasting, and casts medals to commemorate
the sinking of unprotected ships—any nation which does that is
bound to lose the war, no matter how badly things may look at the
present time." It was nothing but that unflinching faith in the power of right which kept our men so steadfast. Right is after all only
another name for the will of God. Men who knew no theology,
who professed no creed, who even pretended to great indifference
about the venture of eternity, were unalterably fixed in their faith
in the power of right. It gives one a great opportunity of building
the higher edifice of religion when one discovers the rock foundation in a man's convictions.

When we reached Vlamertinghe we found that a school house
had been taken over by the 2nd Field Ambulance.

There was a terrible shortage of stretchers and blankets, as most
of the equipment had been lost at Ypres. All that day and night
the furious battle raged, and many fresh British battalions passed
up to reinforce the line. As soon as it was dark, the wounded began
to come in, and by midnight the schoolhouse was filled to overflowing. The men were lying out in rows on the cold stone
floor with nothing under them. Ambulances were coming and
going as hour after hour passed by. I went among the sufferers,
many of whom I knew. The sergeant would come to me and tell
me where the worst cases were. He whispered to me once, "There
is a dying man over here." We trod softly between the prostrate
forms till we came to one poor fellow who looked up with white

face under the candle light. I saw he was dying. He belonged to one of the British battalions that I had passed on the road. I asked him if he would like to receive the Holy Communion. He was pleased when I told him I could give it to him. He had been a chorister in England, and he felt so far from the ministrations of his church now. He made his confession and I pronounced the absolution. Then I gave him the Blessed Sacrament. Like many severely wounded men, he was not suffering much, but was dying of shock. We were now compelled to use the church and it also soon became a scene of suffering. The building to-day is a ruin, but then it had been untouched by shells and was large and impressive. We had only a few candles with which to light it. The wounded were laid out, some on the floor, some on chairs, and some sat up waiting for the convoys of ambulances that were to take them to the Base. It was a strange scene. In the distance we heard the roar of the battle, and here, in the dim light of the hollow-sounding aisles, were shadowy figures huddled up on chairs or lying on the floor. Once the silence was broken by a loud voice shouting out with startling suddenness, "O God! stop it." I went over to the man. He was a British sergeant. He would not speak, but I think in his terrible suffering he meant the exclamation as a kind of prayer. I thought it might help the men to have a talk with them, so I told them what great things were being done that night and what a noble part they had played in holding back the German advance and how all the world would honour them in after times. Then I said, "Boys, let us have a prayer for our comrades up in that roar of battle at the front. When I say the Lord's Prayer join in with me, but not too loudly as we don't want to disturb those who are trying to sleep." I had a short service and they all joined in the Lord's Prayer. It was most impressive in that large, dim church, to hear the voices, not loudly, but quite distinctly, repeating the words from different parts of the building, for some of the men had gone over to corners where they might be by themselves. After the Lord's Prayer I pronounced the Benediction, and then I said, "Boys, the Curé won't mind your smoking in the church tonight, so I am going to pass round some cigarettes." Luckily I had a box of five hundred which had been sent to me by post. These I handed round and lit them. Voices from different parts would say, "May I have one, Sir?" It was really delightful to feel that a moment's comfort could be given to men in their condition. A man arrived that night with both his eyes gone, and even he asked for a cigarette. I had to put the cigarette into his mouth and light it for him. "It's so dark, Sir," he said, "I can't see." I was not going to tell him he would never see again, so I said, "Your head is all bandaged up. Of course you can't." He was one of the first to be taken off in the ambulance, and I do not know whether he is alive or dead. Our Canadians still held on with grim determination, and they deserved the tribute which Marshal Foch has paid them of saving the day at Ypres.

When they came out of the line, and I was living once again among them, going from battalion to battalion, it was most amusing to hear them tell of all their adventures during the great attack. The English newspapers reached us and they were loud in their praise of "the gallant Canadians." The King, General Joffre, and Sir Robert Borden, sent messages to our troops. One man said, amid the laughter of his comrades, "All I can remember, Sir, was that I was in a blooming old funk for about three days and three nights and now I am told I am a hero. Isn't that fine?" Certainly they deserved all the praise they got. In a battle there is always the mixture of the serious and the comic. One Turco, more gallant than his fellows, refused to leave the line and joined the 16th Battalion. He fought so well that they decided to reward him by turning him into a Highlander. He consented to don the kilt, but would not give up his trousers as they concealed his black legs.

The Second Battle of Ypres was the making of what grew to be the Canadian Corps. Up to that time, Canadians were looked upon, and looked upon themselves, merely as troops that might be expected to hold the line and do useful spade work, but from then onward the men felt they could rise to any emergency, and the army knew they could be depended upon. The pace then set was followed by the other divisions and, at the end, the Corps did not disappoint the expectations of General Foch. What higher praise could be desired?

My billet in Vlamertinghe was in a neat little cottage owned by an old maid, who took great pride in making everything shine. The paymaster of one of our battalions and I had a cheerful home there when the poor old lady fled. Her home however did not long survive her absence, for, some days after she left, it was levelled by a shell. The church too was struck and ruined. Beside it is the military cemetery within which lie the mortal remains of many gallant men, amongst them the two Grenfells, one of whom got the V. C. There I buried poor Duffy and many more. The other chaplains laid to rest men under their care.

One picture always comes to my mind when I think of Vlamertinghe. In the road near the church was a Crucifix. The figure was life size and hung on a cross planted upon a rocky mound. One night when the sun had set and a great red glow burnt along the horizon, I saw the large black cross silhouetted against the crimson sky, and before it knelt an aged woman with grey hair falling from beneath the kerchief that was tied about her head. It was dangerous at all times to stay at that place, yet she knelt there silently in prayer. She seemed to be the embodiment of the old life and quiet contented religious hope which must have been the spirit of Vlamertinghe in the past. The village was an absolute ruin a few days later, and even the Sisters had to flee from their convent. The Crucifix, however, stood for a long time after the place was destroyed, but I never passed by without thinking of the poor old woman who knelt at its foot in the evening light and laid her burden of cares upon the heart of Eternal Pity.

CHAPTER VII.

Festubert and Givenchy

May and June, 1915.

W HEN our men came out of the line, the 2nd Field Ambulance was ordered back for rest and reorganization to a village called Ouderdom, three miles to the Southwest, and their O.C. invited me to follow them. It was late in the evening when I started to walk. The light was fading and, as I had no map, I was not certain where Ouderdom was. I went down the road, delighting in the sweet smells of nature. It was with a sense of unusual freedom that I walked along with all my worldly possessions in my haversack. I thought how convenient it was to lose one's kit. Now I could lie down beside any haystack and feel quite at home. The evening air grew chillier and I thought I had better get some roof over my head for the night. I asked various men that I met where Ouderdom was. None of them knew. I was forced once again to take my solitary journey into the great unknown. It was therefore with much satisfaction that, when quite dark, I came upon some wooden huts and saw a number of men round a little fire in a field. I went up to one of the huts and found in it a very kind and courteous middle-aged lieutenant, who was in charge of a detachment of Indian troops. When he heard I was looking for the Field Ambulance and going towards Ouderdom, he told me it was much too late to continue my journey that night. "You stay with me in my hut, Padré," he said, "and in the morning I will give you a horse to take you to your men." He told me that he had been living by himself and was only too delighted to have a companion to talk to. He treated me as bounteously as circumstances would permit, and after a good dinner, he gave me a blanket and straw bed on the floor of his hut. It was very pleasant to come out of the darkness and loneliness of the road and find such a kind host, and such good hospitality. We discussed many things that night, and the next day I was shown over the camp. Later on, the Lieutenant sent me on horseback to Ouderdom. There I found the Ambulance encamped in a pleasant field beside a large pond, which afforded us the luxury of a bath. I shall never forget those two restful days I spent at Ouderdom.

I blamed the blankets, however, for causing an irritation of the
skin, which lasted till I was able to have another wash and change.

Pleasant as my life was with the Ambulance, I felt I ought to
go back and join my Brigade. I got a ride to the transport at
Brielen, and there, under a waggon cover, had a very happy home.
Near us an Imperial battery fired almost incessantly all night long.
While lying awake one night thinking of the men that had gone,
and wondering what those ardent spirits were now doing, the
lines came to me which were afterwards published in " The
Times";

"REQUIESCANT"

In lonely watches night by night,
Great visions burst upon my sight,
For down the stretches of the sky
The hosts of dead go marching by.

Strange ghostly banners o'er them float,
Strange bugles sound an awful note,
And all their faces and their eyes
Are lit with starlight from the skies.

The anguish and the pain have passed,
And peace hath come to them at last.
But in the stern looks linger still
The iron purpose and the will.

Dear Christ, who reign'st above the flood
Of human tears and human blood,
A weary road these men have trod,
O house them in the home of God.

The Quartermaster of the 3rd Brigade furnished me with a
change of underwear, for which I was most grateful. I felt quite
proud of having some extra clothes again. The battalions were
moved at last out of the area and we were ordered off to rest. Our
first stop was near Vlamertinghe. We reached it in the afternoon,
and, chilly though it was, I determined to have a bath. Murdoch
MacDonald got a bucket of water from a green and slimy pond
and put it on the other side of a hedge, and there I retired to have
a wash and change. I was just in the midst of the process when,
to my confusion, the Germans began to shell the adjoining field,
and splinters of shell fell in the hedge behind me. The transport

men on the other side called out to me to run and take cover with them under the waggons. "I can't, boys", I replied, "I have got no clothes on." They roared with laughter at my plight. Though clothes are not at all an impregnable armour, somehow or other you feel safer when you are dressed. There was nothing for it but to complete my ablutions, which I did so effectually in the cold spring air that I got a chill. That night I was racked with pains as I rode on the horse which the M. O. lent me, on our march to Bailleul.

We arrived in the quaint old town about two in the morning, and I made my way in the dark to the hotel in the Square. I was refused admission on the reasonable plea that every bed was already occupied. I was just turning away, wondering where I could go, for I was hardly able to stand up, when an officer came out and said I might go up to a room on the top storey and get into his bed as he would need it no more. It was quite delightful, not only to find a bed, but one which had been so nicely and wholesomely warmed. I spent a most uncomfortable night, and in the morning I wondered if my batman would find out where I was and come and look after me. About ten o'clock I heard a knock at the door and called out "Come in." To my astonishment, a very smart staff officer, with a brass hat and red badges, made his way into my room, and startled me by saying, "I am the Deputy-Judge-Advocate-General." "Oh", I said, "I was hoping you were my batman." He laughed at that and told me his business. There had been a report that one of our Highlanders had been crucified on the door of a barn. The Roman Catholic Chaplain of the 3rd Brigade and myself had tried to trace the story to its origin. We found that the nearest we could get to it was, that someone had told somebody else about it. One day I managed to discover a Canadian soldier who said he had seen the crucifixion himself. I at once took some paper out of my pocket and a New Testament and told him, "I want you to make that statement on oath and put your signature to it." He said, "It is not necessary." But he had been talking so much about the matter to the men around him that he could not escape. I had kept his sworn testimony in my pocket and it was to obtain this that the Deputy-Judge-Advocate-General had called upon me. I gave it to him and told him that in spite of the oath, I thought the man was not telling the truth. Weeks afterwards I got a letter from the Deputy-Judge telling me he had found the man, who, when confronted by a staff officer, weakened, and said he was mistaken in swearing that he had seen the crucifixion he had only been told about it by someone else. We have no right to charge the Germans with the crime. They have done so many things equally bad, that we do not need to bring charges against them of which we are not quite sure.

The Brigade was quartered in the little village of Steenje. It was a pretty place, and it was delightful to be back in the peaceful country again. May was bringing out the spring flowers and the trees wore fresh green leaves. There was something about the exhilarating life we were leading which made one extremely sensitive to the beauties of nature. I have never cared much for flowers, except in a general way. But now I noticed a great change. A wild flower growing in a ditch by the wayside seemed to me to be almost a living thing, and spoke in its mute way of its life of peace and contentment, and mocked, by its very humility, the world of men which was so full of noise and death. Colour too made a most powerful appeal to the heart. The gleam of sunlight on the moss that covered an old thatched roof gave one a thrill of gladness. The world of nature putting on its fresh spring dress had its message to hearts that were lonely and anxious, and it was a message of calm courage and hope. In Julian Grenfell's beautiful poem "Into Battle," he notes this message of the field and trees. Everything in nature spoke to the fighting man and gave him its own word of cheer.

Of course all the men did not show they were conscious of these emotional suggestions, but I think they felt them nevertheless. The green fields and shining waters around Steenje had a very soothing effect upon minds that had passed through the bitterest ordeal in their life's experience. I remember one morning having a service of Holy Communion in the open air. Everything was wonderful and beautiful. The golden sunlight was streaming across the earth in full radiance. The trees were fresh and green, and hedges marked out the field with walls of living beauty. The grass in the meadow was soft and velvety, and, just behind the spot where I had placed the altar, a silver stream wandered slowly by. When one adds to such a scene, the faces of a group of earnest, well-made and heroic young men, it is easily understood that the beauty of the service was complete. When it was over, I reminded them of the twenty-third Psalm, "He maketh me to lie down in green pastures; He leadeth me beside the still waters." There too was the table prepared before us in the presence of our enemies.

At Steenje, as no billet had been provided for me, the Engineers took me in and treated me right royally. Not only did they give me a pile of straw for a bed in the dormitory upstairs, but they also made me an honorary member of their mess. Of the work of the "Sappers", in the Great War, one cannot speak too highly. Brave and efficient, they were always working and co-operating enthusiastically with the infantry. Every week now that passed was deepening that sense of comradeship which bound our force together. The mean people, the men who thought only of themselves, were either being weeded out or taught that there was no place for selfishness in the army. One great lesson was impressed upon me in the war, and that is, how wonderfully the official repression of wrong thoughts and jealousies tends to their abolition. A man who lets his wild fancies free, and gives rein to his anger and selfishness, is going to become the victim of his own mind. If people at home could only be prevented, as men were in the war, from saying all the bitter and angry things they feel, and from criticising the actions of their neighbours, a different temper of thought would prevail. The comradeship men experienced in the Great War was due to the fact that everyone knew comradeship was essential to our happiness and success. It would be well if all over Canada men realized that the same is true of our happiness and success in times of peace. What might we not accomplish if our national and industrial life were full of mutual sympathy and love!

Our rest at Steenje was not of long duration. Further South another attack was to be made and so one evening, going in the direction whither our troops were ordered, I was motored to the little village of Robecq. There I managed to get a comfortable billet for myself in the house of a carpenter. My bedroom was a tiny compartment which looked out on the backyard. It was quite delightful to lie in a real bed again and as I was enjoying the luxury late in the morning I watched the carpenter making a baby's coffin. Robecq then was a very charming place. The canal, on which was a hospital barge, gave the men an opportunity for a swim, and the spring air and the sunshine put them in high spirits.

It was at Robecq, that I had my first sight of General Haig. I was standing in the Square one afternoon when I saw the men on the opposite side spring suddenly to attention. I felt that something was going to happen. To my astonishment, I saw a man ride up carrying a flag on a lance. He was followed by several other mounted men. It was so like a pageant that I said to myself, "Hello, here comes Joan of Arc." Then a general appeared with his brilliant staff. The General advanced and we all saluted, but he, spying my chaplain's collar, rode over to me and shook hands and asked if I had come over with the Canadians. I told him I had. Then he said, "I am so glad you have all come into my Army." I did not know who he was or what army we were in, or in fact what the phrase meant, but I thought it was wise to say nice things to a general, so I told him we were all very glad too. He seemed gratified and rode off in all the pomp and circumstance of war. I heard afterwards that he was General Haig, who at that time commanded the First Army. He had from the start, the respect of all in the British Expeditionary Force.

A sudden call "to stand to", however, reminded us that the war was not yet won. The Brigadier told me that we had to move the next morning at five. Then he asked me how I was going and I quoted my favourite text, "The Lord will provide." My breakfast at 3.30 next morning consisted of a tin of green peas without bread or other adulterations and a cup of coffee. At five a. m. I started to walk, but it was not long before I was overtaken by the car of an artillery officer, and carried, in great glory, past the General and his staff, whose horses we nearly pushed into the ditch on the narrow road. The Brigadier waved his hand and congratulated me upon the way in which Providence was looking after me. That afternoon our brigade was settled in reserve trenches at Lacouture. There were a number of Ghurka regiments in the neighbourhood, as well as some Guards battalions. I had a service for the bomb-throwers in a little orchard that evening, and I found a billet with the officers of the unit in a particularly small and dirty house by the wayside.

Some of us lay on the floor and I made my bed on three chairs— a style of bed which I said I would patent on my return to Canada. The chairs, with the middle one facing in the opposite direction to prevent one rolling off, were placed at certain distances where the body needed special support, and made a very comfortable resting place, free from those inhabitants which infested the ordinary places of repose. Of course we did not sleep much, and somebody, amid roars of laughter called for breakfast about two-thirty a. m. The cook who was sleeping in the same room got up and prepared bacon and coffee, and we had quite an enjoyable meal, which did not prevent our having a later one about nine a. m., after which, I beguiled the time by reading aloud Leacock's "Arcadian Adventures with the Idle Rich." Later in the day, I marched off with our men who were going into the trenches, for the battle of Festubert. We passed the place called Indian Village and went to the trenches just beyond.

We met a bearer-party bringing out a young German prisoner who was badly wounded. I went over to him and offered him a cigarette. This he declined, but asked for some water, putting out his dry tongue to show how parched it was. I called to some of our men to know if they could spare him a drink. Several gladly ran across and offered their water-bottles. They were always kind to wounded prisoners. "If thine enemy thirst give him drink." Just before the men went into the trenches, I shook hands with one or two and then, as they passed up, half the battalion shook hands with me. I was glad they did, but at the same time I felt then that it was not wise for a chaplain to do anything which looked as if he were taking matters too seriously. It was the duty of everyone to forget private feelings in the one absorbing desire to kill off the enemy. I saw the different battalions going up and was returning towards headquarters when whom should I meet but the dreaded Brigadier coming up the road with his staff. It was impossible to dodge him; I could see already that he was making towards me. When he came up to me, he asked me what I was doing there, and ordered me back to Headquarters on pain of a speedy return to No. 2 General Hospital. "If you come east of my Headquarters," he said, "you will be sent back absolutely certainly." That night I took my revenge by sleeping in his deserted bed, and found it very comfortable.

Our Brigade Headquarters were at Le Touret in a large farm surrounded by a moat. We were quite happy, but on the next day, which I spent in censoring the letters of the 13th Battalion, I was told that the 2nd Brigade were coming to occupy the billet and that I had to get out and forage for myself. At half past six in the evening I saw from my window the giant form of General Currie followed by his staff, riding across the bridge over the moat. He looked very imposing, but I knew it meant that the bed I had slept in was no longer mine. I called my friend Murdoch MacDonald and I got him to pack my haversack. "Murdoch", I said, "once more we have to face the big, black world alone, but—'the Lord will provide'". The sun had set, the air was cool and scented richly with the fermented manure spread upon the land. Many units were scattered through the fields. We went from one place to another, but alas there was no billet for us. It was tiring work, and both Murdoch and I were getting very hungry and also very grumpy. The prospect of sleeping under the stars in the chilly night was not pleasant. I am ashamed to say my faith began to waver, and I said to Murdoch MacDonald, "Murdoch, my friend, the Lord is a long time providing for us tonight." We made our way back to the main road and there I saw an Imperial Officer who was acting as a point man and directing traffic. I told him my difficulty and implored him, as it was now getting on towards eleven p. m., to tell me where I could get a lodging for the night. He thought for a while and then said, "I think you may find a bed for yourself and your man in the prison." The words had an ominous sound, but I remembered how often people at home found refuge for the night in the police station. He told me to go down the road to the third farmhouse, where I should find the quarters of some Highland officers and men. The farm was called the prison, because it was the place in which captured Germans were to be held until they were sent down the line. Followed by Murdoch, I made my way again down the busy road now crowded with transports, troops and ambulances. It was hard to dodge them in the mud and dark. I found the farmhouse, passed the sentry, and was admitted to the presence of two young officers of the Glasgow Highlanders. I told them who I was and how I had been bidden by the patrol officer to seek refuge with them. They received me most cordially and told me they had a spare heap of straw in the room. They not only said they would arrange for me for the night, but they called their servant and told him to get me some supper. They said I looked worn out. A good dish of ham and eggs and a cup of strong tea at that time were most refreshing and when I had finished eating, seeing a copy of the Oxford Book of Verse on the table, I began to read it to them, and finally, and quite naturally, found myself later on, about one a. m., reciting my own poems. It was most interesting meeting another set of men. The barn, which was kept as a prison for Germans was large and commodious.

6

As we took only five or six prisoners at that time, it was more than
sufficient for the purpose. The officers told me that the reason why
so few prisoners turned up was that the Canadians got tired of
their charges before they arrived at the prison, and only handed
over a few as souvenirs. I really think the Scotsmen believed
it. The Glasgow men moved away and were succeeded by a company of Argyle and Sutherland Highlanders. The tables were now
turned, for as I had kept on inhabiting the large room with the
three heaps of straw in it, the two officers who came "to take over"
asked my permission to make their billet in the prison.

In the meantime, the fighting in the trenches was very fierce.
I spent my days in parish visiting and my nights at the various
dressing stations. The batteries of artillery were all round us
in the fields and orchards, and there was great concentration of
British and Canadian guns. In spite of the brigadier's orders, I
often went east of Headquarters. One lovely Sunday evening
I had a late service for men of the 16th Battalion in an orchard.
They were going off later into No Man's Land on a working party.
The service, which was a voluntary one, had therefore an underlying pathos in it. Shells were falling in the fields on both sides of
us. The great red sunset glowed in the west and the trees overhead cast an artistic gray green light upon the scene. The men
were facing the sunset, and I told them as usual that there lay Canada. The last hymn was "Abide with Me", and the words, "Hold
Thou Thy Cross before my closing eyes", were peculiarly touching
in view of the fact that the working party was to start as soon as
the service was ended. At Festubert our Cavalry Brigade, now
deprived of their horses, joined us, and I remember one morning
seeing Colonel, now General, Macdonell, coming out of the line
at the head of his men. They were few in number and were very
tired, for they had had a hard time and had lost many of their comrades. The Colonel, however, told them to whistle and keep step
to the tune, which they were doing with a gallantry which showed
that, in spite of the loss of their horses, the spirit of the old squadron was still undaunted.

Our batteries round Le Touret were very heavily and systemat-
ically shelled, and of course rumour had it that there were spies in
the neighborhood. The French Police were searching for Germans in British uniforms, and everyone felt that some of the inhabitants might be housing emissaries from the German lines.

FESTUBERT AND GIVENCHY

Some said lights were seen flashing from farmhouses; others a-verred that the French peasants signalled to the enemy by the way they ploughed their fields and by the colour of the horses used. In Belgium we were told that the arrangement of the arms of wind-mills gave away the location of our troops. At any rate everyone had a bad attack of spy-fever, and I did not escape it. One night about half past ten I was going down a dark road to get my letters from the post office, when an officer on a bicycle came up to me and, dismounting, asked me where a certain British Artillery Brigade was. I was not concerned with the number of the brigade, but I was horrified to hear the officer pronounce his "rs" in the back of his throat. Of course, when we are not at war with Germany, a man may pronounce his "rs" however he pleases, but when we are at war with the great guttural hordes of Teutons it is different. The moment I heard the sepulchral "r" I said, "This man is a Ger-man". He told me he had come from the Indian Army and had a message for the artillery brigade. I took him by subtlety, think-ing all was fair in war, and I asked him to come with me. I made for the billet of our signallers and told the sentry that the officer wanted a British brigade. At the same time I whispered to the man to call out the guard, because I thought the stranger was a spy.

The sentry went into the house, and in a few seconds eager Cana-dians with fixed bayonets came out of the building and surrounded the unfortunate officer. Canadians were always ready for a bit of sport. When I saw my man surrounded, I asked him for his pass. He appeared very much confused and said he had none, but had come from the Indian Army. What made us all the more suspic-ious was the fact that he displayed a squared map as an evidence of his official character. I told him that anybody could get a squar-ed map. "Do you take me for a spy?" he said. I replied gently that we did, and that he would have to come to Headquarters and be identified. He had an ugly looking revolver in his belt, but he submitted very tamely to his temporary arrest. I was taking him off to our Headquarters, where strange officers were often brought for purposes of identification, when a young Highland Captain of diminutive stature, but unbounded dignity, appeared on the scene with four patrol men. He told me that as he was patrolling the roads for the capture of spies, he would take over the custody of my victim. The Canadians were loath to lose their prey. So we all followed down the road. After going a short distance, the signallers had to return to their quarters, much to my regret, for it seemed to me that the safety of the whole British Army depended on our capturing the spy, and I knew I could depend upon the Canadians. However I made up my mind that I would follow to the bitter end.

The Highlander put the officer between us and, followed by the four patrol men, we went off down a lonely road. The moon had now risen. After walking about half a mile we came to a large barn, outside of which stood a sentry. It was the billet of a battalion of Highlanders. I told the man privately, that we had arrested the officer under suspicion of his being a spy, and if the sentry on duty should see him coming back along the road, he was to detain him and have him identified. As we walked along, a number of men who had been concealed in the ditches on each side of the road rose up and followed us. They were men of the patrol commanded by the young Highlander on the other side of our prisoner. It was a delightfully weird experience. There was the long quiet moonlit road and the desolate fields all around us. While I was talking to one of the men, the patrol officer, unknown to me, allowed the spy to go off on his wheel, and to my astonishment when I turned I saw him going off down the road as hard as he could. I asked the officer why he had let him go. He said he thought it was all right and the man would be looked after. Saying this, he called his patrol about him and marched back again. The thing made me very angry. It seemed to me that the whole war might depend on our capturing the spy. At least, I owed it to the British Army to do my best to be certain the man was all right before I let him go. So I continued to follow him by myself down the road. The next farm I came to was about a mile off. There I was halted by a sentry, and on telling my business I was shown into a large barn, where the sergeant-major of a Scottish battalion got out of the straw and came to talk to me. He told me that an officer riding a wheel had passed sometime before, asking his way to a certain artillery brigade. I told the sergeant-major my suspicions and while we were talking, to our astonishment, the sentry announced that the officer, accompanied by a Black Watch despatch rider, had turned up again, having heard that the brigade he wanted was in the other direction.

The sergeant and I went out and challenged him and said that he had to come to the colonel and be identified. The colonel was in the back room of a little cottage on the other side of the road. I made my way through the garden and entered the house. The col-

onel, an oldish man, was sitting at a table. In front of him was
an empty glass and an empty whisky bottle. It struck me from
a superficial glance that the colonel was the only full thing in the
room. He seemed surprised at having so late a visitor. I told him
my suspicions. "Show the man in, Padré," he said, and I did.
The spy seemed worried and excited and his "rs" were more guttural than ever. The old Colonel, who had himself been in India,
at once put the suspect through his facings in Hindustani. Then
the Colonel came out to me, and taking me aside said, "It's all right,
Padré, he can talk Hindustani. I never met a German who could
do that." Though still not quite satisfied, I said "Good night," and
went out into the garden to return home. Immediately the young
despatch rider came up to me and said, "Who are you, who are
stopping a British officer in the performance of his duty? I arrest
you. You must come in to the Colonel and be identified." This
was a turning of the tables with a vengeance, and as I had recently laid stress on its being the duty of every officer to prove his
identity whenever called upon, I had nothing to do but to go back
into the presence of the Colonel and be questioned. I noticed this
time that a full bottle of whiskey and another tumbler had been provided for the entertainment of the Indian Officer. The despatch
rider saluted the Colonel and said, "I have brought in this officer,
Sir, to be identified. He says he is a Canadian chaplain but I
should like to make sure on the point." I stood there feeling rather disconcerted. The Colonel called to his adjutant who was sleeping in a bed in the next room. He came out in a not very agree-
able frame of mind and began to ask me who I was. I immediately told my name, showed my identification disc and engraved silver cigarette case and some cablegrams that I had just received
from home. The Colonel looked up with bleary eyes and said,
"Shall I put him in the guard-room?" but the adjutant had been
convinced by my papers that I was innocent and he said, "I think
we can let him go, Sir." It was a great relief to me, because
guard-rooms were not very clean. I was just making my way
from the garden when out came the young despatch rider. I
bore him no malice for his patriotic zeal. I felt that his heart was
in the right place, so I said to him, "You have taken the part of
:. .a officer, and now that you are sure I am all right,
may I ask you what you know about him?" "I don't know anything", he said, "only that I met him and he asked me the way to

the Brigade, and as I was going there myself I told him I would act as his guide." "Well", I said, "we are told that there are spies in the neighborhood reporting the location of our batteries to the Germans, so we ought to be very careful how we give these locations away." "I tell you what, Sir," he replied, "I'll go and examine his wheel and see what the make is; I know a good deal about the wheels used in the army." We went over to the wheel and by the aid of my flashlight he examined it thoroughly and then said, "This is not an English wheel, I have never seen one like it before. This wheel was never in use in our army." The despatch rider now got an attack of spy-fever. It was decided that he should ride on to the Brigade Headquarters and find out if an Indian officer was expected there. He promised to come back as soon as possible and meet me in the road. We trusted that the bottle of whiskey in the Colonel's billet would cause sufficient delay for this to be accomplished. The night was cool and beautiful and the sense of an adventure added charm to the situation. I had not gone far down the road when to my horror I heard a wheel coming behind me, and turning, I saw my spy coming towards me as fast as he could. I was not of course going to let him get past. The added information as to the character of the wheel gave me even greater determination to see that everything was done to protect the army from the machinations of a German spy.

I stood in the road and stopped the wheel. The poor man had to dismount and walk beside me. I wished to delay him long enough for the despatch rider to return with his message from the Brigade. Our conversation was a trifle forced, and I remember thinking that if my friend was really a British officer he would not have submitted quite so tamely to the interference of a Padré. Then I looked at the revolver in his belt, and I thought that, if, on the other hand, he was a German spy he would probably use his weapon in that lonely road and get rid of the man who was impeding his movements. We went on till we came to the sentry whom I had warned at first. At once, we were challenged, "Halt, who are you?" and the suspected spy replied "Indian Army." But the sentry was not satisfied, and to my delight he said, "You will both have to come in and be identified". We were taken into the guard-room and told that we should have to stay there for the night. My friend got very restless and said it was too bad to be held up like this. I looked anxiously down the road to see if there were any signs of the returning despatch rider. The sentries were obdurate and said they woudn't let us go till we could be identified in the morning. Then the officer requested that he might be sent to the Brigade under escort. The sergeant asked me if that would meet with my approval. I said, "Certainly", and so, turning out three members of the guard with fixed bayonets, they marched us off towards the Brigade. The spy had a man with a fixed bayonet on each side of him: they gave me only one. I felt that this was a slight upon my manhood, and asked why they did not put a soldier on each side of me too, as I was as good a man as the other. It was a queer procession in the moonlight. At last we came to the orchard in which stood the billet of the General commanding the Artillery Brigade. I was delighted to find that some Canadian Batteries were there, and told the men what my mission was. They instantly, as true Canadians, became fired with interest and spy-fever. When we got to the house I asked to see the General. He was asleep in a little room off the kitchen. I was shown in, and he lit a candle and proceeded to get up. I had never seen a general in bed before, so was much interested in discovering what he looked like and how he was dressed. I found that a general in war time goes to bed in his underclothes, like an ordinary private. The General got up and went outside and put the spy through a series of questions, but he did so in a very sleepy voice, and with a perfunctory manner which seemed to me to indicate that he was more concerned about getting back to bed than he was in saving the army from danger. He told the officer that it was too late then to carry on the business for which he had come, but that he would see about it in the morning. The spy with a guttural voice then said, "I suppose I may go, Sir?" and the General said, "Certainly." Quickly as possible, fearing a further arrest, the stranger went out, took his wheel, and sped down the road. When I went into the garden, I found a number of men from one of our ambulances. They had turned up with stolen rifles and were waiting with the keenest delight to join in "Canon Scott's spy hunt." Imagine therefore, their disappointment when the officer came out a free man, answered the sentry's challenge on the road, and disappeared in the distance.

On the following day, the French military police came to my billet and asked for particulars about the Indian officer. They told Murdoch MacDonald that they were on the lookout for a German spy who was reported to be going about through our lines dressed in a British uniform. He had been seen at an observation post, and was making enquiries which aroused suspicions. This of course made me more sorry than ever that I had allowed the spy to get through my fingers. Like the man the French police were after, the officer was fair, had a light moustache and was of good size and heavily built.

My adventures with my friend did not end there. When we had left Festubert and got to the neighbourhood of Bethune, I took two young privates one day to have lunch with me in a French hotel near the Square. We were just beginning our meal when to my astonishment the suspected spy, accompanied by a French interpreter, sat down at an opposite table. He looked towards me but made no sign of recognition—a circumstance which I regarded as being decidedly suspicious. I naturally did not look for any demonstration of affection from him, but I thought he might have shown, if he were an honest man, that he remembered one who had caused him so much inconvenience. Once more the call of duty came to my soul. I felt that this man had dodged the British authorities and was now giving his information to a French interpreter to transmit it at the earliest possible moment to the Germans. I told my young friends to carry on as if nothing had happened, and excusing myself, said I would come back in a few minutes. I went out and inquired my way to the Town Major's office. There, I stated the object of my journey and asked for two policemen to come back with me and mount guard till I identified a suspicious looking officer. I then returned and finished my lunch. When the officer and the interpreter at the conclusion of their meal went out into the passage, I followed them and asked for their identification. The officer made no attempt to disguise or check his temper. He said that there must be an end to this sort of work. But the arrival of the two policemen in the passage showed that he had to do what I asked him. This he did, and the interpreter also, and the police took their names and addresses. Then I let my friends go, and heard them depart into the street hurling denunciations and threats of vengeance upon my devoted and loyal head.

It was about a week or ten days afterwards that I was called into our own Brigadier's office. He held a bundle of letters in his hand stamped with all sorts of official seals. The gist of it all was that the G.O.C. of the Indian Division in France had reported to

FESTUBERT AND GIVENCHY

General Alderson the extraordinary and eccentric conduct of a Canadian Chaplain, who persisted in arresting a certain British officer whenever they happened to meet. He wound up with this cutting comment, "The conduct of this chaplain seems to fit him rather for a lunatic asylum than for the theatre of a great war." Of course explanations were sent back. It was explained to the General that reports had reached us of the presence in our lines of a German spy in British uniform, who from the description given, resembled the Indian officer in all particulars.

It is needless to say that every one was immensely amused at "the Canon's spy story," and I mentally resolved that I would be more careful in the future about being carried away by my suspicions. I told people however that I would rather run the risk of being laughed at over making a mistake than to let one real spy escape.

Festubert made a heavy toll upon our numbers, and we were not sorry when we were ordered out of the line and found ourselves quartered in the neighbourhood of Bethune. Bethune at that time was a delightful place. It was full of people. The shops were well provided with articles for sale, and a restaurant in the quaint Grande Place, with its Spanish tower and Spanish houses, was the common meeting ground of friends. The gardens behind private residences brought back memories of pre-war days. The church was a beautiful one, built in the 16th century. The colours of the windows were especially rich. It was always delightful to enter it and think how it had stood the shock and turmoil of the centuries.

One day when I was there the organ was being played most beautifully. Sitting next to me in a pew, was a Canadian Highlander clad in a very dirty uniform. He told me that a friend of his had been killed beside him drenching him in blood. The Highlander was the grandson of a British Prime Minister. We listened to the music till the recital was over, and then I went up to the gallery and made myself known to the organist. He was a delicate young fellow, quite blind, and was in a state of nervous excitement over his recent efforts. I made a bargain with him to give us a recital on the following evening. At the time appointed, therefore, I brought some of our men with me. The young organist met us at the church and I led him over to a monastery in which a British ambulance was making its headquarters. There, in the chapel, the blind man poured out his soul in the strains of a most beautiful instrument. We sat entranced in the evening light. He transported us into another world. We forgot the shells, the mud, the darkness, the wounded men, the lonely graves, and the hideous fact of war. We wandered free and unanxious down the avenues of thought and emotion which were opened up before us by the genius of him whose eyes were shut to this world. It was with deep regret that, when the concert was over, we heard him close the keyboard. Three years later the organist was killed by a shell while he was sitting at his post in the church he loved so well and had never seen.

When we were at Bethune a very important event in my military career took place. In answer to repeated requests, Headquarters procured me a horse. I am told that the one sent to me came by mistake and was not that which they intended me to have. The one I was to have, I heard, was the traditional padré's horse, heavy, slow, unemotional, and with knees ready at all times to sink in prayer. The animal sent to me, however, was a high-spirited chestnut thoroughbred, very pretty, very lively and neck-reined. It had once belonged to an Indian general, and was partly Arab. Poor Dandy was my constant companion to the end. After the Armistice, to prevent his being sold to the Belgian army, he was mercifully shot, by the orders of our A.D.V.S. Dandy certainly was a beauty, and his lively disposition made him interesting to ride. I was able now to do much more parish visiting, and I was rather amused at the way in which my mount was inspected by the different grooms in our units. I had to stand the fire of much criticism. Evil and covetous eyes were set upon Dandy. I was told he was "gone" in the knees. I was told he had a hump on the back—he had what is known as the "Jumper's bump." Men tickled his back and, because he wriggled, told me he was "gone" in the kidneys. I was told he was no proper horse for a padré, but that a fair exchange was always open to me. I was offered many an old transport hack for Dandy, and once was even asked if I would change him for a pair of mules. I took all the criticisms under consideration, and then when they were repeated I told the men that really I loved to ride a horse with a hump on its back. It was so biblical, just like riding a camel. As for bad kidneys, both Dandy and I were teetotallers and we could arrest disease by our temperance habits. The weakness of knees too was no objection in my eyes. In fact, I had so long, as a parson, sat over weak-kneed congregations that I felt quite at home sitting on a weak-kneed horse.

90

FESTUBERT AND GIVENCHY

Poor dear old Dandy, many were the rides we had together. Many were the jumps we took. Many were the ditches we tumbled into. Many were the unseen barbed wires and over-hanging telephone wires which we broke, you with your chest and I with my nose and forehead. Many were the risks we ran in front of batteries in action which neither of us had observed till we found ourselves deafened with a hideous explosion and wrapped in flame. I loved you dearly, Dandy, and I wish I could pull down your soft face towards mine once again, and talk of the times when you took me down Hill 63 and along Hyde Park corner at Ploegsteert. Had I not been wounded and sent back to England at the end of the war, I would have brought you home with me to show to my family— a friend that not merely uncomplainingly but cheerfully, with prancing feet and arching neck and well groomed skin, bore me safely through dangers and darkness, on crowded roads and untracked fields. What dances we have had together, Dandy, when I have got the bands to play a waltz and you have gone through the twists and turns of a performance in which you took an evident delight! I used to tell the men that Dandy and I always came home together. Sometimes I was on his back and sometimes he was on mine, but we always came home together.

A few days later my establishment was increased by the purchase of a well-bred little white fox-terrier. He rejoiced in the name of Philo and became my inseparable companion. The men called him my curate. Dandy, Philo and I made a family party which was bound together by very close ties of affection. Though none of us could speak the language of the others, yet the sympathy of each enabled us to understand and appreciate one another's opinions. I always knew what Dandy thought and what he would do. I always knew too what Philo was thinking about. Philo had a great horror of shells. I put this down to the fact that he was born at Beuvry, a place which had been long under shell-fire. When he heard a shell coming in his direction, Philo used to go to the door of the dugout and listen for the explosion, and then come back to me in a state of whining terror. He could not even stand the sound of our own guns. It made him run round and round barking and howling furiously.

It was while we were out in rest at Bethune that I was told I could go on a week's leave to London. I was glad of this, not only for the change of scene, but for the sake of getting new clothes. I awoke in the early morning and listened to the French guns pounding away wearily near Souchez. At noon I started with a staff officer in a motor for Boulogne. It was a lovely day, and as we sped down the road through little white unspoilt villages and saw peaceful fields once again, it seemed as if I were waking from a hideous dream. That evening we pulled in to Victoria Station, and heard the Westminster chimes ringing out half past eight.

CHAPTER VIII.

Ploegsteert—A Lull in Operations

July to December, 1915

LEAVE in London during the war never appealed to me. I always felt like a fish out of water. When I went to concerts and theatres, all the time amid the artistic gaiety of the scene I kept thinking of the men in the trenches, their lonely vigils, their dangerous working parties, and the cold rain and mud in which their lives were passed. And I thought too of the wonderful patrol kept up on the dark seas, by heroic and suffering men who guarded the life and liberty of Britain. The gaiety seemed to be a hollow mockery. I was not sorry therefore when my week's leave was over and I went back to the line. A staff officer whom I met on the leave boat informed me that the Division had changed its trenches, and my Brigade had left Bethune. We had a most wonderful run in the staff car from Boulogne, and in two hours arrived at the Brigade Headquarters at Steenje, near Bailleul. There, with my haversacks, I was left by the staff car at midnight and had to find a lodging place. The only light I saw was in the upper windows of the Curé's house, the rest of the village was in complete darkness. I knocked on the door and, after a few minutes, the head and shoulders of a man in pyjamas looked out from the window and asked me who I was and what I wanted. On my giving my name and requesting admission, he very kindly came down and let me in and gave me a bed on the floor. On a mattress beside me was a young officer of the Alberta Dragoons, only nineteen years of age. He afterwards joined the Flying Corps and met his death by jumping out of his machine at an altitude of six thousand feet, when it was hit and burst into flames. The Alberta Dragoons later on became the Canadian Light Horse, and were Corps Troops. At that time, they were part of the 1st Division and were a magnificent body. The practical elimination of cavalry in modern warfare has taken all the romance and chivalry out of fighting. It is just as well however for the world that the old feudal conception of war has passed away. The army will be looked upon in the future as a class of citizens who are performing the necessary and unpleasant task of policing the world, in order that the rational occupations of human life may be carried on without interruption.

Brigade Headquarters now moved to a large farm behind the trenches at Ploegsteert. I bid farewell to my friends of the Alberta Dragoons and found a billet at La Crêche. From thence I moved to Romarin and made my home in a very dirty little French farmhouse. The Roman Catholic chaplain and I had each a heap of straw in an outhouse which was a kind of general workroom. At one end stood a large churn, which was operated, when necessary, by a trained dog, which was kept at other times in a cage. The churn was the breeding place of innumerable blue-bottles, who in spite of its savoury attractions annoyed us very much by alighting on our food and on our faces. I used to say to my friend, the chaplain, when at night we had retired to our straw beds and were reading by the light of candles stuck on bully beef tins, that the lion and the lamb were lying down together. We could never agree as to which of the animals each of us represented. At the head of my heap of straw there was an entrance to the cellar. The ladies of the family, who were shod in wooden shoes, used to clatter round our slumbers in the early morning getting provisions from below. Life under such conditions was peculiarly unpleasant. It was quite impossible too to have a bath. I announced to the family one day that I was going to take one. Murdoch MacDonald provided some kind of large tub which he filled with dishes of steaming water. Instead however of the fact that I was about to have a bath acting as a deterrent to the visits of the ladies, the announcement seemed to have the opposite effect. So great were the activities of the family in the cellar and round the churn that I had to abandon the idea of bathing altogether. I determined therefore to get a tent of my own and plant it in the field. I wrote to England and got a most wonderful little house. It was a small portable tent. When it was set up it covered a piece of ground six feet four inches square. The pole, made in two parts like a fishing rod, was four feet six inches high. The tent itself was brown, and made like a pyramid. One side had to be buttoned up when I had retired. It looked very small as a place for human habitation. On one side of the pole was my Wolseley sleeping bag, on the other a box in which to put my clothes, and on which stood a lantern. When Philo and I retired for the night we were really very comfortable, but we were much annoyed by earwigs and the inquisitiveness of the cows, who never could quite satisfy themselves as to what we were. Many is the time we have been awakened out of sleep in the morning by the sniffings and sighings of a cow, who poked round my tent until I thought she had the intention of swallowing us up after the manner in which the cow disposed of Tom Thumb. At such times I would turn Philo loose upon the intruder. Philo used to suffer at night from the cold, and would wake me up by insisting upon burrowing his way down into my tightly laced valise. There he would sleep till he got so hot that he woke me up again burrowing his way out. It would not be long before once again the cold of the tent drove him to seek refuge in my bed. I hardly ever had a night's complete rest. Once I rolled over on him, and, as he was a very fiery tempered little dog, he got very displeased and began to snap and bark in a most unpleasant manner. As the sleeping bag was tightly laced it was difficult to extract him. Philo waged a kind of submarine warfare there until grasping his snout, I pulled him out and refused all his further appeals for readmission.

My little tent gave me great comfort and a sense of independence. I could go where I pleased and camp in the lines of the battalions when they came out of the trenches. This enabled me to get into closer touch with the men. One young western fellow said that my encampment consisted of a caboose, my tent, a cayouse, which was Dandy, and a papoose, which was my little dog, friend Philo. Now that I had a comfortable billet of my own I determined that Romarin was too far from the men, so I removed my settlement up to the Neuve Eglise road and planted it near some trees in the field just below the row of huts called Bulford Camp. At this time, Murdoch MacDonald went to the transport lines, and his place was taken by my friend Private Ross, of the 16th Battalion, the Canadian Scottish. He stayed with me to the end. We were very comfortable in the field. Ross made himself a bivouac of rubber sheets. Dandy was picketed not far off and, under the trees, my little brown pyramid tent was erected, with a rude bench outside for a toilet table, and a large tin pail for a bath-tub. When the battalions came out of the line and inhabited Bulford Camp and the huts of Court-o-Pyp, I used to arrange a Communion Service for the men every morning. At Bulford Camp the early morning services were specially delightful. Not far off, was the men's washing place, a large ditch full of muddy water in-

to which the men took headers. Beside it were long rows of benches, in front of which the operation of shaving was carried on. The
box I used as an altar was placed under the green trees, and cover-
with the dear old flag, which now hangs in the chancel of my church
in Quebec. On top was a white altar cloth, two candles and a
small crucifix. At these services only about ten or a dozen men
attended, but it was inspiring to minister to them. I used to hear
from time to time that so and so had been killed, and I knew he
had made his last Communion at one of such services. It was
an evidence of the changed attitude towards religion that the men
in general did not count it strange that soldiers should thus come
to Holy Communion in public. No one was ever laughed at or teased for doing so.

Neuve Eglise, at the top of the road, had been badly wrecked
by German shells. I went up there one night with an officer
friend of mine, to see the scene of desolation. We were halted
by some of our cyclists who were patrolling the road. Whenever
they stopped me at night and asked who I was I always said,
"German spy", and they would reply, "Pass, German spy, all's
well." My friend and I went down the street of the broken and
deserted village, which, from its position on the hill, was an easy
mark for shell fire. Not a living thing was stirring except a big
black cat which ran across our path. The moonlight made strange
shadows in the roofless houses. Against the west wall of the
church stood a large crucifix still undamaged. The roof had gone,
and the moonlight flooded the ruins through the broken Gothic windows. To the left, ploughed up with shells, were the tombs of the
civilian cemetery, and the whole place was ghostly and uncanny.

Near the huts, on the hill at Bulford Camp was a hollow in the
ground which made a natural amphitheatre. Here at night concerts were given. All the audience packed together very closely sat
on the ground. Before us, at the end of the hollow, the performers
would appear, and overhead the calm stars looked down. I
always went to these entertainments well provided with Players'
cigarettes. A neat trick was played upon me one night. I
passed my silver cigarette case round to the men and told them that
all I wanted back was the case. In a little while it was passed back
to me. I looked into it to see if a cigarette had been left for
my use, when, to my astonishment, I found that the case had been
filled with De Reszke's, my favourite brand. I thanked my unknown
benefactor for his graceful generosity.

PLOEGSTEERT—A LULL IN OPERATIONS

The field behind the huts at Court-o-Pyp was another of my favourite camping grounds. It was on the Neuve Eglise side of the camp, and beyond us was some barbed wire. About two o'clock one night I was aroused by an excited conversation which was being carried on between my friend Ross in his bivouac, and a soldier who had been dining late and had lost his way. The young fellow had got it into his head that he had wandered into the German lines, and Ross had great difficulty in convincing him that he was quite safe. He was just going off with mind appeased when he caught sight of my pyramid tent on a rise in the ground. "What's that?" he cried in terror, evidently pointing towards my little house. "That's the Rev. Major Canon Scott's billet" said Ross with great dignity from under his rubber sheets, and the man went off in fear of his identity becoming known. He afterwards became an officer and a very gallant one too, and finally lost a leg in the service of his country. But many is the time I have chaffed him about the night he thought he had wandered into the German lines.

One day when I had ridden up to Court-o-Pyp I found that a canteen had just been opened there, and being urged to make a purchase for good luck I bought a large bottle of tomato catsup, which I put into my saddle bag. I noticed that the action was under the observation of the battalion, which had just returned from the trenches and was about to be dismissed. I mounted my horse and went over to the C.O. and asked if I might say a word to the men before he dismissed them. He told me the men were tired, but I promised not to keep them long. He called out, "Men, Canon Scott wants to say a word to you before you are dismissed," and they stood to attention. "All I wanted to say to you, Boys, was this; that was a bottle of tomato catsup which I put in my saddle bag, and not, as you thought, a bottle of whiskey." A roar of laughter went up from all ranks.

It was about this time that our Brigadier was recalled to England to take over the command of a Division. We were all sincerely sorry to lose him from the 3rd Brigade. He was ever a good and true friend, and took a deep interest in his men. But the immediate effect of his departure, as far as I was concerned, was to remove out of my life the hideous spectre of No. 2 General Hospital, and to give me absolute liberty in wandering through the trenches. In fact, as I told him sometime afterwards, I was beginning a little poem, the first line of which was "I never knew what freedom meant until he went away."

THE WAR AS I SAW IT

One day, General Seely invited me to go and stay with him at his Headquarters in Westhof Farm where I had a most delightful time. Not only was the General a most entertaining host, but his staff were very charming. At dinner, we avoided war topics and shop, and talked about things political and literary. The mess was in the farm building and our sleeping quarters were on an island in the moat. My stay here brought me into contact with the Canadian Cavalry Brigade, and a fine lot of men they were.

But a change in my fortunes was awaiting me. The Senior Chaplain of the Division had gone back to England, and General Alderson sent for me one day to go to Nieppe. There he told me he wished me to be Senior Chaplain. I was not altogether pleased at the appointment, because it meant that I should be taken away from my beloved 3rd Brigade. I told the General so, but he assured me I should not have to stay all the time at Headquarters, and could go with the 3rd Brigade as much as I pleased.

This unexpected promotion, after what I had gone through, opened up a life of almost dazzling splendour. I now had to go and live in the village of Nieppe on the Bailleul-Armentieres road. Here were our Headquarters. General Alderson had his house in the Square. Another building was occupied by our officers, and a theatre was at my disposal for Church Services and entertainments. The town was also the Headquarters of a British Division, so we had plenty of men to look after. I got an upper room in a house owned by an old lady. The front room downstairs was my office, and I had a man as a clerk. Round my bedroom window grew a grape vine, and at night when the moon was shining, I could sit on my window-sill, listen to the sound of shells, watch the flare lights behind Armentieres and eat the grapes which hung down in large clusters. Poor Nieppe has shared the fate of Neuve Eglise and Bailleul and is now a ruin. Everyone was exceedingly kind, and I soon found that the added liberty which came to me from having a definite position really increased my chances of getting amongst the men. By leaving my clerk to do the work of Senior Chaplain, I could go off and be lost at the front for a day and a night without ever being missed. I knew that each brigade must now have an equal share of my interest and I was very careful never to show any preference. A chaplain had at all times to be very careful to avoid anything that savoured of favouritism. I was now also formally inducted into the membership of that august body known as "C" mess, where the heads of noncombatant departments met for dining and wining. Somebody asked me one day what "C" mess was. I told him it was a lot of withered old boughs on the great tree of the Canadian Expeditionary Force—a description which was naturally much resented by the other members. I had no difficulty now in arranging for my billets, as that was always done for me by our Camp Commandant.

Life in Nieppe was very delightful and the presence of the British Division gave it an added charm. We had very pleasant services in the Hall, and every Sunday evening I had a choral Evensong. So many of the men who attended had been choristers in England or Canada that the responses were sung in harmony by the entire congregation. On week days we had smoking concerts and entertainments of various kinds. I sometimes had to take duty with the British units. On one occasion, I was invited to hold a service for his men by a very staunch churchman, a Colonel in the Army Service Corps. He told me, before the service, that his unit had to move on the following day, and also that he was accustomed to choose and read the lesson himself. I was delighted to find a layman so full of zeal. But in the midst of the service I was rather distressed at his choice of the lesson. It was hard enough to get the interest of the men as it was, but the Colonel made it more difficult by choosing a long chapter from Deuteronomy narrating the wanderings of the children of Israel in the desert. Of course the C.O. and I knew that the A.S.C. was to move on the following day, but the congregation was not aware of the fact, and they must have been puzzled by the application of the chapter to the religious needs of the men at the front. However the reader was delighted with his choice of subject, and at tea afterwards told me how singularly appropriate the lesson was on this particular occasion. I thought it was wiser to make no comment, but I wondered what spiritual fruit was gathered by the mind of the ordinary British Tommy from a long account of Israel's pitching their tents and perpetually moving to places with extraordinary names.

We had several meetings of chaplains, and I paid a visit to the Deputy Chaplain General, Bishop Gwynne, at his headquarters in St. Omer. He was exceedingly kind and full of human interest in the men. The whole conception of the position of an army chaplain was undergoing a great and beneficial change. The rules which hitherto had fenced off the chaplains, as being officers, from easy intercourse with the men were being relaxed. Chaplains were being looked upon more as parish priests to their battalions. They could be visited freely by the men, and could also have meals with the men when they saw fit. I am convinced that it is a mistake to lay stress upon the chaplain's office as a military one. The chaplain is not a soldier, and has no men, as a doctor has, under his command. His office being a spiritual one ought to be quite outside military rank. To both officers and men, he holds a unique position, enabling him to become the friend and companion of all. Bishop Gwynne upheld the spiritual side of the chaplain's work, and by establishing conferences and religious retreats for the chaplains, endeavoured to keep up the sacred standards which army life tended so much to drag down.

The Cathedral at St. Omer is a very beautiful one, and it was most restful to sit in it and meditate, looking down the long aisles and arches that had stood so many centuries the political changes of Europe. One morning when the sun was flooding the building and casting the colours of the windows in rich patterns on the floor, I sat under the gallery at the west end and read Shelley's great elegy. I remember those wonderful last lines and I thought how, like an unshattered temple, the great works of literature survive the tempests of national strife. My mind was carried far away, beyond the anxieties and sorrows of the present,

> "To where the soul of Adonais like a star
> Beacons from the abode where the Eternal are,"

In the square was a large building which had been used originally as headquarters for the Intelligence Department. Later on, this building was taken by the Bishop and used as the Chaplains' Rest-Home. There is an amusing story told of a despatch rider who came to the place with a message for its original occupants, but when he inquired for the Intelligence Department the orderly answered, "This is the Chaplains' Rest Home, there is no Intelligence here." At St. Omer also was the office of the Principal Chaplain who had under his charge all the Non-Conformist Chaplains at the front. The very best relations existed between the various religious bodies, and it was the endeavour of all the chaplains to see that every man got the religious privileges of his own faith.

We arrived in the Ploegsteert area at a good time for the digging and repairing of the trenches. The clay in Belgium in fine weather is easily worked; consequently a most elaborate and well made system of trenches was established in front of Messines. The brown sides of the trenches became dry and hard in the sun, and the bathmats along them made walking easy. The trenches were named, "Currie Avenue," "McHarg Avenue," "Seely Avenue," and so forth. The men had their cookers and primus stoves, and occupied their spare time in the line by cooking all sorts of dainty dishes. Near the trenches on the other side of Hill 63 were several ruined farm houses, known as "Le Per'du Farm," "Ration Farm," and one, around which hovered a peculiarly unsavoury atmosphere, as "Stinking Farm." Hill 63 was a hill which ran immediately behind our trench area and was covered at its right end with a delightful wood. Here were "Grand Moncque Farm," "Petit Moncque Farm," "Kort Dreuve Farm" and the "Piggeries." All these farms were used as billets by the battalions who were in reserve. In Ploegsteert Wood, "Woodcote Farm," and "Red Lodge," were also used for the same purpose. The wood in those days was a very pleasant place to wander through. Anything that reminded us of the free life of nature acted as a tonic to the nerves, and the little paths among the trees which whispered overhead in the summer breezes made one imagine that one was wandering through the forests in Canada. In the wood were several cemeteries kept by different units, very neatly laid out and carefully fenced in. I met   officer one day who told me he was going up to the trenches one cv. ag past a cemetery in the wood, when he heard the sound of someone sobbing. He looked into the place and there saw a young boy lying beside a newly made grave. He went in and spoke to him and the boy seemed confused that he had been discovered in his sorrow. "It's the grave of my brother, Sir," he said, "He was buried here this afternoon and now I have got to go back to the line without him." The lad dried his eyes, shouldered his rifle and went through the woodland path up to the trenches. No one would know again the inner sorrow that had darkened his life.

The farms behind the wood made really very pleasant homes for awhile. They have all now been levelled to the ground, but at the time I speak of they were in good condition and had many large and commodious buildings. At Kort Dreuve there was a very good private chapel, which the proprietor gave me the use of for my Communion Services. It was quite nice to have a little Gothic chapel with fine altar, and the men who attended always enjoyed the services there. Round the farm was a large moat full of good sized gold-fish, which the men used to catch surreptitiously and fry for their meals. "The Piggeries" was a large building in which the King of the Belgians had kept a fine breed of pigs. It was very long and furnished inside with two rows of styes built solidly of concrete. These were full of straw, and in them the men slept.

I was visiting one of the battalions there one evening, when I heard that they had been ordered to go back to the trenches before Sunday. I told some of the men that I thought that, as they would be in the trenches on Sunday, it would be a good idea if we had a voluntary service that evening. They seemed pleased, so I collected quite a large congregation at one end of the Piggeries, and was leading up to the service by a little overture in the shape of a talk about the war outlook, when I became aware that there was a fight going on at the other end of the low building, and that some of the men on the outskirts of the congregation were beginning to get restive. I knew that a voluntary service could not stand up against the rivalry of a fight, so I thought I had better take the bull by the horns. I said, "Boys, I think there is a fight going on at the other end of the Piggeries, and perhaps it would be well to postpone the service and go and see the fight, and then return and carry on." The men were much relieved and, amid great laughter, my congregation broke loose and ran to the other end of the building, followed by myself. The fight was soon settled by the intervention of a sergeant, and then I said, "Now, Boys, let us go back to the other end and have the service." I thought the change of location might have a good effect upon their minds and souls. So back we went again to the other end of the building and there had a really enthusiastic and devout service. When it was over, I told the men that nothing helped so much to make a service bright and hearty as the inclusion of a fight, and that when I returned to Canada, if at any time my congregation was listless or sleepy, I would arrange a fight on the other side of the street to which we could adjourn and from which we should return with renewed spiritual fervour. I have met many men at different times who look back upon that service with pleasure.

We had a feeling that Ploegsteert was to be our home for a good long time, so we settled down to our life there. We had visits from Sir Sam Hughes and Sir Robert Borden, and also Lord Kitchener. I was not present when the latter inspected the men, but I asked one who was there what it was like. "Oh Sir," he replied, "we stood to attention, and Kitchener passed down the lines very quietly and coldly. He merely looked at us with his steely grey eyes and said to himself, "I wonder how many of these men will be in hell next week," General Hughes' inspection of one of the battalions near Ploegsteert Wood was interrupted by shells and the men were hastily dismissed.

A visit to the trenches was now a delightful expedition. All the way from Nieppe to Hill 63 one came upon the headquarters of some unit. At a large farm called "Lampernise Farm" all the transports of the 3rd Brigade were quartered. I used to have services for them in the open on a Sunday evening. It was very difficult at first to collect a congregation, so I adopted the plan of getting two or three men who could sing, and then going over with them to an open place in the field, and starting some well known hymn. One by one others would come up and hymn-books were distributed. By the time the service was finished, we generally had quite a good congregation, but it took a certain amount of courage and faith to start the service. One felt very much like a little band of Salvationists in a city square.

In spite of having a horse to ride, it was sometimes difficult to cover the ground between the services on Sunday. One afternoon, when I had been to the Cavalry Brigade at Petit Moncque Farm, I had a great scramble to get back in time to the transport lines. In a bag hanging over the front of my saddle, I had five hundred hymn books. Having taken a wrong turn in the road I lost some time which it was necessary to make up, and, in my efforts to make haste, the string of the bag broke and hymn books fluttered out and fell along the road. Dandy took alarm, misunderstanding the nature of the fluttering white things, and started to gallop. With two haversacks on my back it was difficult to hold on to the bag of hymn books and at the same time to prevent their loss. The more the hymn books fluttered out, the harder Dandy bolted, and the harder Dandy bolted, the more the hymn books fluttered out. At last I passed a soldier in the road and asked him to come to my assistance. I managed to rein in the horse, and the man collected as many of the hymn books as were not spoilt by the mud. Knowing how hard it was and how long it took to get hymn books from the Base, it was with regret that I left any behind. But then I reflected that it might be really a scattering of the seed by the wayside. Some poor lone soldier who had been wandering from the paths of recititude might pick up the hymns by chance and be converted. Indulging in such self consolation I arrived just in time for the service.

Services were never things you could be quite sure of until they came off. Often I have gone to bed on Saturday night feeling that everything had been done in the way of arranging for the following day. Battalions had been notified, adjutants had put the hours of service in orders, and places for the gatherings had been carefully located. Then on the following day, to my intense disgust, I would find that all my plans had been frustrated. Some general had taken it into his head to order an inspection, or some paymaster had been asked to come down and pay off the men. The Paymaster's Parade, in the eyes of the men, took precedence of everything else. A Church Service was nowhere in comparison. More often than I can recollect, all my arrangements for services have been upset by a sudden order for the men to go to a bathing parade. Every time this happened, the Adjutant would smile and tell me, as if I had never heard it before, that "cleanliness was next to godliness." A chaplain therefore had his trials, but in spite of them it was the policy of wisdom not to show resentment and to hold one's tongue. I used to look at the Adjutant, and merely remark quietly, in the words of the Psalmist, "I held my tongue with bit and bridle, while the ungodly was in my sight."

People at Headquarters soon got accustomed to my absence and never gave me a thought. I used to take comfort in remembering Poo Bah's song in the Mikado, "He never will be missed, he never will be missed." Sometimes when I have started off from home in the morning my sergeant and Ross have asked me when I was going to return. I told them that if they would go down on their knees and pray for illumination on the subject, they might find out, but that I had not the slightest idea myself. A visit to the trenches was most fascinating. I used to take Philo with me. He found much amusement in hunting for rats, and would often wander off into No Man's Land and come back covered with the blood of his victims. One night I had missed him for sometime, and was whistling for him, when a sentry told me that a white dog had been "captured" by one of the men with the thought that it was a German police dog, and he had carried it off to company headquarters under sentence of death. I hurried up the trench and was just in time to save poor little Philo from a court martial. There had been a warning in orders that day against the admission of dogs from the German lines.

The men were always glad of a visit, and I used to distribute little bronze crucifixes as I went along. I had them sent to me from London, and have given away hundreds of them. I told the men that if anyone asked them why they were at the war, that little cross with the patient figure of self-sacrifice upon it, would be the answer. The widow of an officer who was killed at Albert told me the cross which I gave her husband was taken from his dead body, and she now had it, and would wear it to her dying day. I was much surprised and touched to see the value which the men set upon these tokens of their faith. I told them to try to never think, say or do anything which would make them want to take off the cross from their necks.

The dugouts in which the officers made their homes were quite comfortable, and very merry parties we have had in the little earth houses which were then on the surface of the ground. One night when some new officers had arrived to take over the line, one of the companies gave them a dinner, consisting of five or six courses, very nicely cooked. We were never far however, from the presence of the dark Angel, and our host on that occasion was killed the next night. Our casualties at this time were not heavy, although every day there were some men wounded or killed. The shells occasionally made direct hits upon the trenches. I came upon a place once which was terribly messed about, and two men were sitting by roaring with laughter. They said their dinner was all prepared in their dugout, and they had gone off to get some wood for the fire, when a shell landed and knocked their home into ruins. They were preparing to dig for their kit and so much of their dinner as would still be eatable. As they took the whole matter as a joke, I joined with them in the laugh. One day as I was going up the line, a young sapper was carried out on a sitting stretcher. He was hit through the chest, and all the way along the bath mats was the trail of the poor boy's blood. He was only nineteen years of age, and had done splendid work and won the admiration of all the men in his company. I had a short prayer with him, and then saw him carried off to the dressing station, where not long after he died. The sergeant who was with him was exceedingly kind, and looked after the boy like a father. As

the war went on, the men were being united more and more closely
in the bonds of a common sympathy and a tender helpfulness. To
the enemy, until he was captured, they were flint and iron; to one
another they were friends and brothers.

It always took a long time to pass down the trenches. There
were so many men I knew and I could not pass them without a
short conversation. Time, in the line had really no meaning, except in the matter of "standing to" or "changing guard". On fine
days, the life was not unpleasant. I remember, however, on one
dark rainy night, being in a trench in front of Wulverghem. The
enemy trenches were at that point only thirty-five yards away. I
was squeezed into a little muddy dugout with an officer, when the
corporal came and asked for a tot of rum for his men. They had
been lying out on patrol duty in the mud and rain in front of our
trench for two hours.

Dandy was still the envy of our men in the transport lines, and
one day I nearly lost him. I rode up to Hill 63. Just behind it
was an orchard, and in it there were two batteries of British Artillery, which were attached to our Division. I was going up to the
trenches that afternoon, so I gave the horse some oats and tied him
to a tree near the officers' billet. I then went up over the hill down
to Ration Farm, and from thence into the line. It was quite late
in the afternoon, but walking through the trenches was easy when
it was not raining. I was returning about 10 o'clock, when the
second in command of the 16th Battalion asked me to wait for him
and we would come out together over the open. It must have been
about midnight when I started with the Major, and another officer.
The night was dark and it was rather a scramble, but the German
flare lights would go up now and then and show us our course.
Suddenly a machine gun opened up, and we had to lie on our faces
listening to the swish of the flying bullets just overhead. I turned
to the officer next to me and asked him how long he had been at
the front. He said he had only arrived that afternoon at four o'
clock. I told him it wasn't always like this, and we laughed over
the curious life to which he had been so recently introduced. We
finally made our way to Ration Farm and as I had a long ride before
me, I determined to go back. I was very hungry, as I had had
nothing to eat since luncheon. I went into a cellar at Ration Farm
and there found one of the men reading by the light of a candle supported on tins of bully-beef. I asked him for one of these and he

gladly gave it to me. As I started up the hill on the long straight road with trees on either side, I tried to open the tin with the key, but as usual it broke and left only a little crack through which with my penknife I extracted strings of beef. I could not use my flashlight, as the hill was in sight of the enemy, so I had to content myself with what nourishment I was able to obtain. Half way up the hill I noticed a tall figure standing by one of the trees. I thought he might be a spy but I accosted him and found he was one of the Strathcona Horse who had a working party in the trenches that night. I told him my difficulty, and he got his knife and very kindly took off the top of the tin. By this time a drizzling rain was falling and the night was decidedly uncomfortable. I went over the hill and down to the orchard, and made my way to the tree to which poor old Dandy had been tied so many hours before. There, I found the tree just where I had left it—it was of no use to me, as, like the barren fig tree, it had no fruit upon it, but to my horror the horse, which was so necessary, had disappeared. I scoured the orchard in vain looking for my faithful friend, and then I went over to the Artillery officers' house and told them my trouble. We all decided that it was too late to search any longer, I was provided with a mackintosh, and determined to make my way over to Petit Moncque Farm where the 3rd Infantry Brigade Headquarters were. It was a long walk and the roads were sloppy. The path I took led through a field of Indian corn. This, though not ripe and not cooked, would remind me of Canada, so with my search-light I hunted for two or three of the hardest ears, and then, fortified with these, made my way over towards the farm.

From past experience, I knew that a sentry was stationed somewhere in the road. The sudden challenge of a sentry in the dark always gave me a fright, so I determined this time to be on the watch and keep from getting a surprise. However when I arrived at the place where the man usually stood, no one challenged me. I thought that perhaps on account of the night being rainy and uncomfortable he had retired to the guard room, and I walked along with a free mind. I was just near the large gateway, however, when a most stentorian voice shouted out, "Halt, who goes there?" and at the same instant in the darkness I saw the sudden flash of a bayonet flourished in my direction. Not expecting such an event, I could not for the moment think of what I ought to say, but I called out in equally stentorian tones, "For heaven's sake, my boy,

don't make such a row; its only Canon Scott and I have lost my
horse." A burst of laughter greeted my announcement, and the
man told me that, seeing somebody with a flashlight at that time of
the night wandering through the fields, and searching for something, he had become convinced that a German spy was at work
cutting the telephone wires that led back to the guns, so he had got
near the guard room where he could obtain assistance, and awaited
my approach in the darkness. It was a great relief to get to headquarters, and the officer on duty kindly lent me his comfortable
sleeping bag. The next morning I made my way back to Nieppe,
and telegraphed to the various units, searching for Dandy. Later
on, in the afternoon, he was brought in by a man of the Strathcona
Horse. His story was that the intelligent animal had untied himself from the tree and followed the working party ome from the
orchard. It is most likely that he had preceded them. Luckily for
me, their quartermaster had recognized him in the Strathcona lines,
and, being an honest man, had sent him back. The incident taught
me a great and useful lesson, and in future I was very careful to
see that my horse was safely guarded whenever I had to leave him.

Our signallers had been active in setting up a wireless telegraph
in a field near Headquarters and were able to get the various com-
muniqués which were sent out during the night by the different
nations. The information was passed round Headquarters every
morning on typewritten sheets and made most interesting reading.
We were able to anticipate the news detailed to us in the papers.
Later on, however. someone in authority put an end to this and we
were deprived of our Daily Chronicle.

About this time we heard that the 2nd Division was coming to
France, and that the two Divisions, which would be joined by a
third, were to be formed into the Canadian Corps. This meant a
very radical change in the status of the old 1st Division. Up to
this time we were "the Canadians"; now we were only to be one
among several divisions. General Alderson was to take command
of the Corps, and the question which was daily asked among the
officers at headquarters was, "Are you going to the Corps?" It
was a sundering of ties amongst our friends, and we felt sorry that
our society would be broken up. One of the staff officers asked me to
write a poem on his departure. I did so. It began—

"He left the war
And went to the Corps,

108

PLOEGSTEERT—A LULL IN OPERATIONS

Our hearts were sore,
We could say no more."

My friend was not at all pleased at the implication contained in the first two lines.

Bailleul was made Corps Headquarters, whither General Alderson moved. His place at the division was taken by General Currie, who afterwards commanded the Corps and led it to victory. The old town now became a great Canadian centre. The General had comfortable quarters in a large house, which was nicely furnished, and had an air of opulence about it. The Grande Place was full of activity, and in the streets one met many friends. The hotel offered an opportunity for afternoon tea and a tolerable dinner. Besides this, there was the officers' tea room, kept by some damsels who provided cakes and served tea on little tables, like a restaurant in London. Here we could be sure of meeting many of our friends and very pleasant such gatherings were. In a large hall a concert took place every evening. We had a very special one attended by several generals with their staffs. The proceeds were given to the Canadian "Prisoners of War Fund". The concerts were most enjoyable and the real, artistic ability of some of the performers, both Canadian and British, was remarkable. It was always pleasant to live in the neighbourhood of a town, and the moment the men came out of the trenches they wanted to clean up and go into Bailleul. After a residence in the muddy and shaky little shacks in and behind the front lines, to enter a real house and sit on a real chair with a table in front of you was a great luxury.

There were several well-equipped hospitals in Bailleul. One large British one had a nice chapel set aside for our use. In it one day we had a Confirmation service which was very impressive, a number of candidates being present.

While Headquarters were at Nieppe the British attack upon Loos was to take place, and it was arranged that the Canadians, in order to keep the Germans busy in the North, were to make an attack. I happened to be visiting "the Piggeries" in the afternoon previous. The 1st Battalion was in the line. I heard the Colonel read out to the officers the orders for the attack. We were not told that the whole thing was what our soldiers call "a fake". As he read the orders for the next morning, they sounded serious, and I was invited to be present, which of course I gladly consented to. The guns were to open fire at 4 a. m. I had been away from Headquarters for some time so I determined to ride back and return later. At three o'clock a. m. my servant woke me up and I had a cup of coffee, and started off on Dandy to go up to "the Piggeries". I took a tin of bully-beef with me, and so was prepared for any eventuality. It was just before dawn and the morning air was fresh and delightful. Dandy had had a good feed of oats and was full of life. He seemed to enjoy the sport as much as I did. We rode up the well known roads, and round their curious curves past the small white farm houses, till we came into the neighbourhood of our batteries. All of a sudden these opened fire. It was a splendid sound. Of all the music I have ever heard in my life, none comes near the glorious organ sound of a barrage. I look back with the greatest pleasure to that early morning ride through the twilight lit up by gun flashes from batteries scattered along our whole front. One great dread I always had, and that was the dread of being killed by our own artillery. On this occasion, I had to ride down roads that looked perilously near batteries in action. When I got to a corner near "the Piggeries", I was just stopped in time from what might have been my finish. There was a concealed battery among the trees by the wayside, and I, not knowing it was there, was about to ride by unconcernedly, when a gunner came out from the bushes and stopped me just in time, telling me that in half a minute the battery was going to open up. Dandy and I waited till the guns had fired and then went on. Along our front line there was much stir and commotion. Bundles of lighted straw making a hideous smoke were poked over the trenches, and the whole night previous, all the limbers available had been driven up and down the roads, making as much noise as possible. The Germans were convinced we were preparing for an attack on a big scale, and that the yellow smoke which they saw coming towards them was some new form of frightfulness. Of course they returned our fire, but our men knew by this time that the whole affair was only a pretence. Far off to the South, however, there was a real battle raging, and the cemeteries which we afterwards saw at Loos bore testimony to the bitter struggle which the British forces endured.

The village of Ploegsteert behind the wood was very much damaged. Like the other villages at the front, it must at one time have been quite a prosperous place. The church, before it was ruined, was well built and capacious. There was a building on the main street which a British chaplain had used as a clubhouse, and handed over to me when his division moved south. It was well stocked with all things necessary to make the men comfortable. It had a kitchen, reading rooms, and upstairs a chapel. Two or three shells, however, had made their way into it, and the holes were covered with canvas. The Mayor's house was on the other side of the street, and he had a young girl there as a servant, who kept the keys of the club. The chaplain who moved away told me that this girl, when the town was being heavily shelled one day, saved the lives of some men who were lying wounded in the house, by carrying them on her back over to a place of safety in a farmhouse. It was a deed that merited recognition, because she had to pass down the road which was then under heavy shell fire. I brought her case before the notice of the military authorities, and General Seely was asked to take the matter up and make an application to the King for a reward for the girl's bravery. There was a doubt as to what award could be given to her. We got the sworn testimony of the Mayor and other eye-witnesses, and the document was finally laid before the King. It was decided that she should receive the bronze medal of the Order of St. John of Jerusalem. Later on General Alderson sent for me and took me to the Mayor's house in Romarin, where we had the ceremony of conferring the medal. It was quite touching in its simplicity. The girl, who had a fine open face, was on the verge of giving way to tears. The Mayor and some other of the chief inhabitants were arrayed in their best clothes, and a Highland regiment lent us their pipers. One of the citizens presented the heroine with a large bouquet of flowers. General Alderson made a nice speech, which was translated to the townsfolk, and then he presented the medal. We were invited into the house, and the girl's health was proposed and drunk by the General in a glass of Romarin Champagne. We heard afterwards that the country people were much impressed by the way the British Army had recognized the gallantry of a poor Belgian maidservant.

One day a German aeroplane was brought down behind our lines, near Ration Farm. Of its two occupants one was killed. On the aeroplane was found a Colt machine-gun, which had been taken by the Germans from the 14th Battalion several months before, in the Second Battle of Ypres. It now came back to the brigade which had lost it. I buried the airman near Ration Farm, in a grave, which the men did up neatly and over which they erected a cross with his name upon it.

111

THE WAR AS I SAW IT

Although our Headquarters were at Nieppe, the village was really
in the British Area, and so we were informed towards the end of
November that we had been ordered to move to St. Jans Cappel. On Monday, November 22nd I started off by car via Bailleul
to my new billet. Although I had left Nieppe and its pleasant society with great regret, I was quite pleased with my new home.
It was a small house belonging to a widow, on the road that led
from St. Jans Cappel up to Mount Kemmel. The house itself was
brick and well built. The landlady's rooms were on one side of
the passage, and mine were on the other. A large garret overhead gave a billet for Ross and my sergeant clerk. In the yard
there was a stable for the horse. So the whole family was quite
comfortably housed, and Ross undertook to do my cooking. The
room which I used as my office in the front of the house had two
large windows in it, and a neat tiled floor. The furniture was
ample. At the back, up some steps, was my bedroom, and the
window from it opened upon the yard. A former occupant of the
house, a Major Murray, of King Edward's Horse, had left a series
of maps on the wall, on which pins were stuck with a bit of red
cord passing through them, to show the position of our front line.
These maps deeply impressed visitors with my military exactness.
In that little office I have received many guests of all ranks. I
always said that the chaplain's house was like a church, and all
men met there on equal terms. Sometimes it was rather difficult
however, to convince them that this was the case. On one occasion two privates and I had just finished luncheon, and were having
a delightful smoke, when a certain general was announced, and
the men seized with panic, fled up the steps to my bedroom and
bolting through my window hurried back to their lines.

The landlady was quite well to do, and was a woman well thought
of in the village. She both paid calls upon her neighbours and received callers in her rooms. Sometimes I used to be invited in to
join these social gatherings and frequently she would bring me in
a nice bowl of soup for dinner. Philo, too, made himself quite
at home, and carefully inspected all visitors on their admission to
the mansion. In front of the house, there was a pleasant view
of the valley through which the road passed up towards Mont des
Cats. Our Headquarters were down in the village in a large
building which was part of the convent. General Currie and his
staff lived in a charming chateau in pleasant grounds, on the

112

hillside. The chateau, although a modern one, was reputed to be haunted, which gave it a more or less romantic interest in the eyes of our men, though as far as I could hear no apparitions disturbed the slumbers of the G. S. O. or the A. A. & Q. M. G.

The road past my house, which was a favourite walk of mine, went over the hill, and at the top a large windmill in a field commanded a fine view of the country for several miles. My garden was very pleasant, and in it was a summer house at the end of a moss-grown walk. One plant which gave me great delight was a large bush of rosemary. The smell of it always carried my mind back to peaceful times. It was like the odour of the middle ages, with that elusive suggestion of incense which reminded me of Gothic fanes and picturesque processions. Many elm trees fringed the fields, and made a welcome shade along the sides of the road. A little stream ran through the village and added its touch of beauty to the landscape. We were only a mile and a half from Bailleul, so we could easily get up to the town either for a concert or for dinner at the hotel. The Camp Commandant allotted me the school house, which I fitted up as a chapel. It was very small, and not particularly clean, but it served its purpose very well.

My only objection to St. Jans Cappel was that it was situated such a long way from our men, for we still held the same front line near Ploegsteert. It was now a ride of twelve miles to Hill 63 whither I frequently had to go to take burial services, the round trip making a journey of nearly twenty-four miles. The Bailleul road, which was my best route, was a pavé road, and was hard on a horse. I did not want poor willing Dandy to suffer from overwork, so I begged the loan of another mount from Headquarters. It was a young horse, but big and heavily built, and had no life in it. I was trotting down the road with him one day when he tumbled down, and I injured my knee, causing me to be laid up with water on the knee for about six weeks. The men used to chaff me about falling off my horse, but I told them that I could sit on a horse as long as he stood up, but I could not sit on the air when the horse lay down. I was very much afraid that the A. D. M. S. would send me off to a hospital, but I got private treatment from a doctor friend, who was acting A. D. C. to General Currie. Luckily for me, things were pretty quiet at the front at that time, and my being confined to the house did not really make much difference. I had a supper in my billet one night for a number of Bishop's

8

College men.　Of those who attended, the majority have since
made the supreme sacrifice, but it was an evening which brought
back many pleasant memories of our Alma Mater.

The roads round St. Jans Cappel were very pretty, and I had
many a pleasant ride in our staff cars, which I, as Senior Chaplain,
was permitted to use.　It was always a great delight to me to pick
up men on the road and give them a ride.　I used to pile them in
and give them as good a joy ride as the chauffeur, acting under
orders, would allow.　One day, in a heavy snowstorm, I picked up
two nuns, whose garments were blowing about in the blizzard in
a hopeless condition.　The sisters were glad of the chance of a ride
to Bailleul, whither they were going on foot through the snow.
It was against orders to drive ladies in our staff cars, but I thought
the circumstances of the case and the evident respectability of my
guests would be a sufficient excuse for a breach of the rule.　The
sisters chatted in French very pleasantly, and I took them to their
convent headquarters in Bailleul.　I could see, as I passed through
the village, how amused our men were at my use of the car.　When
I arrived at the convent door at Bailleul, the good ladies alighted
and then asked me to give them my blessing.　How could I refuse, or enter upon a discussion of the validity of Anglican
Orders?　The nuns with their hands crossed on their bosoms leaned forward, and I stood up and blessed them from the car, and de-
parted leaving them both grateful and gratified.

The village of St. Jans Cappel had been captured by the Germans in their advance in 1914, and we heard some unpleasant tales
of the rudeness of the German officers who took up their quarters
in the convent and compelled the nuns to wait upon them at the
table.　In 1918, when the Germans made their big push round
Mont Kemmel, St. Jans Cappel, along with Bailleul and Meteren,
was captured once more by the enemy, and the village is now in
ruins and its inhabitants scattered.

I do not look back with much pleasure to the cold rides which I
always used to have on my return from the line.　In frosty weather
the pavé roads were very slippery, and I had to walk Dandy most
of the distance, while I got colder and colder, and beguiled the time
by composing poems or limericks on places at the front.　Arriving
at my billet in the small hours of the morning, I would find my
friend Ross not always in the best of humors at being kept up so
late.　The ride back from Wulverghem or Dranoutre, owing to

the narrowness of the road and the amount of transport and lorries upon it, was rather dangerous. It was a matter of ten miles to come back from Wulverghem, and the roads were very dark. One night in particular I had a narrow escape. I had mounted Dandy at the back of a farmhouse, but for some reason or other I seemed to have lost control over him and he was unusually lively. Luckily for me a man offered to lead him out into the road, and just before he let him go discovered that the bit was not in his mouth.

The Alberta Dragoons had billets in a side road that led to Bailleul. It was a quiet and peaceful neighbourhood, and they had good barns for their horses. In the fields they had splendid opportunities for training and exercise. I often took service for them. One Sunday afternoon I had been speaking of the necessity of purifying the commercial life of Canada on our return, and I said something uncomplimentary about land speculators. I was told afterwards that I had caused much amusement in all ranks, for every man in the troop from the officers downwards, or upwards, was a land speculator, and had town lots to sell in the West. In conversations with privates and non-coms., I often found they had left good positions in Canada and not infrequently were men of means. I have given mud-splashed soldiers a ride in the car, and they have talked about their own cars at home. It was quite pathetic to see how much men thought of some little courtesy or act of kindness. A young fellow was brought in on a stretcher to the Red Chateau dressing station one Sunday afternoon at Courcelette. He was terribly wounded and gave me his father's address in Canada so that I might write to him. He was carried away and I heard afterwards he died. Some months later I had a letter from his father, a Presbyterian minister in Ontario, thanking me for writing and telling me how pleased his son had been by my giving him a ride one day in a Headquarters car. I mention this so that people will realize how much the men had given up when they considered such a trifling thing worth mentioning.

The position of a chaplain as the war went on became very different from what it had been at the beginning. The experience through which the army had passed had showed to the military authorities that there was something more subtle, more supernatural behind the life of the men, than one might gather from the King's Regulations. Our chaplains had done splendid work, and I think I may say that, with one or two exceptions, they were idolized by their units. I could tell of one of our chaplains who lived continually at the advanced dressing station in great hardship and discomfort, sharing the danger and privation of his men. The curious thing about a chaplain's popularity was that the men never praised a chaplain whom they knew without adding "It is a pity that all chaplains are not like him". On one occasion when I was going through the Division, I was told by the men of one unit that their chaplain was a prince, and it was a pity that all chaplains were not like him. I went to another unit, and there again I was told that their chaplain was a prince, and it was a pity that all chaplains were not like him. It seems to be a deeply rooted principle in a soldier's mind to beware of praising religion overmuch. But it amused me in a general survey to find that ignorance of the work of other chaplains led to their condemnation. I fancy the same spirit still manifests itself in the British Army and in Canada. I find officers and men eager enough to praise those who were their own chaplains but always adding to it a condemnation of those who were not. An officer said to me one day that the war had enabled chaplains to get to know men. I told him that the war also had enabled men to get to know chaplains. Large numbers of men in ordinary life are very seldom brought into contact with religion. They have the crude notion of it which they carried away as unfledged boys from Sunday School, and a sort of formal bowing acquaintance through the conventions of later life. In the war, when their minds and affections were put to a severe strain, it was a revelation to them to find that there were principles and relationships of divine origin which enabled the ordinary human will easily to surmount difficulties moral and physical, and which gave a quiet strength that nothing merely earthly could supply. Certainly the war gave chaplains a splendid opportunity of bearing witness to the power of Christ. A great deal has been written about the religion of the men at the front. Some have spoken of it in terms of exaggerated optimism, as though by the miracle of the war men had become beings of angelic outlook and temper. Others have taken a despairing attitude, and thought that religion has lost its real power over the world. The truth is, I think, that there was a revelation to most men, in a broad way, of a mysterious soul life within, and of a huge responsibility to an infinite and eternal Being above. There was a revelation also, wide and deep, to many individual men, of the living force and example of Him who is both

God and Brother-man. Where the associations of church and home had been clean and helpful, men under the batterings of war felt consciously the power of religion. In the life at the front, no doubt there was much evil thinking, evil talking and evil doing, but there was, underlying all this, the splendid manifestation in human nature of that image of God in which man was made. As one looks back upon it, the surface things of that life have drifted away, and the great things that one remembers are the self-sacrifice, the living comradeship, and the unquestioning faith in the eternal rightness of right and duty which characterized those who were striving to the death for the salvation of the world. This glorious vision of the nobility of human nature sustained the chaplain through many discouragements and difficulties. I have often sat on my horse on rainy nights near Hill 63, and watched the battalions going up to the line. With wet rubber sheets hanging over their huge packs and with rifles on their shoulders, the men marched up through the mud and cold and darkness, to face wounds and death. At such times, the sordid life has been transfigured before me. The hill was no longer Hill 63, but it was the hill of Calvary. The burden laid upon the men was no longer the heavy soldier's pack, but it was the cross of Christ, and, as the weary tramp of the men splashed in the mud, I said to myself "Each one has fulfilled the law of life, and has taken up his cross and is following Christ."

I told the men this one day on church parade; and a corporal sometime afterwards said that, when next their battalion was moving up into the line, a young fellow beside him was swearing very hard over the amount of stuff he had to carry. My friend went over to him and said, "Don't you know that Canon Scott told us that this really isn't a pack, but it's the Cross of Christ?" The lad stopped swearing at once, and took up his burden without a word.

CHAPTER. IX

OUR FIRST CHRISTMAS IN FRANCE.

THE 25th of December 1915, was to be our first Christmas in France, and as the day approached there was much speculation among our men as to which Battalions would be in the line. At last orders came out that the 13th and 16th Battalions would relieve the 14th and 15th on Christmas Eve. I determined, therefore, to spend my Christmas with the former two. Our trenches at that time were in front of Ploegsteert. The 16th was on the right and the 13th on the left. Taking my bag with communion vessels and as many hymn books as I could carry, and with a haversack over my shoulder containing requisites for the night, I was motored over on Christmas Eve to the 3rd Brigade Headquarters at Petit Moncque Farm. The day was rainy and so was not calculated to improve the spirits and temper of the men who were going to spend their first Christmas in the line. At dusk I walked up the road to Hill 63, and then down on the other side to Le Plus Douve Farm. It was not a cheerful Christmas Eve. The roads were flooded with water, and the transports that were waiting for the relief were continually getting tangled up with one another in the darkness. To make matters worse, I was met by a Sergeant who told me he had some men to be buried, and a burial party was waiting on the side of the road. We went into the field which was used as a cemetery and there we laid the bodies to rest.

The Germans had dammed the river Douve, and it had flooded some of the fields and old Battalion Headquarters. It was hard to find one's way in the dark, and I should never have done so without assistance. The men had acquired the power of seeing in the dark, like cats.

A Battalion was coming out and the men were wet and muddy. I stood by the bridge watching them pass and, thinking it was the right and conventional thing to do, wished them all a Merry Christmas. My intentions were of the best, but I was afterwards told that it sounded to the men like the voice of one mocking them in their misery. However, as it turned out, the wish was fulfilled on the next day.

As soon as I could cross the bridge, I made my way to the trench-

OUR FIRST CHRISTMAS IN FRANCE

es which the 16th Battalion were taking over. They were at a higher level and were not in a bad condition. Further up the line there was a barn known as St. Quentin's Farm, which for some reason or other, although it was in sight of the enemy, had not been demolished and was used as a billet. I determined therefore to have a service of Holy Communion at midnight, when the men would all have come into the line and settled down. About eleven o'clock I got things ready. The officers and men had been notified of the service and began to assemble. The barn was a fair size and had dark red brick walls. The roof was low and supported by big rafters. The floor was covered with yellow straw about two feet in depth. The men proceeded to search for a box which I could use as an altar. All they could get were three large empty biscuit tins. These we covered with my Union Jack and white linen cloth. A row of candles was stuck against the wall, which I was careful to see were prevented from setting fire to the straw. The dull red tint of the brick walls, the clean yellow straw, and the bright radiance of our glorious Union Jack made a splendid combination of colour. It would have been a fitting setting for a tableau of the Nativity.

The Highlanders assembled in two rows and I handed out hymn books. There were many candles in the building so the men were able to read. It was wonderful to hear in such a place and on such an occasion, the beautiful old hymns, "While Shepherds Watched their Flocks by Night," "Hark the Herald Angels Sing," and "O Come All Ye Faithful." The men sang them lustily and many and varied were the memories of past Christmases that welled up in their thoughts at that time.

I had a comfortable bunk in one of the dugouts that night, and was up next morning early to spend the day among the men in the line. I was delighted to find that the weather had changed and a most glorious day was lighting up the face of nature. The sky overhead was blue and only a few drifting clouds told of the rain that had gone. The sun was beating down warm and strong, as if anxious to make up for his past neglect. The men, of course, were in high spirits, and the glad hand-shake and the words "A Merry Christmas" had got back their old-time meaning.

The Colonel had given orders to the men not to fire on the enemy that day unless they fired on us. The Germans had evidently come to the same resolution. Early in the morning some of them had

119

come over to our wire and left two bottles of beer behind as a peace offering. The men were allowed to go back to their trenches unmolested, but the two bottles of beer quite naturally and without any difficulty continued their journey to our lines. When I got up to the front trench, I found our boys standing on the parapet and looking over at the enemy. I climbed up, and there, to my astonishment, I saw the Germans moving about in their trenches apparently quite indifferent to the fact that we were gazing at them. One man was sawing wood. Between us and them lay that mass of wire and iron posts which is known as the mysterious "No Man's Land." Further down the hill we saw the trenches of the 13th Battalion, where apparently intermittent "Straffing" was still going on. Where we were, however, there was nothing to disturb our Christmas peace and joy. I actually got out into "No Mans Land" and wandered down it. Many Christmas parcels had arrived and the men were making merry with their friends, and enjoying the soft spring-like air, and the warm sunshine. When I got down to the 13th Battalion however, I found that I had to take cover, as the German snipers and guns were active. I did not have any service for that Battalion then, as I was going to them on the following Sunday, but at evening I held another midnight service for those of the 16th who were on duty the night before.

The only place available was the billet of the Machine Gun Officer in the second trench. It was the cellar of a ruined building and the entrance was down some broken steps. One of the sergeants had cleaned up the place and a shelf on the wall illuminated by candles was converted into an altar, and the dear old flag, the symbol of liberty, equality and fraternity, was once again my altar cloth. The Machine Gun Officer, owing to our close proximity to the enemy, was a little doubtful as to the wisdom of our singing hymns, but finally allowed us to do so. The tiny room and the passage outside were crowded with stalwart young soldiers, whose voices sang out the old hymns as though the Germans were miles away. Our quarters were so cramped that the men had difficulty in squeezing into the room for communion and could not kneel down. The service was rich and beautiful in the heartfelt devotion of men to whom, in their great need, religion was a real and vital thing. Not long after midnight, once again the pounding of the old war was resumed, and as I went to bed in the dugout that night, I felt from what a sublime height the world had dropped. We had two more war Christmases in France, but I always look back upon that first one as something unique in its beauty and simplicity.

When I stood on the parapet that day looking over at the Germans in their trenches, and thought how two great nations were held back for a time in their fierce struggle for supremacy, by their devotion to a little Child born in a stable in Bethlehem two thousand years before, I felt that there was still promise of a regenerated world. The Angels had not sung in vain their wonderful hymn "Glory to God in the Highest and on Earth Peace, Good Will towards men."

CHAPTER X

Spring, 1916.

AT the end of March our Division was ordered back to the Salient, and so Headquarters left St. Jans Cappel. It was with great regret that I bid good-by to the little place which had been such a pleasant home for several months. The tide of war since then has no doubt swept away many of the pastoral charms of the scenery, but the green fields and the hillsides will be reclothed in beauty as time goes on. We stopped for a few days at Flêtre, and while there I made the acquaintance of the Australians, and visited the battalions which were billeted in the neighbourhood.

It was always delightful to have the Division out in rest. As long as the men were in the line one could not be completely happy. But when they came out and one went amongst them, there was nothing to overcloud the pleasure of our intercourse. One day I rode over to a battalion and found a lot of men sitting round the cookhouse. We had a long talk about the war, and they asked me to recite my war limericks. I spent the evening with the O.C. of a battery and the night, on my return, was very dark. One of the battalions had been paid off that afternoon, and the men, who as usual had been celebrating the event in an estaminet, were in boisterous spirits. It was so hard to make my way through the crowd that Dandy got nervous and unmanageable. A young fellow who recognized me in the dark came up and asked me if I should like him to lead the horse down the road. I gratefully accepted his offer. He walked beside me till we came to a bridge, and then he told me that he had been very much interested in religion since he came to the war, and was rather troubled over the fact that he had never been baptised. He said he had listened to my limericks that day, and while he was listening had determined to speak to me about his baptism. I arranged to prepare him, and, before the battalion started north, I baptised him in the C.O's. room in a farmhouse. The Adjutant acted as his godfather. I do not know where the lad is now, or how he fared in the war, but someday I hope I shall hear from him again. It was often very difficult, owing to the numbers of men one was meeting, and the many changes that were continually taking place, to keep track of the lives of individuals.

The revelations of the religious experiences and the needs of the human soul, which came over and over again from conversations with men, were always of the greatest help to a chaplain, and made him feel that, in spite of many discouragements and much indifference, there was always some soul asking for spiritual help.

The Headquarters of our Division were now at a place called Hooggraaf. It consisted of a few small houses and a large school kept by nuns. Huts were run up for the officers and, at a little distance down the road, a home was built for "C" mess. At one side were some Armstrong canvas huts, one of which was mine. It was a pleasant place, and being back from the road was free from dust. Green fields, rich in grain, spread in all directions. It was at Hooggraaf that the Engineers built me a church, and a big sign over the door proclaimed it to be "St. George's Church." It was first used on Easter Day, which in 1916 fell on the Festival of St. George, and we had very hearty services.

Poperinghe, only two miles away, became our city of refuge. Many of our units had their headquarters there, and the streets were filled with our friends. We had many pleasant gatherings there in an estaminet which became a meeting place for officers. The Guards Division, among other troops, were stationed in Poperinghe, so there was much variety of life and interest in the town. "Talbot House," for the men, and the new Officer's Club, presided over by Neville Talbot, were centres of interest. The gardens at the back made very pleasant places for an after-dinner smoke. There were very good entertainments in a theatre every evening, where "The Follies," a theatrical company of Imperial soldiers, used to perform. Poperinghe was even at that time damaged by shells, but since then it has suffered more severely. The graceful spire, which stood up over the plain with its outline against the sky, has luckily been preserved. We had some very good rest billets for the men in the area around Hooggraaf. They consisted of collections of large wooden huts situated in different places, and called by special names. "Scottish Lines," "Connaught Lines," and "Patricia Lines," were probably the most comfortable. In fact, all along the various roads which ran through our area different units made their homes.

Our military prison was in a barn about a mile from Headquarters. I used to go there for service every Monday afternoon at six o' clock. By that time, the men had come back from work.

They slept on shelves, one over another. The barn was poorly lighted, and got dark early in the afternoon. The first time I took service there, I was particularly anxious that everything should be done as nicely as possible, so that the men would not think they had come under the ban of the church. Most of their offences were military ones. The men therefore were not criminals in the ordinary sense of the term. I brought my surplice, scarf and hymn books, and I told the men that I wanted them to sing. They lay on the shelves with only their heads and shoulders visible. I told them that I wanted the service to be hearty, and asked them to choose the first hymn. A voice from one of the shelves said—

"Here we suffer grief and pain."

A roar of laughter went up from the prisoners, in which I joined heartily.

At the front, we held Hill 60 and the trenches to the south of it. In a railway embankment, a series of dugouts furnished the Brigade that was in the line with comfortable billets. The Brigadier's abode had a fire-place in it. One of the dugouts was used as a morgue, in which bodies were kept till they could be buried. A man told me that one night when he had come down from the line very late, he found a dugout full of men wrapped in their blankets, every one apparently asleep. Without more ado, he crawled in amongst them and slept soundly till morning. When he awoke, he found to his horror that he had slept all night among the dead men in the morgue. There was a cemetery at Railway Dugouts, which was carefully laid out. Beyond this there was another line of sandbag homes on one side of a large pond called "Zillebeke Lake." They were used by other divisions.

From Railway Dugouts, by paths and then by communication trenches, one made one's way up to Hill 60 and the other parts of the front line, where the remains of a railway crossed the hill. Our dugouts were on the east side of it, and the line itself was called "Lover's Lane". The brick arch of a bridge which crossed the line was part of our front.

One day I was asked by a British chaplain, who was ordered south, to accompany him on a trip he was making to his brother's grave at Hooge. He wished to mark it by a cross. As the place was in full view of the Germans, we had to visit it before dawn. I met my friend at 2.30 a.m. in the large dugout under the Ramparts at Ypres. We started off with two runners, but one managed most conveniently to lose us and returned home. The other accompanied us all the way. It was a weird expedition. The night was partly cloudy, and faint moonlight struggled through the mist which shrouded us. The runner went first, and the Padré, who was a tall man, followed, carrying the cross on his shoulder. I brought up the rear. In the dim light, my friend looked like some allegorical figure from "Pilgrim's Progress". Occasionally we heard the hammering of a machine-gun, and we would lie down till the danger was past. We skirted the grim borders of Sanctuary Wood, and made our way to Hooge. There my friend got out his map to find, if possible, the place where he had buried his brother. He sat down in a large shell hole, and turned his flashlight upon the paper. It was difficult to find the location, because the place had recently been the scene of a hard struggle. The guide and I looked over the ground and we found a line of graves marked by broken crosses. The night was fast passing and in the grey of the eastern sky the stars were going out one by one. At last my friend found the spot he was looking for and there he set up the cross, and had a short memorial service for the dead. On our return, we passed once more by Sanctuary Wood, and in the daylight looked into the place torn and battered by shells and reeking with the odours of unburied bodies.

We parted at Zillebeke Bund, and I made my way to Railway Dugouts. It was a lovely morning and the air was so fresh that although I had been walking all night I did not feel tired. The 3rd Battalion was holding the line just behind a piece of ground which was called the "Bean and Pollock." It was supposed that the Germans had mined the place and that an explosion might be expected at any minute. One company had built a rustic arbour, which they used as their mess-room. The bright sun shone through the green boughs overhead. There was intermittent shelling, but nothing to cause us any worry. I stayed till late in the afternoon, when I made my way towards the rear of Hill 60. There I found the 14th Battalion which was in reserve. They told me that the 16th Battalion in the line was going to blow up a mine that night, and offered to give me a dugout if I would stay for the festivities. I gladly accepted, and just before midnight made my way to a dugout that had just been completed. I was told that there was a bed in it with a wire mattress. When I got into the dugout, I lit a candle, and found to my astonishment that the place was full of men lying on the bed and the floor. They offered to get out but I told them not to think of it. So we lit another candle, and had a very pleasant time until the mine went up. We heard a fearful explosion, and the ground rocked as it does in an earthquake. It was not long before the Germans retaliated, and we heard the shells falling round us. At daybreak I went up to the line to see the result of the explosion. A large crater had been made in No Man's Land, but for some reason or other the side of our trench had been blown back upon our own men and there were many casualties.

I stayed in the trenches all afternoon, and on my way back went to an artillery observation post on a hill which was crowned by the ruins of an old mill. The place was called Verbranden Molen. Here I found a young artillery officer on duty. The day was so clear that we were able to spread out a map before us on the ground and with our glasses look up every point named on the sheet. We looked far over to the North and saw the ruins of Wieltje. Ypres lay to the left, and we could see Zillebeke, Sanctuary Wood, High Wood, Square Wood, and Hooge. The light reflected from our glasses must have been seen by some German sniper, for suddenly we heard the crack of bullets in the hedge behind us and we hastily withdrew to the dugout. As I walked back down the road I came to one of the posts of the motor-machine-gunners who were there on guard. They were just having tea outside and kindly invited me to join them. We had a delightful conversation on poetry and literature, but were prepared to beat a hasty retreat into the dugout in case the Germans took to shelling the road, which they did every evening.

Railway Dugouts was always a pleasant place to visit, there were so many men there. As one passed up and down the wooden walk which ran the length of the embankment there were many opportunities of meeting one's friends. On the other side of it, however, which was exposed to the German shells, the men frequently had a hard time in getting up to the line.

There were several interesting chateaus in the neighbourhood. That nearest to the front was called Bedford House, and stood in what must have been once very beautiful grounds. The upper part of the house was in ruins, but the cellars were deep and capacious and formed a good billet for the officers and men. At one side there was a dressing station and in the garden were some huts protected by piles of sand bags.

SPRING, 1916

A chateau that was well-known in the Salient lay a little to the west of Bedford House. It was called Swan Chateau, from the fact that a large white swan lived on the artificial lake in the grounds. I never saw the swan myself, but the men said it had been wounded in the wing and had lost an eye. It was long an object of interest to many battalions that at different times were housed in the chateau. One day the swan disappeared. It was rumoured that a hungry Canadian battalion had killed it for food. On the other hand, it was said that it had been taken to some place of safety to prevent its being killed. There was something very poetical in the idea of this beautiful bird living on through the scene of desolation, like the spirit of the world that had passed away. It brought back memories of the life that had gone, and the splendour of an age which had left Ypres forever.

CHAPTER XI.

THE ATTACK ON MOUNT SORREL

Summer, 1916.

EASTER Day, 1916, fell on the 23rd of April, and a great many interesting facts were connected with it. The 23rd of April is St. George's Day. It is also the anniversary of Shakespeare's birth and of his death, and also of the 2nd Battle of Ypres. The day was a glorious one. The air was sweet and fresh, the grass was the brightest green, hedgerows and trees were in leaf, and everybody was in high spirits. After services in St. George's church I rode over to Poperinghe and attended a memorial service which the 1st Brigade were holding in the Cinema. General Mercer, who himself was killed not long afterwards, was one of the speakers, The building was crowded with men, and the service was very solemn.

Life at this time was very pleasant, except for the fact that we never knew what might happen when we were in the Salient. We always felt that it was a death-trap, and that the Germans would never give up trying to capture Ypres. I was kept busy riding about, visiting the different units. Round about Hooggraaf the spring roads were very attractive, and the numerous short cuts through the fields and under the overhanging trees reminded one of country life at home.

One day Dandy bolted as I was mounting him, and I fell on some bath mats breaking a bone in my hand and cutting my face in several places. This necessitated my being sent up to the British C. C. S. at Mont des Cats. Mont des Cats was a picturesque hill which overlooked the Flanders Plain, and could be seen from all parts of the Salient. On the top there was a Trappist monastery. The buildings were modern and covered a large extent of ground. They were solidly built of brick and stone and the chapel was a beautiful building with a high vaulted roof. From the top of the hill, a magnificent view of the country could be obtained, to the North as far as the sea, and to the East as far as our trenches, where we could see the shells bursting.

Mont des Cats hospital was a most delightful temporary home. There was a large ward full of young officers, who were more or less ill or damaged. In another part of the building were wards for the men. From the O. C. downwards everyone in the C. C. S. was the soul of kindness, and the beautiful buildings with their pleasant grounds gave a peculiar charm to the life. My room was not far from the chapel, and every night at two a. m. I could hear the old monks chanting their offices. Most of the monks had been conscripted and were fighting in the French army; only a few of the older ones remained. But by day and night at stated intervals the volume of their prayer and praise rose up above the noise of war, just as it had risen through the centuries of the past. There were beautiful gardens which the monks tended carefully, and also many grape vines on the walls. We used to watch the silent old men doing their daily work and making signs to one another instead of speaking. In the evening I would make my way up the spiral staircase to the west-end gallery, which looked down upon the chapel. The red altar lamp cast a. dim light in the sacred building, and every now and then in the stillness I could hear, like the roar of a distant sea, the sound of shells falling at the front. The mysterious silence of the lofty building, with the far off reverberations of war thrilling it now and then, was a solace to the soul.

A smaller chapel in the monastery, with a well-appointed altar, was allotted by the monks to the chaplain for his services. While I was at Mont des Cats we heard of the death of Lord Kitchener. The news came to the Army with the force of a stunning blow; but thank God, the British character is hardened and strengthened by adversity, and while we all felt his loss keenly and looked forward to the future with anxiety, the determination to go on to victory was made stronger by the catastrophe. As the chaplain of the hospital was away at the time, I held a memorial service in the large refectory. Following upon the death of Lord Kitchener came another disaster. The Germans in the beginning of June launched a fierce attack upon the 3rd Division, causing many casualties and capturing many prisoners. General Mercer was killed, and a brigadier was wounded and taken prisoner. To make matters worse, we heard of the battle of Jutland, the first report of which was certainly disconcerting. We gathered from it that our navy had suffered a great reverse. The death of Lord Kitchener, the naval reverse, and the fierce attack on our front, following one another in such a short space of time, called for great steadiness of nerve and coolness of head. I felt that the hospital was no place for me when Canadians were meeting reverses at the front, especially as the First Division was ordered to recapture the lost trenches. I telephoned to my good friend, Colonel Brutenell, the C. O. of the Motor Machine-Gun Brigade, and asked him to send me a side-car to take me forward. He had always in the past shown me much kindness in supplying me with means of locomotion. Colonel Brutenell was an old country Frenchman with the most courteous manners. When I first discovered that he was the possessor of side-cars, I used to obtain them by going over to him and saying, "Colonel, if you will give me a side-car I will recite you one of my poems." He was too polite at first to decline to enter into the bargain, but, as time went on, I found that the price I offered began to lose its value, and sometimes the side-cars were not forthcoming. It then became necessary to change my plan of campaign, so I hit upon another device. I used to walk into the orderly room and say in a raucous voice, "Colonel, if you *don't* give me a side-car I will recite one of my poems." I found that in the long run this was the most effectual method. On the present occasion, therefore, the side-car was sent to me, and I made my way to Wippenhoek and from thence up to the dressing station at Vlamertinghe. Here our wounded were pouring in. Once again Canada was reddening the soil of the Salient with her best blood. It was indeed an anxious time. That evening, however, a telegram was received by the O. C. of the Ambulance saying that the British fleet had sunk twenty or thirty German vessels, and implying that what we had thought was a naval reverse was really a magnificent naval victory. I do not know who sent the telegram, or on what foundation in fact it was based. I think that somebody in authority considered it would be well to cheer up our men with a piece of good news. At any rate all who were at the dressing station believed it, and I determined to carry a copy of the telegram with me up to the men in the line. I started off on one of the ambulances for Railway Dugouts. Those ambulance journeys through the town of Ypres after midnight were things to be remembered. The desolate ruins of the city stood up black and grim. The road was crowded with men, lorries, ambulances, transports and motorcycles. Every now and then the scene of desolation would be lit up by gun flashes. Occasionally the crash of a shell would shake the already sorely smitten city. I can never cease to admire the pluck of those ambulance drivers, who night after

130

night, backwards and forwards, threaded their way in the darkness through the ghost-haunted streets. One night when the enemy's guns were particularly active, I was being driven by a young boy only eighteen years of age. Sitting beside him on the front seat, I told him how much I admired his nerve and coolness. He turned to me quite simply and said that he was not afraid. He just put himself in God's hands and didn't worry. When he came afterwards to Headquarters and drove our side-car he never minded where he went or how far towards the front he took it. I do not know where he is in Canada, but I know that Canada will be the better for having such a boy as one of her citizens.

When I arrived at Railway Dugouts, I found that there was great activity on all sides, but my message about our naval victory had a most stimulating effect and I had the courage to wake up no less than three generals to tell them the good news. They said they didn't care how often they were awakened for news like that. I then got a runner, and was making my way up to the men in the front line when the Germans put on an attack. The trench that I was in became very hot, and, as I had my arm in a sling and could not walk very comfortably or do much in the way of dodging, the runner and I thought it would be wiser to return, especially as we could not expect the men, then so fully occupied, to listen to our message of cheer. We made our way back as best we could to Railway Dugouts, and telephoned the news to the various battalion headquarters. The telegram was never confirmed, and I was accused of having made it up myself. It certainly had a wholesome effect upon our men at a critical and anxious moment.

We had a hard time in retaking the lost ground. Gallant were the charges which were made in broad daylight in the face of heavy machine-gun fire. In preparation for the attack, our men had to lie under the cover of broken hedges for twenty-four hours, living only on the iron rations which they carried with them. I went up one morning when one of our battalions had just come out after a hard fight. The men were in a shallow trench, ankle deep in mud and water. As they had lost very heavily, the Colonel put me in charge of a burial party. We buried a number of bodies but were stopped at last at the entrance of Armagh Wood, which the Germans were at the time heavily shelling, and we had to postpone the performance of our sad duty till things were quieter.

THE WAR AS I SAW IT

Still in spite of reverses, the spirits of our men never declined. They were full of rebound, and quickly recovered themselves. As one looks back to that period of our experience, all sorts of pictures, bright and sombre, crowd the mind—the Square at Poperinghe in the evening, the Guards' fife and drum bands playing tattoo in the old town while hundreds of men looked on; the dark station of Poperinghe in the evening, and the battalions being sent up to the front in railway trucks; the old mill at Vlamertinghe with the reception room for the wounded, and the white tables on which the bleeding forms were laid; the dark streets of Ypres, rank with the poisonous odours of shell gas; the rickety horse-ambulances bearing their living freight over the shell broken roads from Bedford House and Railway Dugouts; the walking wounded, with bandaged arms and heads, making their way slowly and painfully down the dangerous foot-paths; all these pictures flash before the mind's eye, each with its own appeal, as one looks back upon those awful days. The end was not in sight then. The war, we were told, was going to be a war of attrition. It was to be a case of "dogged does it." Under the wheels of the car of the great Juggernaut our men had to throw themselves, till the progress of the car was stayed. How peaceful were the little cemeteries where lay those warriors who had entered into rest. But how stern was the voice from the sleeping dead to carry on undismayed.

The Canadian Corps seemed to have taken root in the Salient, and, after the severe fighting had ended, things went on as if we were to have a long residence round Ypres. In looking over the notes in my diary for June and July, I see a great many records of visits to different units. How well one remembers the keen active life which made that region a second Canada. There was the small town of Abeele, where our Corps Headquarters were, and where our new commander, General Byng, had his house. Not far away, up the road, was the grenade school where the troops were instructed in the gentle art of bomb-throwing. We had our divisional rest-camp in a pleasant spot, where our men were sent to recuperate. The following is a typical Sunday's work at this time:—Celebration of Holy Communion at St. George's Church at eight a. m., Parade Service for the Division at nine fifteen a. m., followed by a second Celebration of Holy Communion at ten a. m., Parade Service followed by Holy Communion for a Battalion at Connaught lines at eleven a. m., service for the divisional rest-camp at three p. m., service at the Grenade School at four p. m., service outside St. George's Church for the Divisional Train six-thirty p. m., service for the 3rd Field Ambulance and convalescent camp at eight-forty-five p. m. On week-days too, we had to arrange many services for units which had come out of the line. It was really a life full of activity and interest. It filled one with a thrill of delight to be able to get round among the men in the trenches, where the familiar scenery of Sanctuary Wood, Armagh Wood, Maple Copse and the Ravine will always remain impressed upon one's memory. Often when I have returned to my hut at night, I have stood outside in the darkness, looking over the fields towards the front, and as I saw the German flares going up, I said to myself, "Those are the foot-lights of the stage on which the world's greatest drama is being enacted." One seemed to be taking part, however humbly, in the making of human history. But it was a grievous thing to think of the toll of life that the war forced upon us and the suffering that it involved. The brave patient hearts of those at home were continually in our thoughts, and we always felt that the hardest burden was laid upon them. They had no excitement; they knew not the comradeship and the exaltation of feeling which came to those who were in the thick of things at the front. They had to go on day by day bearing their burden of anxiety, quietly and patiently in faith and courage. To them our men were always ready to give the palm of the victors.

CHAPTER XII.

The Battle of the Somme

Autumn, 1916

IT always happened that just when we were beginning to feel settled in a place, orders came for us to move. At the end of July we heard of the attack at the Somme. Rumours began to circulate that we were to go South, and signs of the approaching pilgrimage began to manifest themselves. On August 10th all my superfluous baggage was sent back to England, and on the following day I bid good-bye to my comfortable little hut at Hooggraaf and started to ride to our new Divisional Headquarters which were to be for the time near St. Omer. After an early breakfast with my friend General Thacker, I started off on Dandy for the long ride. I passed through Abeele and Steenvoorde, where I paid my respects at the Chateau, overtaking many of our units, either on the march or in the fields by the wayside, and that night I arrived at Cassel and put up at the hotel. The town never looked more beautiful than at sunset on that lovely summer evening. It had about it the spell of the old world, and the quiet life which had gone on through the centuries in a kind of dream. One did hope that the attack to the South would be the beginning of the end and that peace would be restored to the shattered world. On that day, the King had arrived on a flying visit to the front, and some of his staff were billeted at the hotel. The following day I visited the Second Army Headquarters in the Casino Building, and met some of our old friends who had gone there from the Canadian Corps. In the afternoon I rode off to St. Omer, little Philo running beside me full of life and spirits. It was a hot and dusty ride. I put up at the Hotel du Commerce, where I met several Canadian officers and many airmen. The next day was Sunday so I attended the service in the military church. After it was over, I went with a young flying officer into the old cathedral. The service had ended and we were alone in the building, but the sunlight flooded it and brought out the richness of contrast in light and shadow, and the air was still fragrant with the smell of incense. My friend and I were talking, as we sat there, about the effect the war had had upon religion. Turning to me he said,

THE BATTLE OF THE SOMME

"The great thing I find when I am in a tight place in the air is to pray to Jesus Christ. Many and many a time when I have been in difficulties and thought that I really must be brought down, I have prayed to Him and He has preserved me." I looked at the boy as he spoke. He was very young, but had a keen, earnest face, and I thought how often I had seen fights in the air and how little I had imagined that the human hearts in those little craft, which looked like tiny flies among the clouds, were praying to God for help and protection. I told him how glad I was to hear his testimony to the power of Christ. When we got back to the hotel, one of the airmen came up to him and said, "Congratulations, old chap, here's your telegram." The telegram was an order for him to join a squadron which held what the airmen considered to be, from it's exceeding danger, the post of honour at the Somme front. I often wonder if the boy came through the fierce ordeal alive.

It was pleasant to meet Bishop Gwynne and his staff once again. There was always something spiritually bracing in visiting the Headquarters of our Chaplain Service at St. Omer. On the Monday I rode off to our Divisional Headquarters, which were in a fine old chateau at Tilques. I had a pleasant billet in a comfortable house at the entrance to the town, and the different units of the Division were encamped in the quaint villages round about. After their experience in the Salient, the men were glad to have a little peace and rest; although they knew they were on their journey to bigger and harder things. The country around St. Omer was so fresh and beautiful that the change of scene did everyone good. The people too were exceedingly kind and wherever we went we found that the Canadians were extremely popular. There were many interesting old places near by which brought back memories of French history. However, the day came when we had to move. From various points the battalions entrained for the South. On Monday, August 28th, I travelled by train with the 3rd Field Company of Engineers and finally found myself in a billet at Canaples. After two or three days we settled at a place called Rubempré. Here I had a clean billet beside a very malodorous pond which the village cows used as their drinking place. The country round us was quite different in character from what it had been further north. Wide stretches of open ground and rolling hills, with here and there patches of green woods, made up a very pleasant landscape. I rode one day to Amiens and visited the glorious cathedral

135

which I had not seen since I came there as a boy thirty-three years before. I attended the service of Benediction that evening at six o'clock. The sunlight was streaming through the glorious windows, and the whole place was filled with a beauty that seemed to be not of earth. There was a large congregation present and it was made up of a varied lot of people. There were women in deep mourning, Sisters of Charity and young children. There were soldiers and old men. But they were all one in their spirit of humble adoration and intercession. The organ pealed out its noble strains until the whole place was vibrant with devotion. I shall never forget the impression that service made upon me. The next time I saw the cathedral, Amiens was deserted of its inhabitants, four shells had pierced the sacred fane itself, and the long aisles, covered with bits of broken glass, were desolate and silent.

From Rubempré we moved to Albert, where we were billeted in a small house on a back street. Our Battle Headquarters were in the Bapaume road in trenches and dugouts, on a rise in the ground which was called Tara Hill. By the side of the road was a little cemetery which had been laid out by the British, and was henceforth to be the last resting place of many Canadians. Our battalions were billeted in different places in the damaged town, and in the brick-fields near by. Our chief dressing station was in an old school-house not far from the Cathedral. Albert must have been a pleasant town in pre-war days, but now the people had deserted it and every building had either been shattered or damaged by shells. From the spire of the Cathedral hung at right angles the beautiful bronze image of the Blessed Virgin, holding up her child above her head for the adoration of the world. It seemed to me as if there was something appropriate in the strange position the statue now occupied, for, as the battalions marched past the church, it looked as if they were receiving a parting benediction from the Infant Saviour.

The character of the war had now completely changed. For months and months, we seemed to have reached a deadlock. Now we had broken through and were to push on and on into the enemy's territory. As we passed over the ground which had already been won from the Germans, we were amazed at the wonderful dugouts which they had built, and the huge craters made by the explosion of our mines. The dugouts were deep in the ground, lined with wood and lighted by electric light. Bits of handsome furniture, too, had found their way there from the captured villages, which showed that the Germans must have lived in great comfort. We were certainly glad of the homes they had made for us, for our division was in the line three times during the battle of the Somme, going back to Rubempré and Canaples when we came out for the necessary rest between the attacks.

Looking back to those terrible days of fierce fighting, the mind is so crowded with memories and pictures that it is hard to disentangle them. How well one remembers the trips up the Bapaume road to La Boisselle and Pozières. The country rolled off into the distance in vast billows, and bore marks of the fierce fighting which had occurred here when the British made their great advance. When one rode out from our rear headquarters at the end of the town one passed some brick houses more or less damaged and went on to Tara Hill. There by the wayside was a dressing station. On the hill itself there was the waste of pale yellow mud, and the piles of white chalk which marked the side of the trench in which were deep dugouts. There were many wooden huts, too, which were used as offices. The road went on down the slope on the other side of the hill to La Boisselle, where it forked into two—one going to Contalmaison, the other on the left to Pozières and finally to Bapaume. La Boisselle stood, or rather used to stand, on the point of ground where the roads parted. When we saw it, it was simply a mass of broken ground, which showed the ironwork round the former church, some broken tombstones, and the red dust and bricks of what had been houses. There were still some cellars left in which men found shelter. A well there was used by the men for some time, until cases of illness provoked an investigation and a dead German was discovered at the bottom. The whole district was at all times the scene of great activity. Men were marching to or from the line; lorries, limbers, motorcycles, ambulances and staff cars were passing or following one another on the muddy and broken way. Along the road at various points batteries were concealed, and frequently, by a sudden burst of fire, gave one an unpleasant surprise. If one took the turn to the right, which led to Contalmaison, one passed up a gradual rise in the ground and saw the long, dreary waste of landscape which told the story, by shell-ploughed roads and blackened woods, of the deadly presence of war. One of the depressions among the hills was called Sausage Valley. In it were many batteries and some cemeteries, and trenches where our brigade headquarters were. At the corner of a branch road, just above the ruins of Contalmaison, our engineers put up a little shack, and this was used by our Chaplains' Service as a distributing place for coffee and biscuits. Some men were kept there night and day boiling huge tins of water over a smoky fire in the corner. A hundred and twenty-five gallons of coffee were given away every twenty-four hours. Good strong coffee it was too, most bracing in effect. The cups used were cigarette tins, and the troops going up to the trenches or coming back from them, used to stop and have some coffee and some biscuits to cheer them on their way. The place in the road was called Casualty Corner, and was not supposed to be a very "healthy" resting place, but we did not lose any men in front of the little canteen. The work had been started by the Senior Chaplain of the Australian Division which we had relieved, and he handed it over to us.

Under our Chaplains' Service the canteen became a most helpful institution; not only was coffee given away, but many other things, including cigarettes. Many a man has told me that that drink of coffee saved his life when he was quite used up.

In Contalmaison itself, there had once been a very fine chateau. It, like the rest of the village, survived only as a heap of bricks and rubbish, but the cellars, which the Germans had used as a dressing station, were very large and from them branched off deep dugouts lined with planed boards and lit by electric light.

The road which turned to the left led down to a waste of weary ground in a wide valley where many different units were stationed in dugouts and holes in the ground. Towards the Pozières road there was a famous chalk pit. In the hill-side were large dugouts, used by battalions when out of the line. There was also a light railway, and many huts and shacks of various kinds. Pozières looked very much like La Boisselle. Some heaps or rubbish and earth reddened by bricks and brick-dust alone showed where the village had been. At Pozières the Y.M.C.A. had another coffee-stall, where coffee was given away free. These coffee-stalls were a great institution, and in addition to the bracing effect of the drink provided, the rude shack with its cheery fire always made a pleasant place for rest and conversation.

After Courcelette was taken by the 2nd Division, our front line lay beyond it past Death Valley on the slope leading down to Regina Trench, and onward to the villages of Pys and Miraumont. Over all this stretch of country, waste and dreary as it got to be towards the end of September, our various fighting units were scattered, and along that front line, as we pushed the enemy back, our men made the bitter sacrifice of life and limb. It was a time of iron resolve and hard work. There was no opportunity now for amusement and social gatherings. When one spoke to staff officers, they answered in monosyllables. When one rode in their cars, one had very fixed and definite times at which to start and to return. The army had set its teeth and was out to battle in grim earnest. It was a time, however, of hope and encouragement. When, as we advanced, we saw what the German defences had been, we were filled with admiration for the splendid British attack in July which had forced the enemy to retreat. If that had been done once it could be done again, and so we pressed on. But the price we had to pay for victory was indeed costly and one's heart ached for the poor men in their awful struggle in that region of gloom and death. This was war indeed, and one wondered how long it was to last. Gradually the sad consciousness came that our advance was checked, but still the sacrifice was not in vain, for our gallant men were using up the forces of the enemy.

Ghastly were the stories which we heard from time to time. One man told me that he had counted three hundred bodies hanging on the wire which we had failed to cut in preparation for the attack. An officer met me one day and told me how his company had had to hold on in a trench, hour after hour, under terrific bombardment. He was sitting in his dugout, expecting every moment to be blown up, when a young lad came in and asked if he might stay with him. The boy was only eighteen years of age and his nerve had utterly gone. He came into the dugout, and, like a child clinging to his mother clasped the officer with his arms. The latter could not be angry with the lad. There was nothing to do at that point but to hold on and wait, so, as he said to me, "I looked at the boy and thought of his mother, and just leaned down and gave him a kiss. Not long afterwards a shell struck the dugout and the boy was killed, and when we retired I had to leave his body there." Wonderful deeds were done; some were known and received well merited rewards, others were noted only by the Recording Angel. A piper won the V.C. for his gallantry in marching up and down in front of the wire playing his pipes while the men were struggling through it in their attack upon Regina Trench. He was killed going back to hunt for his pipes which he had left in helping a wounded man to a place of safety. One cannot write of that awful time unmoved, for there come up before the mind faces of friends that one will see no more, faces of men who were strong, brave and even joyous in the midst of that burning fiery furnace, from which their lives passed, we trust into regions where there shall be no more death, neither sorrow nor crying, and where the sound of war is hushed forever.

One new feature which was introduced into the war at this time was the "Tank." A large family of these curious and newly developed instruments of battle was congregated in a wood on the outskirts of the town, and awoke great interest on all sides. At that time we were doubtful how far they would be able to fulfill the hopes that were entertained of them. Some of them had already been knocked out near Courcelette. One lay partly in the ditch by the road. It had been hit by a shell, and the petrol had burst into flames burning up the crew within, whose charred bones were taken out when an opportunity offered, and were reverently buried. The tank was often visited by our men, and for that reason the Germans made it a mark for their shell-fire. It was wise to give it a wide berth.

Our chaplains were working manfully and took their duties at the different dressing-stations night and day in relays. The main dressing-station was the school-house in Albert which I have already described. It was a good sized building and there were several large rooms in it. Many is the night that I have passed there, and I see it now distinctly in my mind. In the largest room, there were the tables neatly prepared, white and clean, for the hours of active work which began towards midnight when the ambulances brought back the wounded from the front. The orderlies would be lying about taking a rest until their services were needed, and the doctors with their white aprons on would be sitting in the room or in their mess near by. The windows were entirely darkened, but in the building was the bright light and the persistent smell of acetylene gas. Innumerable bandages and various instruments were piled neatly on the white covered tables; and in the outer room, which was used as the office, were the record books and tags with which the wounded were labelled as they were sent off to the Base. Far off we could hear the noise of the shells, and occasionally one would fall in the town. When the ambulances arrived everyone would be on the alert. I used to go out and stand in the darkness, and see the stretchers carried in gently and tenderly by the bearers, who laid them on the floor of the outer room. Torn and broken forms, racked with suffering, cold and wet with rain and mud, hidden under muddy blankets, lay there in rows upon the brick floor. Sometimes the heads were entirely covered; sometimes the eyes were bandaged; sometimes the pale faces, crowned with matted, muddy hair, turned restlessly from side to side, and parched lips asked for a sip of water. Then one by one the stretchers with their human burden would be carried to the tables in the dressing room. Long before these cases could be disposed of, other ambulances had arrived, and the floor of the outer room once more became covered with stretchers. Now and then the sufferers could not repress their groans. One night a man was brought in who looked very pale and asked me piteously to get him some water. I told him I could not do so until the doctor had seen his wound. I got him taken into the dressing room, and turned away for a moment to look after some fresh arrivals. Then I went back towards the table whereon the poor fellow was lying. They had uncovered him and, from the look on the faces of the attendants round about, I saw that some specially ghastly wound was disclosed. I went over to the table, and there I saw a sight too horrible to be described. A shell had burst at his feet, and his body from the waist down was shattered. Beyond this awful sight I saw the white face turning from side to side, and the parched lips asking for water. The man, thank God, did not suffer very acutely, as the shock had been so great, but he was perfectly conscious. The case was hopeless, so they kindly and tenderly covered him up, and he was carried out into the room set apart for the dying. When he was left alone, I knelt down beside him and talked to him. He was a French Canadian and a Roman Catholic, and, as there happened to be no Roman Catholic Chaplain present at the moment, I got him to repeat the "Lord's Prayer" and the "Hail Mary," and gave him the benediction. He died about half an hour afterwards. When the sergeant came in to have the body removed to the morgue, he drew the man's paybook from his pocket, and there we found that for some offence he had been given a long period of field punishment, and his pay was cut down to seventy cents a day. For seventy cents a day he had come as a voluntary soldier to fight in the great war, and for seventy cents a day he had died this horrible death. I told the sergeant that I felt like dipping that page of the man's paybook in his blood to blot out the memory of the past. The doctor who attended the case told me that that was the worst sight he had ever seen.

One night a young German was brought in. He was perfectly conscious, but was reported to be seriously wounded. He was laid out on one of the tables and when his torn uniform was ripped off, we found he had been hit by shrapnel and had ten or twelve wounds in his body and limbs. I never saw anyone more brave. He was a beautifully developed man, with very white skin, and on the grey blanket looked like a marble statue, marked here and there by red, bleeding wounds. He never gave a sign by sound or movement of what he was suffering; but his white face showed the approach of death. He was tended carefully, and then carried over to a quiet corner in the room. I went over to him, and pointing to my collar said, "Pasteur." I knelt beside him and started the Lord's Prayer in German, which he finished adding some other prayer. I gave him the benediction and made the sign of the cross on his forehead, for the sign of the cross belongs to the universal language of men. Then the dying, friendless enemy, who had made expiation in his blood for the sins of his guilty nation, drew his hand from under the blanket and taking mine said, "Thank you." They carried him off to an ambulance, but I was told he would probably die long before he got to his destination.

On the 26th of September I spent the night in a dressing station in the sunken road near Courcelette. I had walked from Pozières down to the railway track, where in the dark I met a company of the Canadian Cyclist Corps, who were being used as stretcher bearers. We went in single file along the railway and then across the fields which were being shelled. At last we came to the dressing station. Beside the entrance, was a little shelter covered with corrugated iron, and there were laid a number of wounded, while some were lying on stretchers in the open road. Among these were several German prisoners and the bodies of dead men. The dressing station had once been the dugout of an enemy battery and its openings, therefore, were on the side of the road facing the Germans, who knew its location exactly. When I went down into it I found it crowded with men who were being tended by the doctor and his staff. It had three openings to the road. One of them had had a direct hit that night, and mid the debris which blocked it were the fragments of a human body. The Germans gave the place no rest, and all along the road shells were falling, and bits would clatter upon the corrugated iron which roofed the shelter by the wayside. There was no room in the dugout for any but those who were being actually treated by the doctor, so the wounded had to wait up above till they could be borne off by the bearer parties. It was a trying experience for them, and it was hard to make them forget the danger they were in. I found a young officer lying in the road, who was badly hit in the leg. I had prayers with him and at his request I gave him the Holy Communion. On the stretcher next to him, lay the body of a dead man wrapped in a blanket. After I had finished the service, the officer asked for some water. I went down and got him a mouthful very strongly flavoured with petrol from the tin in which it was carried. He took it gladly, but, just as I had finished giving him the drink, a shell burst and there was a loud crack by his side. "Oh," he cried, "they have got my other leg." I took my electric torch, and, allowing only a small streak of light to shine through my fingers, I made an examination of the stretcher, and there I found against it a shattered rum jar which had just been hit by a large piece of shell. The thing had saved him from another wound, and I told him that he owed his salvation to a rum jar. He was quite relieved to find that his good leg had not been hit. I got the bearer party to take him off as soon as possible down the long path across the fields which led to the light railway, where he could be put on a truck. Once while I was talking to the men in the shelter, a shell burst by the side of the road and ignited a pile of German ammunition. At once there were explosions, a weird red light lit up the whole place, and volumes of red smoke rolled off into the starlit sky. To my surprise, from a ditch on the other side of the road, a company of Highlanders emerged and ran further away from the danger of the exploding shells. It was one of the most theatrical sights I have ever seen. With the lurid light and the broken road in the foreground, and the hurrying figures carrying their rifles, it was just like a scene on the stage.

The stars were always a great comfort to me. Above the gun-flashes or the bursting of shells and shrapnel, they would stand out calm and clear, twinkling just as merrily as I have seen them do on many a pleasant sleigh-drive in Canada. I had seen Orion for the first time that year, rising over the broken Cathedral at Albert.

I always felt when he arrived for his winter visit to the sky, that he came as an old friend, and was waiting like us for the wretched war to end. On that September night, when the hours were beginning to draw towards dawn, it gave me great pleasure to see him hanging in the East, while Sirius with undiminished courage merrily twinkled above the smoke-fringed horizon and told us of the eternal quietness of space.

With dawn the enemy's artillery became less active and we sent off the wounded. Those who could walk were compelled to follow the bearer parties. One man, who was not badly hit, had lost his nerve and refused to leave. The doctor had to tell him sharply that he need not expect to be carried, as there were too many serious cases to be attended to. I went over to him and offered him my arm. At first he refused to come, and then I explained to him that he was in great danger and the thing to do was to get back as quickly as possible, if he did not wish to be wounded again. At last I got him going at a slow pace, and I was afraid I should have to drag him along. Suddenly a shell landed near us, and his movements were filled with alacrity. It was a great relief to me. After a little while he found he could walk quite well and whenever a whiz-bang came near us his limbs seemed to get additional strength. I took him down to a place were a battalion was camped, and there I had to stop and bury some men in a shell hole. While I was taking the service however, my companion persuaded some men to carry him, and I suppose finally reached a place of safety.

There was a large dressing station in the cellars of the Red Chateau in Courcelette, whither I made my way on a Sunday morning in September. The fighting at the time was very heavy and I met many ambulances bringing out the wounded. I passed Pozières and turned down the sunken road towards Courcelette.

Beside the road was a dugout and shelter, where the wounded, who were carried in on stretchers from Courcelette, were kept until they could be shipped off in the ambulances. A doctor and some men were in charge of the post. The bearers, many of whom were German prisoners, were bringing out the wounded over the fields and laying them by the roadside. I went with some of the bearers past "Dead Man's Trench," where were many German bodies. Every now and then we came upon a trench where men were in reserve, and we saw also many machine gun emplacements, for the rise in the ground gave the gun a fine sweep for its activity.

The whole neighbourhood, however, was decidedly unhealthy, and it was risky work for the men to go over the open. When we got to the ruins of Courcelette, we turned down a path which skirted the old cemetery and what remained of the church. Several shells fell near us, and one of the men got a bit nervous, so I repeated to him the verse of the psalm:

"A thousand shall fall beside thee, and ten thousand at
thy right hand, but it shall not come nigh thee."

We had hardly arrived at the heaps of rubbish which surrounded the entrance to the dressing station, beside which lay the blackened body of a dead man, when a shell burst, and one of the bits broke the leg of the young fellow I was talking to. "What's the matter with your text now, Canon?" he said. "The text is all right, old man, you have only got a good Blighty and are lucky to get it," I replied. The cellars below had been used as a dressing station by the enemy before Courcelette was taken and consisted of several large rooms, which were now being used by our two divisions in the line. Beyond the room used for operations, there was one dark cellar fitted up with two long shelves, whereon lay scores of stretcher bearers and cyclists, and at the end of that, down some steps, there was another, in which more bearers awaited their call. Only two candles lit up the darkness. As there must have been between three and four hundred men in the Red Chateau, the air was not particularly fresh. Our choice lay, however, between foul air within and enemy shells without, for the Germans were making direct hits upon the debris overhead. Naturally we preferred the foul air. It showed how one had grown accustomed to the gruesome sights of war, that I was able to eat my meals in a place where rags saturated in human blood were lying on the floor in front of me. Two years before it would have been impossible. The stretcher bearers were doing noble work. When each case had been attended to, they were called out of the back cellar and entrusted with their burden, which they had to carry for more than a mile over those dangerous fields to the ambulances waiting in the sunken road. Again and again a bearer would be brought back on a stretcher himself, having been wounded while on the errand of mercy. Once a party, on their return, told me that one of their number had disappeared, blown to atoms by a shell.

About four o'clock, though time had little meaning to us, because the only light we had was from the candles and acetylene lamps, I went into the cellar where the bearers lay, and, reminding them that it was Sunday, asked if they would not like to have a service. One of them handed me a candle, so we had prayers and a reading, and sang "Nearer My God to Thee," and some other hymns. When the service was over, I asked those who would like to make their Communion to come to the lower cellar at the end, where there was more room. We appropriated one of the corners and there I had seven or eight communicants. More than a year afterwards, in London, I met a young soldier in the Underground Railway, and he told me that he had made his communion on that day, and that when he was lying on the ground wounded at midnight, the shells falling round him, he thought what a comfort it was to know that he had received the Sacrament. I did not leave the Red Chateau till late the following afternoon, when I went back with a ration-party.

The most unpleasant things at Albert were the air raids, which occurred every fine night. One moonlight night I lay on my bed, which was in the top storey of our house, and listened to some German planes dropping bombs upon the town. The machines were flying low and trying to get the roads. Crash would follow crash with great regularity. They came nearer and nearer, and I was just waiting for the house to be struck when, to my great relief, the planes went off in another direction. Next day a sentry told me that he had heard a hundred bombs burst, and, as far as he knew, not one of them had done any damage, all having fallen among the ruined houses and gardens of the town.

I had been asked to look up the grave of a young officer of a Scottish battalion, who had been killed in the July advance. I rode over to Mametz and saw all that historic fighting ground. The village was a heap of ruins, but from out of a cellar came a smartly-dressed lieutenant, who told me that he had the great privilege and honour of being the Town Major of Mametz. We laughed as we surveyed his very smelly and unattractive little kingdom. I found the grave, and near it were several crosses over the last resting places of some of our Canadian Dragoons, who had been in the great advance. All that region was one of waste and lonely country-side, blown bare by the tempest of war.

It was during our last visit to Albert that the 4th Division arrived to take over the line from us. I had the great joy, therefore, of having my second son near me for six days. His battalion, the 87th, was camped on a piece of high ground to the right of "Tara Hill," and from my window I could see the officers and men walking about in their lines. It was a great privilege to have his battalion so near me, for I had many friends among all ranks.

The Sunday before I left I had service for them and a celebration of the Holy Communion, after which one of the sergeants came and was baptized. Our Divisional Headquarters left Albert for good on October 17th. We made our way to our abode at Canaples. We only stayed there two days and then went on to Bernaville and Frohen Le Grand, spending a night in each place, and on Sunday arrived at the Chateau of Le Cauroy, which we were afterwards to make our headquarters in the last year of the war. I was billeted in a filthy little room in a sort of farm building and passed one of the most dreary days I have ever known. It was rainy and cold, and every one was tired and ill-humoured. I had a strange feeling of gloom about me which I could not shake off, so I went over to the Curé's house at the end of the avenue and asked him if I might come in and sit beside the fire in his kitchen. He was very kind, and it was quite nice to have someone to talk to who was not in the war. We were able to understand each other pretty well, and he gave me an insight into the feelings of the French. On the next morning, the weather had cleared and the A. D. M. S. motored me to our new halting place at Roellencourt, where I was given a billet in the Curé's house. He was a dear old man and received me very kindly, and gave me a comfortable room overlooking his garden. Downstairs his aged and invalid mother sat in her chair, tended kindly by her son and daughter. Roellencourt was a pleasant place on the St. Pol Road, and quite a number of our men were billeted there. I went to St. Pol to lunch at the hotel and spent the day buying some souvenirs. On my return in the afternoon I made my way to the Curé's house, where I found my room neatly arranged for me. Suddenly I heard a knock at the door, and there stood the old man with a letter in his hand. I thought he looked somewhat strange. He handed me the letter, and then taking my hand, he said to me in French, "My brother, have courage, it is very sad." At once the truth flashed upon me and I said, "My son is dead." He shook my hand, and said again, "Have courage, my brother." I went downstairs later on and found his old mother sitting in her chair with the tears streaming down her cheeks. I shall never cease to be grateful to those kind, simple people for their sympathy at that time. The next morning the General sent me in his car to Albert, and Colonel Ironside took me up to the chalk-pit where the 87th were resting. They had suffered very heavy losses, and I heard the account of my son's death. On the morning of October 21st, he was leading his company and another to the attack on Regina Trench. They had advanced, as the barrage lifted, and he was kneeling in a shell hole looking at his watch waiting for the moment to charge again, when a machine gun opened fire and he was hit in the head and killed instantly. As he still kept kneeling looking at his watch, no one knew that anything had happened. The barrage lifted again behind the German trench; still he gave no sign. The Germans stood up and turned their machine-guns on our men. Then the officer next in command went over to see what had happened, and, finding my son dead, gave the order to advance. Suffering heavy casualties, the men charged with determination and took the trench, completely routing the enemy. When the battalion was relieved the dead had to be left unburied, but several men volunteered to go and get my son's body. This I would not hear of, for the fighting was still severe, and I did not believe in living men risking their lives to bring out the dead. I looked far over into the murky distance, where I saw long ridges of brown land, now wet with a drizzling rain, and thought how gloriously consecrated was that soil, and how worthy to be the last resting place of those who had died for their country. Resolving to come back later on when things were quieter, and make my final search, I bid good-bye to the officers and men of the battalion and was motored back to my Headquarters.

In the little church of Roellencourt hangs a crucifix which I gave the Curé in memory of my son. It is near the chancel-arch in the place which the old man chose for it. Some day I hope I may re-visit my kind friends at the Presbytére and talk over the sad events of the past in the light of the peace that has come through victory.

CHAPTER XIII.

Our Home at Camblain L'Abbe

November and December, 1916

FROM Roellencourt we moved up to our new headquarters in the Chateau at Camblain L'Abbe, which, after we left it in December, was long the home of the Canadian Corps. I had an Armstrong hut under the trees in the garden, and after it was lined with green canvas, and divided into two by green canvas curtains, it was quite artistic and very comfortable. Opposite the Chateau we had a large French hut which was arranged as a cinema. The band of the 3rd Battalion was stationed in town and gave us a concert every evening, also playing at our services on Sundays. After the concert was over I used to announce a "rum issue" at half-past nine in the building. The men knew what it meant, and a good number would stay behind. Then I would give them a talk on temperance, astronomy, literature or any subject about which I thought my audience knew less than I. We generally finished up by singing some well-known evening hymn. Very pleasant were the entertainments we had in that old cinema. One night, before a battalion was going up to the line, I proposed we should have a dance. The band furnished the music, and the men had one of the most enjoyable evenings they had ever had. Camblain L'Abbe was not a large place, so we were cramped for room, and a Nissen hut had to be built for "C" mess.

My little friend Philo had been stolen on our march, so his place was taken now by a brindle bull terrier which had been born in Albert. I called her "Alberta" and as time went on she became a well-known figure in the First Division. She often accompanied me on my walks to the trenches, and one day was out in No Man's Land when a minnenwerfer burst. Alberta did not wait for the bits to come down, but made one dive into the trench, to the amusement of the men, who said she knew the use of the trenches. She was my constant companion till her untimely end in 1918.

The country round about Camblain l'Abbe was very peaceful and pretty, and the road to the left from the Chateau gave one a fine view of the towers of Mont St. Eloi, which were not then damaged by shells. The two towers and the front wall of the old abbey were a striking object against the horizon, and could be seen for miles around. They made a beautiful picture in the distance when seen at sunset from the trenches beyond Arras. Those two towers must stand out in the foreground of all the memories which Canadians have of that region which was so long their war-home. As far as I could learn, Mont St. Eloi had been the site of an old monastery which had been destroyed in the French Revolution, the towers and the walls of the church alone surviving. The farms of the monastery had passed to secular ownership, but were rich and well cultivated. A spiral stone staircase led up to an observation post at the top of one of the towers. The place was visible from the German lines, and till we had taken Vimy Ridge no one was allowed to climb the tower unless on duty.

Our trenches now were extremely quiet, and were a pleasant contrast to those we had left on the Somme. The whole Corps had only a few casualties each day. The spirits of the men, who had been under a heavy strain, were now completely restored. Our Corps Headquarters at this time were at the beautiful Chateau of Ranchicourt, where they were very comfortably settled, the country round about being hilly, richly wooded and well watered. We had church parades in the cinema, and I often wished that the people at home could have heard the singing of the men when we had some favourite hymn which the band accompanied. Every morning I had a celebration of the Holy Communion there, and sometimes had a good congregation. One night I was talking to some men in a cook-house on the opposite side of the village and I announced the service. When I was leaving, one of the men followed me and asked me if I would speak to his officer for him and get him sent back to some quiet job. He told me that he had once had an attack of nervous prostration, caused by the shock of his father's sudden death, and that he could not stand life in the trenches. He seemed very much upset, and I felt that perhaps it would be wise to get him out of the line, but I could not avoid a sense of disappointment in the midst of my pity. He told me that he had been confirmed, but had never made his Communion and was coming to my service the next morning. I promised I would speak to his officer and went off.

The next morning, the man was at the service, and after the others left, waited to speak to me. I thought he wanted to remind me of my promise. But, instead of that, he came up and said to

me, "I don't want you to speak to my officer, Sir, God has given
me strength to carry on. I have determined to do so and go over
the top with the others." I was delighted to see the change in him.
It meant everything to him and was one of the turning points in
his life. Whatever the future had in store, it was the man's victory over himself, and I gave him a glad hand-shake and told him
how proud I was of him. Months afterwards, after the taking of
Vimy Ridge, I was passing down the lines of his battalion, which
was in tents near the La Targette road, when the young fellow came
running up to me, his face radiant with smiles, and told me he had
been through all the fighting and had gone over the top with the
boys, and that it wasn't half so bad as he had thought. In the
spring of 1919, I was going into the Beaver Hut in the Strand one
day, when a young fellow came up to me and thanked me for what
I had done for him in the war. I did not recognize him and asked
him what I had done for him, and he told me he was the man who
had been at that service in Camblain L'Abbe and had been through
all the fighting ever since and had come out without a scratch.
I met similar instances in which the human will, by the help of God,
was able to master itself and come out victorious. Once at Bracquemont a man came to my billet and asked me to get him taken out
of his battalion, and sent to some work behind the lines. He told
me his mother and sisters knew his nerves were weak and had
always taken special care of him. He said that up to this time God
had been very good to him in answering his prayer that he might
not have to go over the parapet. I asked him what right he had
to pray such a prayer. He was really asking God to make another
man do what he would not do himself. The prayer was selfish and
wrong, and he could not expect God to answer it. The right prayer
to pray was that, if he was called to go over the parapet God would
give him strength to do his duty. He seemed quite surprised at
the new light which was thus thrown upon the performance of
what he considered his religious duties. Then I told him that he
had the chance of his life to make himself a man. If in the past
he had been more or less a weakling, he could now, by the help of
God, rise up in the strength of his manhood and become a hero.
His mother and sisters no doubt had loved him and taken care of
him in the past, but they would love him far more if he did his
duty now, "For", I said, "All women love a brave man." I told
him to take as his text, "I can do all things through Christ which

strengtheneth me," and I made him repeat it after me several times. I saw that the young fellow was pulling himself together, and he shook hands with me and told me he would go up to the line and take his chance with the rest—and he did. Later on, he was invalided to the Base with some organic disease. I do not know where he is now, but he conquered; and like many another soldier in the great crusade will be the better for all eternity for his self-mastery.

On the road which led to Ranchicourt there was an interesting old chateau at a place called Ohlain, which is mentioned by Dumas in "The Three Musketeers." The chateau is surrounded by a large moat, and was built in medieval times. It has a very fine tower, and some other old buildings surrounding a little courtyard with a garden. The place is entered by a drawbridge which in olden days used to be raised up against the massive gateway by chains. One night I had service in the courtyard at sunset, with the 16th Battalion. One could hardly imagine a more picturesque setting for a war service in dear old France. At one point, however, we were disturbed by the arrival of three men who had been dining in an estaminet in the village, and coming unexpectedly upon a church service were a little too hearty in their religious fervour. They had to be guided to some quiet spot where they might work it off in solitude. Incidents of that kind during voluntary services were always a little embarrassing, for officers and men felt, as well as myself, that under the softening influences of religion we could not be over-hard on the transgressions of frail mortality. Nothing but the direst necessity would compel us at such times to resort to the process of military discipline.

Near Camblain l'Abbe, our ambulances were set up on an elevation of the ground where two roads crossed. The place rejoiced in the name of "The Four Winds", and anyone who has resided there for any length of time feels that the title is an appropriate one. At times the wind would sweep over the place, and, when rain was mingled with the gale, it was rather an unpleasant corner. But the ambulances were comfortable, and the patients were well looked after. Near by is the little cemetery, where the bodies of many Canadians lie in peace.

Our life at Camblain l'Abbe, after the hard fighting at the Somme, was really very pleasant, and the battalions were filled up with new drafts from the Base. We felt that as the winter was approaching there would probably be no hard fighting for some months. Special pains were taken to provide concert parties in the different battalions, so that the men might have amusement in the evening. It was wonderful what talent was discovered in the various units. As I look back upon some of those entertainments at the front I think I never enjoyed anything more. Not only were the performers clever and resourceful, but the audience was one that it was thrilling to sit amongst. In the cinema the stage was well appointed and lighted with electric lights; the costumes of the men, especially those who took the part of ladies, were good and well made. The music, vocal and instrumental, was all that could be desired. But the audience, composed of hundreds of strong, keen, young men who had endured hard things, and perhaps, in a few hours after the show, would be once again facing death in the front trenches, was a sight never to be forgotten. Could any performer ask for a more sympathetic hearing? Not a joke was lost upon the men, not a gesture was unobserved; and when some song with a well-known chorus was started, through the murky atmosphere of cigarette smoke would rise a volume of harmony which would fairly shake the building. I have often stood at the back and listened to a splendid burst of song, which to me had an added charm from the deep unconscious pathos of it all. Some of those men that were joining in the rollicking ragtime tune were dying men. Some of the eyes kindling with laughter at the broad farce of the play, within a few hours would be gazing upon the mysteries behind the screen of mortal life. The pathetic chorus of "A Long, Long Trail" always moved me, and I wondered how many of those brave young hearts in the crowded hall, now on "the long, long trail," would ever see again the land of their dreams. I took good care not to let the men know that I was ever moved by such sentimentalism. We were out to fight the Germans, and on that one object we had to concentrate all our thoughts to the obliteration of private emotions.

CHAPTER XIV.

My Search is Rewarded

WE had now reached the middle of November, and the 4th Division was expected to come north very soon. My only chance of finding my son's body lay in my making a journey to Albert before his battalion moved away. I woke up one morning and determined that I would start that day. I told Ross to get my trench clothes and long boots ready, for I was going to Albert. At luncheon my friends asked me how I proposed to travel, for Albert was nearly fifty miles away. I told them that the Lord would provide, and sallied off down the road with my knapsack, thoroughly confident that I should be able to achieve my purpose. An ambulance picked me up and took me to the Four Winds cross-roads, and then a lorry carried me to Aubigny. I went to the field canteen to get some cigarettes, and while there I met a Canadian Engineer officer whom I knew. We talked about many things, and as we were leaving I told him that I was going forth in faith as I hoped to get to Albert that evening. I said, "You know my motto is 'The Lord will provide'." As we walked along we came to a turn in the road, where we saw at a little distance a side-car with a driver all ready. I said to my friend, "It is just the thing I want. I think I will go to the owner of that car and say to him that the Lord has provided it for me." He burst out laughing and said, "I am the owner of that car, and you may have it." I thanked him and started off. It was a long ride, and at the end a very wet and muddy one, but I got to Tara Hill that evening and had dinner at General Thacker's Headquarters. I told the officers there of the purpose of my visit, that I was going up to the front line the next morning, and asked if they would telephone to one of the batteries and tell the O. C. that I should arrive some time in the middle of the night. The Brigade Major of course tried to dissuade me, but I told him that I was going in any case, that he was not responsible for my actions, but that if he liked to make thing easier for me he could. He quite understood the point, and telephoned to the 11th Battery. I then went back to the reserve headquarters of the 4th Division in the town, and prepared myself for the journey. When I had to make an early start in the morning, I always shaved the night before, because I thought that, of all the officers, the chaplain should look the freshest and cleanest. I was in the middle of the process of shaving, and some staff officers were making chocolate for our supper, when a German plane came over and dropped a huge bomb in the garden. It was about one a.m., and we could not help laughing at the surprise the Germans would have felt if they could have seen our occupation going on quite undisturbed by their attempt to murder us.

About half-past one, I started up the street which led to the Bapaume road. The moon was shining, and I could see every object distinctly. Near our old Headquarters I got a lift in a lorry, which took me almost to Pozières. There I got out and proceeded on my way alone. I entered the Y. M. C. A. hut and had a good strong cup of coffee, and started off afresh. That lonely region in the moonlight with the ruined village to one side and the fields stretching far away on either hand gave me an eerie feeling. I came upon four dead horses which had been killed that evening. To add to the strangeness of the situation, there was a strong scent of tear-gas in the air, which made my eyes water. Not a living soul could I see in the long white road.

Suddenly I heard behind me the sound of a troop of horses. I turned and saw coming towards me one of the strangest sights I have ever seen, and one which fitted in well with the ghostly character of the surroundings. It was a troop of mounted men carrying ammunition. They wore their gas masks, and as they came nearer, and I could see them more distinctly in the moonlight, the long masks with their two big glass eye-pieces gave the men a horse-like appearance. They looked like horses upon horses, and did not seem to be like human beings at all. I was quite glad when they had passed. I walked on till I came to what was known as Centre Way. It was a path, sometimes with bath-mats on it, which led across the fields down to the battery positions in the valley. Huge shell holes, half filled with water, pitted the fields in every direction, and on the slippery wood I had great difficulty to keep from sliding into those which were skirted by the path. Far off beyond Courcellette I saw the German flare-lights and the bursting of shells. It was a scene of vast desolation, weird beyond description. I had some difficulty when I got into the trench at the end of Centre Way, in finding the 11th Battery. The ground had been ploughed by shells and the trenches were heavy with soft and clinging mud.

At last I met a sentry who told me where the O. C.'s dugout was. It was then about half-past three in the morning, but I went down the steps, and there, having been kindly welcomed, was given a blanket on the floor. I started at 6 a. m. with a young sergeant for Death Valley, where I was to get a runner to take me to Regina Trench. The sergeant was a splendid young fellow from Montreal who had won the D.C.M., and was most highly thought of in the battery. He was afterwards killed on Vimy Ridge, where I buried him in the cemetery near Thélus. I had been warned that we were going to make a bombardment of the enemy's lines that morning, and that I ought to be out of the way before that began. I left the sergeant near Courcellette and made my way over to the Brigade Headquarters which were in a dugout in Death Valley. There with the permission of his O. C., a runner volunteered to come with me. He brought a spade, and we started down the trench to the front line. When I got into Regina Trench, I found that it was impossible to pass along it, as one sank down so deeply into the heavy mud. I had brought a little sketch with me of the trenches, which showed the shell hole where it was supposed that the body had been buried. The previous night a cross had been placed there by a corporal of the battalion before it left the front line. No one I spoke to, however, could tell me the exact map location of the place where it stood. I looked over the trenches, and on all sides spread a waste of brown mud, made more desolate by the morning mist which clung over everything. I was determined, however, not to be baffled in my search, and told the runner who was with me that, if I stayed there six months, I was not going to leave till I had found that grave. We walked back along the communication trench and turned into one on the right, peering over the top every now and then to see if we could recognize anything corresponding to the marks on our map. Suddenly the runner, who was looking over the top, pointed far away to a lonely white cross that stood at a point where the ground sloped down through the mist towards Regina Trench. At once we climbed out of the trench and made our way over the slippery ground and past the deep shell holes to where the white cross stood out in the solitude. We passed many bodies which were still unburied, and here and there were bits of accoutrement which had been lost during the advance. When we came up to the cross I read my son's name upon it, and knew that I had reached the object I had in view. As the corporal who had

placed the cross there had not been quite sure that it was actually
on the place of burial, I got the runner to dig the ground in front
of it. He did so, but we discovered nothing but a large piece of a
shell. Then I got him to try in another place, and still we could
find nothing. I tried once again, and after he had dug a little
while he came upon something white. It was my son's left hand,
with his signet ring upon it. They had removed his identification
disc, revolver and pocket-book, so the signet ring was the only
thing which could have led to his identification. It was really quite
miraculous that we should have made the discovery. The mist
was lifting now, and the sun to the East was beginning to light
up the ground. We heard the crack of bullets, for the Germans
were sniping us. I made the runner go down into a shell hole,
while I read the burial service, and then took off the ring. I looked
over the ground where the charge had been made. There lay Regina Trench, and far beyond it, standing out against the morning
light, I saw the villages of Pys and Miraumont which were our
objective. It was a strange scene of desolation, for the November rains had made the battle fields a dreary, sodden waste. How
many of our brave men had laid down their lives as the purchase
price of that consecrated soil! Through the centuries to come it
must always remain sacred to the hearts of Canadians. We made
a small mound where the body lay, and then by quick dashes from
shell hole to shell hole we got back at last to the communication
trench, and I was indeed thankful to feel that my mission had been
successful. I have received letters since I returned to Canada from
the kind young fellow, who accompanied me on the journey, and I
shall never cease to be grateful to him. I left him at his headquarters in Death Valley, and made my way past Courcellette towards the road. As the trench was very muddy, I got out of it,
and was walking along the top when I came across something red
on the ground. It was a piece of a man's lung with the windpipe
attached. I suppose some poor lad had had a direct hit from a
shell and his body had been blown to pieces. The Germans were
shelling the road, so with some men I met we made a detour
through the fields and joined it further on, and finally got to the
chalk-pit where the 87th Battalion was waiting to go in again to the
final attack. I was delighted to see my friends once more, and they
were thankful that I had been able to find the grave. Not many
days afterwards, some of those whom I then met were called them-

selves to make the supreme sacrifice. I spent that night at the Rear Headquarters of the 4th Division, and they kindly sent me back the next day to Camblain l'Abbe in one of their cars.

On November 24th I received a telegram saying that a working party of one of the battalions of the 4th Division had brought my son's body back, and so on the following day I motored once again to Albert and laid my dear boy to rest in the little cemetery on Tara Hill, which he and I had seen when he was encamped near it, and in which now were the bodies of some of his friends whom I had met on my last visit. I was thankful to have been able to have him buried in a place which is known and can be visited, but I would say to the many parents whose sons lie now in unknown graves, that, after all, the grave seems to be a small and minor thing in view of the glorious victory and triumphant life which is all that really matters. If I had not been successful in my quest, I should not have vexed my soul with anxious thought as to what had become of that which is merely the earthly house of the immortal spirit which goes forth into the eternal. Let those whose dear ones lie in unrecorded graves remember that the strong, glad spirits—like Valiant for Truth in "Pilgrim's Progress"—have passed through the turbulent waters of the river of death, and "all the trumpets have sounded for them on the other side."

In June of the following year, when the Germans had retired after our victory at Vimy Ridge, I paid one more visit to Regina Trench. The early summer had clothed the waste land in fresh and living green. Larks were singing gaily in the sunny sky. No sound of shell or gun disturbed the whisper of the breeze as it passed over the sweet-smelling fields. Even the trenches were filling up and Mother Nature was trying to hide the cruel wounds which the war had made upon her loving breast. One could hardly recall the visions of gloom and darkness which had once shrouded that scene of battle. In the healing process of time all mortal agonies, thank God, will be finally obliterated.

CHAPTER XV.

A TIME OF PREPARATION

Christmas, 1916, to April, 1917

IT was certain now that all serious fighting was at an end till next spring, so everyone settled down to his work with a sense of relief and tried to make the best of things. A few days after my return from Albert I went to England.

On my return to France, I heard with some regret that our Divisional Headquarters were going to move, and that the Corps would make Camblain l'Abbe their headquarters. On December 20th we moved back to the town of Bruay, where we were to stay till after the New Year. Bruay in comparison with Camblain l'Abbe is a large and thriving town, all the inhabitants being more or less connected with the mines in the neighbourhood. Our Headquarters were in the administration building of the Mining Company, in a square, and I had a billet in a street near by. There was a good theatre in the place, which our 1st Divisional Concert party took over, and where I had services on Sunday. In and around the town were several of the battalions; the rest of the division were in the villages near by. Bruay had not been shelled, and the mines were being worked as in pre-war days. It was a comfort to have the men out of the line once again, and the roads round about were very pleasant, the country being hilly and unspoilt. Bethune was within easy reach, and a visit to the quaint town made a pleasant afternoon's ride.

Rumours were abroad that with the opening of Spring we were to begin an offensive, and it was generally believed that towards the close of the next year we might hope for the end of hostilities. Our men were being trained, when weather permitted, in open warfare, and the time of so-called rest was really a period of constant activity. The chief hotel in the place became an officers' club, and very pleasant were the reunions we had there. I was glad we were going to spend Christmas out of the line, and determined to take advantage of the theatre as a place for Christmas services. The 8th and 14th Battalions were quartered in the town, besides some smaller units, so we had a good many men to draw upon for a congregation. On Christmas Eve, at half-past eleven, I had a celebration of the

Holy Communion. We had a splendid band to play the Christmas hymns, and a large number of men attended. The stage was made to look as much as possible like a chancel, and the service was very hearty. Many made their communion. I also had a watch-night service on New Year's Eve. The theatre was almost filled with men —there were rows of them even in the gallery. It was an inspiring sight, and we all felt we were beginning a year that was to decide the destinies of the Empire. I told the men that somewhere in the pages of the book which we were opening that night lay hidden the tremendous secret of our success or failure. At ten minutes to twelve we sat in silence, while the band played Chopin's Funeral March. It was almost too moving, for once again the vision came before us of the terrible battle-fields of the Somme and the faces that had gone. Then we all rose, and there was a brief moment for silent prayer. At midnight the buglers of the 14th Battalion sounded the Last Post, and at the close the band struck up the hymn "O God our help in ages past." A mighty chorus of voices joined in the well-known strains. After the Benediction, I went down to the door and shook hands with as many of the men as I could and wished them a happy New Year. No one who was at that service will ever forget it. As we found out, the trail before us was longer than we had expected, and the next New Year's Eve found many of us, though, alas, not all, in that theatre once more, still awaiting the issue of the conflict.

In January, I paid a flying visit to the Canadian Cavalry Headquarters at Tully near Abbeville, and saw many old friends. On my return, I had a curious experience which throws a light upon railway travelling at the Front. A friend had motored me to Abbeville that afternoon, just in time to catch a leave-train full of men returning from England. I only wanted to go as far as St. Pol, about thirty miles off, where I hoped to get a car for Bruay. I got into a carriage with four officers, one of whom was a chaplain who had just been decorated with the D.S.O. I had crossed the Channel with him once before, so was glad to renew our acquaintance. The train left Abbeville about four o' clock. We found ourselves in a second-class compartment. The windows were broken, the floor was dirty, and there was no lamp to lighten our darkness. By pulling down the curtains we tried to keep out the cold wind, but the draught was very unpleasant, and we had to trust to the accumulated warmth of our bodies to keep from freezing.

A TIME OF PREPARATION

Instead of going directly to St. Pol, for some reason or other, the train started off to the South. We travelled on and on at a snail's pace, and had frequent and lengthy stops. When the light died away, we should have been in complete darkness if one of the officers had not brought a candle with him. Hour after hour passed by and we began to get hungry. Somebody had some sandwiches and a piece of cake, and this was shared by all the company. It served to stimulate rather than soothe the appetite. About midnight to our astonishment we found we had got to Canaples, where I had stayed when we were going to the Somme. Someone said there had been a railway accident and we had to travel by branch lines. In spite of the cold, we tried to sleep. I sat between my parson friend, who was inclined to be stout, and another officer who was remarkably angular. When I leaned upon my corpulent friend, his frequent fits of coughing made my head bounce as though it were resting on an air-cushion. When I got tired of this and leaned against my angular friend on the other side, the jolting of the carriage scraped my ear against his ribs. I spent the night by leaning first on one companion, and then on the other. The morning found us still travelling, and finally at half-past ten the train drew up once more at our starting point in Abbeville station. Having been eighteen hours without food or drink or the opportunity of a shave, I thought it was about time to retire, and told my companions that life was too short to spend it in railway journeys of that description. So, with a feeling of superiority and independence which made the others green with envy, I bid them good-bye. I never heard any more of my friends, but, although the war has long since ended, I have a sort of dim impression in my mind that they are still travelling round and round and coming back to Abbeville again. I went over to the officers' club and had a good wash and luncheon, and there meeting a very nice engineer officer, I asked him if he could tell me where I could find any lorries going North. I told him my railway experience, and it so moved him that he very kindly sent me off in his own car to St. Pol, where I was picked up by one of our staff cars and taken home in time for dinner. Railway journeys in France were not things to remember with pleasure, and if they were bad for the officers, what must they have been for the poor men in the crowded third-class carriages?

At the end of January, our pleasant life at Bruay came to an end, and we moved off to Barlin which was to be our headquarters

for a month and a half. It was while we were there that I had an
attack of trench-fever, which, like being "crummy," is really part
of a complete war experience. Barlin was not a bad place of residence. There were many men within easy reach, and I had an upper
room in the Town Hall for use as a chapel. The presence of a well
equipped British hospital also gave one opportunities of seeing our
wounded men. We had come to know by this time that the first
task which lay before us in the opening of spring was the taking
of Vimy Ridge, and our life became filled with fresh zest and interest in view of the coming attack.

On the 15th of March our Division moved up to a place called
Ecoivres, where we were billeted in the old Château. The Count who
owned the Château kept some rooms downstairs for himself, but we
occupied all the rest of the building. In the hall upstairs we had a
large model of Vimy Ridge, which all the officers and men of the
battalions visited in turn, in order to study the character of the land
over which they had to charge. In the garden were numerous huts,
and in a large building in a street to the right of the Château was
a billet which held a great number of men. It was almost entirely
filled up with tiers upon tiers of wooden shelves, on which the men
made their beds. They were reached by wooden stairs. Nearly
fifteen hundred men were crowded into the building. On the ground
floor beside the door, there was a high platform which commanded a
view of the whole interior. On this, one of the bands lived and
gave us music in the evening. Every night after dinner, I used to
go to the cinema, as we called the place, and have either a service
or a talk with the men on general subjects. At such times outsiders
would crowd in, and we have had very hearty singing when the
band struck up a hymn. I always tried to have some piece of good
news to announce, and would get the latest reports from the signallers to read aloud. The men were in splendid spirits, and we
were all buoyed up with the hope that we were going to end the
war. I used to speak about the war outlook, and would tell the men
that there were only two issues before us: Victory or Slavery.
When I asked them one night "Which shall it be, Boys?" a loud
shout of "Victory!" went up.

News was not always plentiful, and it was a little hard at times
to find anything particularly interesting to say, and so, one night
I determined to make a variation. I told the men that on the next
evening, if they would bring in questions to me on any subject

which had been troubling them, I should be very glad to try to give an answer. I thought that an entertainment of that kind might be both attractive and helpful. On the next evening, therefore, I ascended the platform as usual and found the place crowded with men. I had my acetylene lamp with me to furnish light for reading any questions that might be sent up. I called the meeting to order, and then asked if any men had any questions to ask. To my great delight, someone at the back held an envelope above the crowd, and it was passed up to me. I tore it open, and, holding my lamp in one hand, without first looking over the letter, I read it aloud to the men, who were hushed in the silence of anticipation. I give it just as it was written:—

"Somewhere in France,
3/4/17.

Dear Sir:—

I am going to ask you a question which has been a load to my little bit of mental capacity for a period of months. Often have I woke up in the old dugout, my hair standing straight up and one eye looking straight into the eyeball of the other, trying to obtain an answer to this burning question. I have kept my weary vigil over the parapet at night, with my rifle in one hand and a couple of bombs in the other, and two or three in each pocket, and still I am pondering over this burning question. I will now ask you the question. When do you think this God dam war will be over, eh?"

I never was so completely taken aback in all my life. A roar of laughter burst from the men, in which I joined heartily. From the tiers of bunks and every part of the building, cheers went up, and we had one of the pleasantest evenings in that old cinema that we had ever experienced. I do not know who the man was who sent the letter, or whether he is alive now. If he is, I wish he would write to me. I want to thank him for giving us all a good, hearty laugh at that time of preparation and anxiety. I keep the letter among my most treasured war souvenirs.

The winter rains had not improved the roads, but still day and night, through mud and water, a constant stream of vehicles of all descriptions passed up towards the front carrying ammunition. Ammunition was everywhere. At certain places it was stacked along the roads. The strain upon the horses was very great, and numbers of them died, and their bodies lay by the wayside for many days, no one having time to bury them.

It was perfectly impossible to get any place in which to hold Communion services, so, with the permission of the family who owned it, I made use of a little Gothic shrine near the church, which stood over a family vault. It was a miniature chapel, and had an altar in it. The glass in the coloured windows had been broken, but we replaced it by canvas. I hung upon the wall outside the board which I used as a sign, with the words "St. George's Church" upon it. In this little building every morning at eight o'clock I had a celebration of Holy Communion, and I always had some men attending.

Our trenches were tolerably quiet, and lay beyond the Arras-Bethune Road. At a place called Maison Blanche there was a large cavern which was used as a billet for one of the battalions in reserve. Some strange stories were told about the fighting that had taken place in it between the French and the Germans at the beginning of the war. I went down into it one evening when the 16th Battalion was there. It was a most picturesque place. The walls and roof were white chalk and the place was cut up by passages and openings which led into other caves. The atmosphere was smoky, and a multitude of candles lit up the strange abode. The men were cooking in their mess tins, some were playing cards, and some were examining the seams of their shirts. I told them I was going to have a service at one end of the cavern and I proceeded thither with a good number following. Some of the card players seemed too interested in their game to care to attend, and so I called out to the men in a loud voice not to make too much noise, lest they should disturb the gamblers. One of the men who was playing cards responded "If you will wait till we have finished this hand, Sir, we will all come too." I made the announcement therefor that we would not begin till the players were ready. The result of this was that in a very little while all the men came and joined in the service.

The possession of the Ridge gave the Germans a great advantage, because it commanded a view of a very large piece of country and several main roads. Further up the road from Maison Blanche there was a place called Arriane Dump, where the Engineers had stored material in preparation for our attack. A long plank road connected it with the Anzin-St. Eloi road. On a dark and rainy night that wooden track was an unpleasant place for a walk. Lorries, wagons, limbers, transports, horses and men crowded it, and the traffic every now and then would get blocked. No flashlights could be used, and it was hard to escape being run over. Yet to step off the boards meant to sink almost to your knees in mud. The language that one heard at such times in the darkness was not quite fit for ears polite. It is well that the horses were not able to understand the uncomplimentary speeches that were addressed to them.

There was a tremendous concentration of artillery in the back area. The town of Anzin, on the bank of the river Scarpe, was filled with heavy batteries. To ride through it was to run the risk of many unpleasant surprises from the sudden firing of big guns by the wayside. Once, I was approaching an apparently harmless hole in a brick wall, when all of a sudden Dandy and I found ourselves enveloped in flame and almost stunned by a huge report. As we bounded past the hole, I saw a large gun moving up and down under the force of its recoil, and with smoke still curling out of its mouth.

The siege battery in which my third son was a gunner had now arrived and taken up its position in a field behind Anzin, where a 15-inch howitzer sent forth its deadly missives to the Germans every fifteen minutes and in return drew their fire. One day a shell burst in a hut used by some Railway Troops. A large number of them were wounded and eleven killed, whom I buried in a row on the hillside.

On the 4th of April, we received news that America had declared war upon Germany. I thanked God in my heart that at last the English-speaking world had been drawn together, and I knew that the effect upon the Germans would be disastrous. I rode out that afternoon to give the good news to our men. I met a British Battalion coming out of the line, looking very tired and hungry. They were resting by the roadside, and I passed along and cheered them by telling them that the United States had now come in definitely as one of our Allies, and that I thought the effect would be the shortening of the war. America's decision could not have come at a better time. The year was opening out before us, and the initiative was coming into our hands. The prospect was bright and our men were keen for the encounter.

April 6th was Good Friday. It was impossible to have service at Ecoivres, as everyone was so busy, so I rode over to Anzin and had service for the 7th Siege Battery in an empty Nissen hut. Most of the men of the battery were present, and I had forty communicants. The place was lit by candles which every now and then were extinguished by the firing of the fifteen-inch gun nearby. Easter Day was originally intended to be the day for our attack, but it had been postponed till Monday. We could not do much in the way of observing the great feast. Every room and shed in the town was filled, and men were lying out under rubber sheets in the fields. I had two celebrations of the Holy Communion in the Y.M.C.A. hut, the floor of which was covered with sleeping men. I managed to clear a little space on the stage for the altar. Of course, not many attended, but at one of the services was an officer who had won the V.C. and the D.S.O. and had a foreign Decoration as well. In the afternoon I visited and gave an address to one of the battalions moving up the line. I also had a service in the cinema that evening.

It was a time of mingled anxiety and exhilaration. What did the next twenty-four hours hold in store for us? Was it to be a true Easter for the world, and a resurrection to a new and better life? If death awaited us, what nobler passage could there be to Eternity than such a death in such a cause? Never was the spirit of comradeship higher in the Canadian Corps. Never was there a greater sense of unity. The task laid upon us was a tremendous one, but in the heart of each man, from private to general, was the determination that it should be performed. On that Easter night, the battalions took their places in the line. The men at the guns, which had hitherto been concealed and kept silent, were ready to open fire at zero hour, and all along that front the eager heart of Canada waited impatiently for the dawn.

CHAPTER XVI.

THE CAPTURE OF VIMY RIDGE

April 9th, 1917

MY alarm clock went off at four a.m. on the great day of April 9th, which will always shine brightly in the annals of the war. I got up and ate the breakfast which I had prepared the night before, and taking with me my tin of bully-beef, I started off to see the opening barrage. It was quite dark when I emerged from the door of the Chateau and passed the sentry at the gate. I went through the village of Ecoivres, past the Crucifix by the cemetery, and then turning to the right went on to a path which led up to Bray Hill on the St. Eloi road. I found some men of one of our battalions bent on the same enterprise. We got into the field and climbed the hill, and there on the top of it waited for the attack to begin. The sky was overcast, but towards the east the grey light of approaching dawn was beginning to appear. It was a thrilling moment. Human lives were at stake. The honour of our country was at stake. The fate of civilization was at stake.

Far over the dark fields, I looked towards the German lines, and, now and then, in the distance I saw a flarelight appear for a moment and then die away. Now and again, along our nine-mile front, I saw the flash of a gun and heard the distant report of a shell. It looked as if the war had gone to sleep, but we knew that all along the line our trenches were bristling with energy and filled with men animated with one resolve, with one fierce determination. It is no wonder that to those who have been in the war and passed through such moments, ordinary life and literature seem very tame. The thrill of such a moment is worth years of peace-time existence. To the watcher of a spectacle so awful and sublime, even human companionship struck a jarring note. I went over to a place by myself where I could not hear the other men talking, and there I waited. I watched the luminous hands of my watch get nearer and nearer to the fateful moment, for the barrage was to open at five-thirty. At five-fifteen the sky was getting lighter and already one could make out objects distinctly in the fields below. The long hand of my watch was at five-twenty-five. The fields, the roads, and the hedges were beginning to show the difference of colour in the early light. Five-twenty-seven! In three minutes the rain of death was to begin. In the awful silence around it seemed as if Nature were holding her breath in expectation of the staggering moment. Five-twenty-nine! God help our men! Five-thirty! With crisp sharp reports the iron throats of a battery nearby crashed forth their message of death to the Germans, and from three thousand guns at that moment the tempest of death swept through the air. It was a wonderful sound. The flashes of guns in all directions made lightnings in the dawn. The swish of shells through the air was continuous, and far over on the German trenches I saw the bursts of flame and smoke in a long continuous line, and, above the smoke, the white, red and green lights, which were the S. O. S. signals from the terrified enemy. In an instant his artillery replied, and against the morning clouds the bursting shrapnel flashed. Now and then our shells would hit a German ammunition dump, and, for a moment, a dull red light behind the clouds of smoke, added to the grandeur of the scene. I knelt on the ground and prayed to the God of Battles to guard our noble men in that awful line of death and destruction, and to give them victory, and I am not ashamed to confess that it was with the greatest difficulty I kept back my tears. There was so much human suffering and sorrow, there were such tremendous issues involved in that fierce attack, there was such splendour of human character being manifested now in that "far flung line," where smoke and flame mocked the calm of the morning sky, that the watcher felt he was gazing upon eternal things.

When it got thoroughly light I determined to go on up the road to the 3rd Artillery Brigade which was to press on after the infantry. I found both officers and men very keen and preparing to advance. For weeks at night, they had been making bridges over the trenches, so that the guns could be moved forward rapidly on the day of the attack. I had breakfast with the O. C. of one of the batteries, a young fellow only twenty-three years of age who had left McGill to enter the war. He was afterwards killed in front of Arras. After breakfast I went on up the line till I came to the 3rd Artillery Brigade Headquarters, and there asked for the latest reports of progress. They were feeling anxious because the advancing battalions had given no signal for some time, and it was thought that they might have been held up. Someone, however looked at his watch and then at the schedule time of attack, and found that at that particular moment the men were to rest for ten minutes before pressing on. The instant the time for advance came, rockets were sent up to show that our men were still going ahead. I went up the road to Neuville St. Vaast, where there was an aid post, and there I saw the wounded coming in, some walking, with bandaged arms and heads, and some being brought in on stretchers. They were all in high spirits and said that the attack had been a great success. Of course, the walking wounded were the first to appear, the more serious cases came afterwards, but still there was the note of triumph in all the accounts of the fighting which I heard. I moved on to a track near Maison Blanche, and then followed up the men. The ridge by this time was secured and our front line was still pressing forward on the heels of the retreating Germans. It was a glorious moment. The attack which we had looked forward to and prepared for so long had been successful. The Germans had been taken by surprise and the important strategic point which guarded the rich coal fields of Northern France was in our possession.

The sight of the German trenches was something never to be forgotten. They had been strongly held and had been fortified with an immense maze of wire. But now they were ploughed and shattered by enormous shell holes. The wire was twisted and torn and the whole of that region looked as if a volcanic upheaval had broken the crust of the earth. Hundreds of men were now walking over the open in all directions. German prisoners were being hurried back in scores. Wounded men, stretcher-bearers and men following up the advance were seen on all sides, and on the ground lay the bodies of friends and foes who had passed to the Great Beyond. I met a British staff officer coming back from the front, who told me he belonged to Army Headquarters. He asked me if I was a Canadian, and when I replied that I was, he said, "I congratulate you upon it." I reminded him that British artillery were also engaged in the attack and should share in the glory. "That may be", he said, "but, never since the world began have men made a charge with finer spirit. It was a magnificent achievement."

Our burial parties were hard at work collecting the bodies of those who had fallen, and the chaplains were with them. I met some of the battalions, who, having done their part in the fighting, were coming back. Many of them had suffered heavily and the mingled feelings of loss and gain chastened their exaltation and tempered their sorrow. I made my way over to the ruins of the village of Thélus on our left, and there I had my lunch in a shell hole with some men, who were laughing over an incident of the attack. So sudden had been our advance that a German artillery officer who had a comfortable dugout in Thélus, had to run away before he was dressed. Two of our men had gone down into the dugout and there they found the water in the wash-basin still warm and many things scattered about in confusion. They took possession of everything that might be of use including some German war maps, and were just trying to get a very fine telephone when two other of our men hearing voices in the dugout and thinking the enemy might still be there, threw down a smoke bomb which set fire to the place. The invaders had to relinquish their pursuit of the telephone and beat a hasty retreat. Smoke was still rising from the dugout when I saw it and continued to do so for a day or two.

Our signallers were following up the infantry and laying wires over the open. Everyone was in high spirits. By this time the retreating Germans had got well beyond the crest of the Ridge and across the valley. It was about six o'clock in the evening when I reached our final objective, which was just below the edge of the hill. There our men were digging themselves in. It was no pleasant task, because the wind was cold and it was beginning to snow. The prospect of spending a night there was not an attractive one, and every man was anxious to make the best home for himself he could in the ground. It was wonderful to look over the valley. I saw the villages of Willerval, Arleux and Bailleul-sur-Berthouit. They looked so peaceful in the green plain which had not been disturbed as yet by shells. The church spires stood up undamaged like those of some quiet hamlet in England. I thought, "If we could only follow up our advance and keep the Germans on the move," but the day was at an end and the snow was getting heavier. I saw far off in the valley, numbers of little grey figures who seemed to be gradually gathering together, and I heard an officer say he thought the Germans were preparing for a counter-attack. Our men, however, paid little attention to them. The pressing question of the moment was how to get a comfortable and advantageous position for the night. Canadians never showed up better than at such times. They were so quiet and determined and bore their hardships with a spirit

of good nature which rested on something sounder and more funda-
mental than even pleasure in achieving victory. About half-past six,
when I started back, I met our Intelligence Officer, V.C., D.S.O.,
coming up to look over the line. He was a man who did much but
said little and generally looked very solemn. I went up to him and
said, "Major, far be it from me, as a man of peace and a man of
God, to say anything suggestive of slaughter, but, if I were a combatant officer, I would drop some shrapnel in that valley in front of
our lines." Just the faint flicker of a smile passed over his countenance and he replied, "We are shelling the valley." "No," I said,
"Our shells are going over the valley into the villages beyond, and the
Germans in the plain are getting ready for a counter-attack. I
could see them with my naked eyes." "Well." he replied, "I will go
and look."

Later on when I was down in a German dugout which had been
turned into the headquarters of our advanced artillery brigade,
and was eating the half tin of cold baked beans which my friend,
the C.O. had failed to consume, I had the satisfaction of hearing
the message come through on the wires, that our artillery had
to concentrate its fire on the valley, as the Germans were preparing
for a counter-attack. When I left the warm comfortable dugout,
I found that it was quite dark and still snowing. My flashlight
was of little use for it only lit up the snowflakes immediately in
front of me, and threw no light upon my path. I did not know
how I should be able to get back in the darkness through the maze
of shell holes and broken wire. Luckily a signaller came up to me
and seeing my plight led me over to a light railway track which
had just been laid, and told me that if I kept on it I should ultimately get back to the Arras-Bethune road. It was a hard
scramble, for the track was narrow and very slippery, and had
to be felt with the feet rather than seen with the eyes. I was
terribly tired, for I had had a long walk and the excitement of
the day and talking to such numbers of men had been very fatiguing. To add to my difficulties, our batteries lay between me
and the road and were now in full action. My old dread of being
killed by our own guns seemed to be justified on the present occasion. Gun flashes came every few seconds with a blinding effect, and I thought I should never get behind those confounded
batteries. I had several tumbles in the snow-covered mud, but
there was nothing to be done except to struggle on and trust to

good luck to get through. When at last I reached the road I was devoutly thankful to be there and I made my way to the dugout of the signallers, where I was most kindly received and hospitably entertained, in spite of the fact that I kept dropping asleep in the midst of the conversation. One of our signal officers, in the morning, had gone over with some men in the first wave of the attack. He made directly for the German signallers' dugout and went down with his followers, and, finding about forty men there, told them they were his prisoners. They were astonished at his appearance, but he took possession of the switch-board and told them that the Canadians had captured the Ridge. One of the Germans was sent up to find out, and returned with the report that the Canadians held the ground. Our men at once took possession of all the telegraph instruments and prevented information being sent back to the enemy in the rear lines. Having done this, our gallant Canadians ordered the prisoners out of the dugout and then sat down and ate the breakfast which they had just prepared. This was only one of many deeds of cool daring done that day. On one occasion the Germans were running so fast in front of one of our battalions that our men could not resist following them. They were actually rushing into the zone of our own fire in order to get at them. A gallant young lieutenant, who afterwards won the V. C., seeing the danger, with great pluck, ran in front of the men and halted them with the words, "Stop, Boys, give the barrage a chance."

In spite of the numbers of wounded and dying men which I had seen, the victory was such a complete and splendid one that April 9th, 1917, was one of the happiest days in my life, and when I started out from the signallers dugout on my way back to Ecoivres, and passed the hill where I had seen the opening of the great drama in the early morning, my heart was full of thankfulness to Almighty God for his blessing on our arms. I arrived at my room in the Chateau at about half past two a.m., very tired and very happy. I made myself a large cup of strong coffee, on my primus stove, ate a whole tin of cold baked beans, and then turned in to a sound slumber, filled with dreams of victory and glory, and awoke well and fit in the morning, more than ever proud of the grand old First Division which, as General Horne told us later, had made a new record in British war annals by taking every objective on the scheduled dot of the clock.

CHAPTER XVII.

A Month on the Ridge

April to May, 1917.

THE great drawback to a victory in a war of movement, which we were told we were now engaged in, is that, after an advance, one has to follow up the line, and consequently, comfortable billets have to be exchanged for broken down shacks in the forward area. Not many days after our men had taken Vimy Ridge, Divisional Headquarters had to move up to the Arras-Bethune road and occupy a chalk cave which was known as the Labyrinth. It had once been the scene of fierce fighting between the French and the Germans. Deep down, in passages scooped out of the chalk were the various offices of the division and the billets for the staff. The place was very much crowded, and I quickly perceived that the last person whose society was wanted there was the Senior Chaplain. Having taken the situation in at a glance, I made my way to my friend the Staff Captain of the Artillery, and he very kindly invited me to share with him and another officer, the little dugout he had chosen for himself. It was entered by a narrow passage cut through the chalk in the side of the trench, and the roof consisted of a large semi-circular piece of iron under the ground. We had three beds and a table, and so were comfortable. When one stood on the earth which covered our roof, it was impossible to see any suggestion of a home underneath. Nothing was in sight but the wide expanse of rolling country cut up on all sides by trenches and shell holes, and wearing a sort of khaki uniform of light brown mud. To the east of us, lay the road bordered with leafless and battered trees, past which went an interminable line of lorries, guns and limbers. We were very comfortable, and at night when the winds were blowing and the rain was coming down in sheets, it was not half bad after dinner to read aloud Tennyson's "Ulysses" or other of my favourite poems. I am not sure that I did not at times, relying upon the inclemency of the weather overhead, recite some of my own. I know that one morning, when I had awakened at about four o' clock, I turned on the light of a storage battery which I had found in a German dugout, and sitting up wrote the verses which I

173

called "The Silent Toast" and which my artillery friends approved of when I recited them at breakfast.

The aftermath of victory is of course very sad. Many were the gallant men whose bodies were laid to rest in the little cemetery at Ecoivres. The cemetery is well kept and very prettily situated. The relatives of those who are buried there will be pleased to find the graves so carefully preserved. The large crucifix which stands on a mound near the gate is most picturesquely surrounded by trees. In the mound some soldier, probably a Frenchman, had once made a dugout. The site was evidently chosen with the idea that crucifixes were untouched by shells, and therefore places of refuge from danger. I often thought, as I looked at the crucifix with the human shelter beneath it, that it might stand as a symbol of the hymn:—

> "Rock of Ages cleft for me
> Let me hide myself in Thee."

The engineers had had a dump for their material near the Bethune-Arras road, and when they moved it forward to a place called the "Nine Elms," the engineer officer gave me his dugout, which was partly beside the road and partly under it. It consisted of several rooms, one of which contained a bed, and had steps going down to a deep chamber whither one could retire in case of shelling. It was good to have such a large and comfortable establishment, and when Alberta was chained up in her corner and I had strapped myself into my kit bag at night, we both felt very snug. The only trouble was that visitors kept coming at all hours to ask for engineering materials, not knowing that the character of the abode had changed. Early one morning, an officer came in a great hurry, and waking me up, asked if there were any winches there,—he pronounced the word like wenches. I sat up in bed and looked at him sternly, and said, "Young man, this is a religious establishment, I am the Senior Chaplain, and there are no wenches here." He did not know quite what to make of the situation. "I mean wooden ones," he said. I replied, "Young man, there are no wenches here, either wooden or any other kind; the engineers have gone forward." He apologized and left. On another occasion, in the darkness of middle night, an Imperial soldier who had lost his way came down the steps and put his head into my door and began to stammer and hiss in such an extraordinary way that Alberta was roused and barked furiously. I woke up with a start and asked what the matter was, but all I could get from the poor man was a series of noises and hisses. I turned on my flashlight, and a very muddy face covered with a shock of red hair looked in at the door of my little room, and with many contortions and winkings, emitted a series of incomprehensible noises. What with the stammering man and the barking dog, I was at my wits end to find out the trouble. At last by a process of synthesis, I pieced the various sounds together and found that the man wanted the location of a certain British battery. I gave him the best information I could.

Not far from me, at Arriane Dump, the Chaplain's Service established a coffee stall, and there men who were going up to or coming from the line could get coffee, biscuits and cigarettes at all hours. The neighborhood had now become so safe that little huts were being run up in various places. I asked our C. R. E. to build me a church, and, to my great joy, an officer and some men were detailed to put up a little structure of corrugated iron. At one end, over the entrance door, there was a belfry in which was hung a good sized German gas bell found in the trenches on our advance. Surmounting the belfry, was a cross painted with luminous paint. Inside the church, I had an altar with crucifix and candlesticks, and the Union Jack for a frontal. I also had a lectern and portable organ. The oiled linen in the windows let in a sufficient quantity of light, and the whole place was thoroughly church-like. I shall never forget the first service we held in it when the building was completed. It was in the evening and the sun was just setting. The air was balmy and spring-like and there was no shelling in the front line. The bell was rung and the congregation began to collect. I went over to the church and there I found, lying wrapped in a blanket on a stretcher beside the building, the body of a poor lad of the 2nd Division. It could not be buried until word had been received from his battalion. I got some of the men to carry the stretcher in and lay it in the aisle. I put on my cassock and surplice, lit the candles, and we had choral evensong, my organist playing the responses. The little church was filled, and there, in the midst of us, was one who had entered into his rest. It seemed to me that the most suitable hymn was :—

> "Let saints on earth in concert sing
> With those whose work is done,

THE WAR AS I SAW IT

For all the servants of our King
In heaven and earth are one.

One army of the living God
To His command we bow;
Part of the host have crossed the flood,
And part are crossing now."

All present sang the hymn most heartily, and we felt its appropriateness. I never hear it now without thinking of that evening service in St. George's Church at Arriane Dump. To those at home, I suppose, it will appear strange that an incident of that kind would not be almost too moving. At the front, however, death did not seem to be such a terrible thing—it was part of our life and something to be expected and met uncomplainingly. Every morning, until we moved, I had a Celebration of the Holy Communion in the church at eight o'clock, and every evening I had Evensong at six. I was told long afterwards that when General Horne paid his first visit to our Battle Headquarters, he pointed to the little iron structure with its belfry and white cross, and asked what it was. When they told him it was a church, he said, "A church! Now I know why the Canadians won Vimy Ridge." Unfortunately, the point of the observation was lost by the fact that the church was built, not before, but after we had taken the Ridge.

When we left Arriane Dump, I handed over the church to the Senior Chaplain of the British division which took our place, and he had the building taken down, put in lorries, and re-erected in the village of Roclincourt, where he adorned it with a painted window of St. George and the Dragon.

Along the Arras-Bethune road are various cemeteries where the men of the different battalions are buried. The greatest care was taken in collecting the dead and making their last resting place as neat and comely as possible. A plank road was constructed to connect the Bethune-Arras road with the Lens-Arras road further foward, It lay in a straight line over the broken ground cut up by trenches and huge craters, and brought one to the headquarters of the siege battery in which my son was a gunner. On all sides stretched the plain which our men had won. Far off, on clear days, one could see in the distance the little hamlets behind the German lines.

We had taken the Ridge, but there were villages in the plain which were not yet in our hands. I heard there was to be an attack one morning early. So the night before, I left my dugout at one a.m. It was a strange, weird walk along the plank road and then down the railway track to Farbus wood. The barrage was to open at four-thirty, and at four-ten a.m. I walked into the dugout where the Headquarters of the 3rd Artillery Brigade were. We waited till four twenty-five, and then I went up to see the barrage. Before us lay the plain, and all round us on the hillside, except in the space before us, were trees of Farbus Wood. At four-thirty the barrage opened, and we had a fine view of the line of bursting shells along the enemy's front. For a time our fire was very intense, and when it eased off I started down the hill to the town of Willerval, where in a dugout I found the officers of one of our battalions regaling themselves with the bottles of wine and mineral water which the Germans had left behind them in their well-stocked cellars. Willerval was badly smashed, but enough was left to show what a charming place it must have been in the days before the war. In the shell-ploughed gardens, spring flowers were putting up inquiring faces, and asking for the smiles and admiration of the flower-lovers who would tread those broken paths no more. I sat in a quiet place by a ruined brick wall and tried to disentangle the curious sensations which passed through the mind, as I felt the breeze lightly fanning my face, smelt the scent of flowers, heard the skylarks singing, saw the broken houses and conservatories, and listened to the shells which every now and then fell on the road to the east of the village. That super-sensitiveness to the charms of nature, which I have mentioned before, thrilled me with delight. The warm spring sun beat down from a cloudless sky, and the glorious romance of being out in the war-zone added to the charm.

One of our ambulances had a dressing station in the cellars of the Château, and there were a number of German prisoners there who were waiting their turn as stretcher bearers. From Willerval I went to the dressing station in the sunken road, where one of our chaplains was hard at work rendering assistance to the wounded. We had taken Arleux, but of course had to pay the price, and over the fields in different directions one could see stretchers being carried, bearing their loads of broken and suffering bodies. Our grand old Division never failed in taking its objective, and later on, we advanced from Arleux to Fresnoy, which completed

177

THE WAR AS I SAW IT

for us our campaign on Vimy Ridge. The Divisions on each side of us were held up, but when we left the Ridge we handed over Fresnoy to our successors in the line. Later, they were obliged to relinquish it.

There is something splendid in the esprit-de-corps of a Division, and none could be greater than that which animated all the units of the 1st Canadian Division, or as we were called, "the boys of the old red patch," from the red patch which we wore as a distinguishing mark upon our arms.

On May 4th, orders came to us that we had to move, and at night I walked over the old plank road to say good-bye to my son—for their battery was to retain its position—and on the next day, followed by little Alberta, I rode from Arriane Dump to my old billet in Bruay, breaking the journey by a visit to the 87th Battalion at Château de la Haie. We had returned to our old quarters covered with glory, and, on all sides, the French people were sincere in their admiration for what the Canadian Corps had done. It was certainly delightful to get back to clean billets, and to be able to enjoy the charming spring weather on roads that were not shelled and in fields that were rich in the promise of summer. Our Headquarters once again made their home in the Administration Building in the square, and the usual round of entertaining went on. During the day-time, battalions practised the noble art of open warfare. The sense of "Something accomplished, something done," inspired our men with the ardour of military life, and bound us all even closer together in the spirit of valiant comradeship.

CHAPTER XVIII

A Well-Earned Rest

May and June. 1917

THREE days after we had settled at Bruay I was invited by one of our staff officers and the Colonel of one of our battalions to accompany them on a visit to our old trenches on the Somme. We left in the morning and went south, over the roads and past the little villages which we knew so well, till we came to Albert. We went up the Bapaume road, now deserted and lonely. Our front line was some miles to the east, and so all that waste of country over which we had fought was now without inhabitants. We left the motor near Courcellette and walked over the fields to the old trenches where the First Brigade had made their attack. It was a dreary day. Low clouds hung over the sky and a cold wind blew from the east. Spring had made very little advance in those wide fields of death, and the grass was hardly green, where there was any grass. We walked over the well-known tracks reviewing incidents of the great battle. We crossed Death Valley and saw our old lines. The place was so solemn that by mutual agreement we did not talk, but each went off by himself. I found a number of Canadian and German bodies still unburied, and all over the fields were rifles and mess tins, spades and bits of accoutrement. One could hardly imagine a scene more desolate and forlorn. Every inch of that ground had been fought over and bought with the price of human blood. The moan of the wind over the fields seemed like the great lament of Nature for her sons who had gone. It was impossible to identify the bodies we found, but we knew that burial parties would soon set to work to collect them. Over each poor brown and muddy form I held a short service and used the form of committal from the burial office in our prayer-book.

It was with a sense of relief that we walked back up the road, past the ruins of Courcelette, and rejoined the motor. The scene was too painful. and made too great a pull upon the heart-strings. In the great army of the slain that lay beneath that waste of mud were many whom we had known and loved with that peculiar love which binds comrades in the fighting line to one another—

179

THE WAR AS I SAW IT

"God rest you valiant Gentlemen
Who sleep beneath that ground."

Once more, at the end of the month, I paid another visit to Regina Trench, when I was on my way to place a cross over my son's grave in the cemetery at Tara Hill. By this time, the grass was green, the trenches were filling up and in the cloudless blue sky larks were singing. The impression of dreariness was passing away, and the wounds on the breast of nature were being healed.

Our life at Bruay as usual was exceedingly pleasant, and the men thoroughly enjoyed the beauty and the freshness of the country. Games and sports were indulged in and the nightly entertainments in the theatre given by our concert party were most enjoyable.

I shall never forget the happy rides on Dandy down the roads and across the fields to the various battalions and artillery brigades. At every turn I would meet men whom I knew, and to shake hands with those glorious lads who had done such great things for the world was an honour and a privilege. In looking back to that time faces and places come before me, and I feel once again the warm spring winds over the fields of France, and see the quaint old villages of Houdain, Ruitz and Hallicourt where our various battalions were billetted. Sometimes, at exalted moments, I had meals with generals in their comfortable quarters; sometimes with company officers; sometimes with the non-coms, but I think the most enjoyable were those that I took with the men in dirty cook-houses. With a dish-cloth they would wipe off some old box for a chair, another for a table; then, getting contributions of cutlery, they would cook me a special dinner and provide me with a mess-tin of strong hot tea. When the meal was over and cigarettes had been lighted, general conversation was indulged in, and there would be talks of home, of war experiences, and many discussions of religion and politics. One question which was asked me again and again in trenches and dugouts and billets was—"Are we winning the war?" It may be hard for people at home to realize how little our men knew of what was happening. The majority of them never saw the newspapers, and of course the monotony of our life and the apparent hopelessness of making any great advance was a puzzle to them. I never failed to take the question seriously and give them, as far as I was able, a general idea of the aspect of the war on the various fronts. In order to be able to do this I read "The Times" daily with great care. It was really the only paper that one could depend on, and its marvellous influence on the conduct of the campaign completely justified its claim to be still the exponent of British policy, and its inherited right to the title of "The Thunderer,"

Our artillery were still in the line along the Ridge, but our infantry brigades were all at rest. It was proposed that we should have a thanksgiving service for victory with each brigade. The Senior Chaplain of the Corps took the matter in hand with the Senior Chaplain of the Army. A form of service was printed on slips of paper, and on Sunday, May 13th, we had services for the three infantry brigades. It was a lovely warm day, and the services were held at the most convenient points. The 2nd Brigade were assembled at Ruitz. It was a splendid sight. The 5th, 7th, 8th and 10th Battalions were drawn up in a great square, generals and staff officers were present; a band played the hymns and the army chaplain gave us a most stirring address. The next service was with the 1st Brigade in a field near Coupigny, where the 1st, 2nd, 3rd and 4th Battalions were drawn up, making a magnificent show of young, ardent and stalwart manhood. The moment it was over the general and staff were motored over to the 3rd Brigade at Chateau-de-la-Haie. Here were assembled the 13th, 14th, 15th and 16th Battalions. General Horne attended this Service, and, after the religious ceremony was over, gave an address. His admiration for the achievement of our men was evidently sincere, and he always showed the deepest interest in everything connected with the welfare of the Canadians.

Near Bruay on the way to Houdain were some large aerodromes and the headquarters of the squadron. I had met their chaplain before at Armentiéres when he was attached to the infantry. He very kindly invited me up to his quarters, and several times I dined with him at the officers' mess. He was the chaplain of several squadrons, and had to fly from one to another to take services on Sundays after the manner of a true "sky pilot." He told me some splendid tales of the gallantry of the young men to whom he had to minister. On one occasion the order was given that six German observation balloons along the front line had to be brought down, for we were about to make an advance. Six men were therefore, told off for this important but dangerous duty. The chaplain told me that at once the question arose as to how they were to dress for the encounter. Should they wear old clothes or should they be arrayed in their best? They decided that if they were brought down they would like, by their appearance, to do most credit to their squadron, and so it was determined that they should wear their newest uniforms. He told me that to him, who knew the dangers underlying the enterprise, it was most pathetic to see the young fellows in the highest spirits getting themselves polished up as if they were going to an investiture at Buckingham Palace. He had thought of having a service of Holy Communion for them, but there was no time, so he saw them start off on their voyage telling them that he would follow them with his prayers. The danger of such an undertaking was very great, as the planes had to fly low over the German trenches and then rise up and attack the balloons. That night six young airmen came to dinner in the mess as usual, but there were six observation balloons less in the German lines.

One night when I went to dinner with the officers of the squadron I was placed at the right hand of the O.C. He was late in arriving, and I wondered what sort of man would come to fill the vacant chair. To my surprise, when we were half way through dinner, a young officer, not much more than a boy came and took the seat and welcomed me to the mess. I asked him if he were the Major. He said he was, and on his left breast were several decorations. I was just going to make some remark about his youthful appearance when he said, "Now don't say it, Padré, don't say I look young, I really can't help it." I had a long and interesting talk with him about his work. He was full of enthusiasm, and his knowledge of men impressed me deeply. There was a large number of officers at the table all under his command. I thought it was wonderful that a man so young should have such a knowledge of human character. This war has certainly shown that mellowed age is not such a necessary qualification for right judgment as we thought it was. Old age has had its day, and the young world, that has just been born in the anguish and travail of the old, must be "run" by young men who unite in themselves the qualities of judgment and the love of adventure. The hut used as a mess-room was most artistically decorated, and made a fine setting for the noble young fellows, who sat round the table chaffing one another and laughing as if they never had to face death in the blinding mists of morning or the blazing sun of noon, with the rain of shells and machine gun fire falling round them, as they climbed higher and higher like skylarks into the wide vault of heaven.

On the first of June, we were ordered back to the line, and our Divisional Headquarters was to be divided. The General and staff were to be at the advanced position in the huts and dugouts on the La Targette road, and the non-combatant officers were to be billetted near Villers au Bois in Chateau d'Acq, a comfortable modern house with a large garden on one side and a pleasant tree-covered hill at the back. Here, to my surprise and delight, I found myself in possession of a large front room with furniture in it that appeared almost gorgeous. I had one comfortable night's sleep in it, but alas only one. On the next evening, when the full moon was shining with that fateful power which she has of turning night into day and of guiding the flight of hostile bombers, we were sitting smoking our cigars after dinner at the artillery headquarters in the La Targette road, when suddenly we heard the pulsating buzzing of a German plane. At once someone called out, "A Boche plane, put out the lights." In an instant the lights were out, but the fatal moonlight shone with clear and cruel lustre. There was a huge crash, then another, then another, then another, and someone said, "It has discharged its load." For a few moments we waited in silence, then we heard the sound of voices and men calling for help. I went across the open to the huts where the staff officers and the clerks lived. The German plane kept buzzing round and round at a low altitude, the observer evidently trying to find out what mischief he had done. To my dismay, I found that sixteen persons including the A. D. M. S. and the Assistant to the A. P. M., had been wounded, two of them fatally. We could not use the lights in attending to the wounded for the German airman was on the watch, and it was not until he went away that we could get ambulances to carry them off.

The General did not think it was worth while to risk a second attack by remaining at the place, so, in the middle of the night, with great dispatch the headquarters was moved back to the Chateau, and instead of my occupying the mahogany bed in the front room, I found myself on the floor of one of the huts in the garden. The General quite rightly and naturally taking to himself the bed which I had left.

Chateau d'Acq was for many weeks and at different times our comfortable and delightful home. There were many Nissen huts round the Chateau and under the beautiful trees on the hillside. Here the different branches of the service had their offices, and the engineers built for me a little house of tar paper lined with green canvas, over the door of which was painted the sign "St. George's Rectory." The C. R. E. also built me a new St. George's Church on the other side of the road. It was to be the chef d'oeuvre of his architectural skill, and to be made as complete and perfect as possible. A compass was brought and the true east and west found. The material of which the church was to be built was tar paper and scantling. The roof was to be covered with corrugated iron. The belfry was to be hung this time with two German gas bells, which were dignified with the title of a chime of bells. The windows, filled with oiled linen, were to be pointed after the manner of Gothic architecture. The church was to be cruciform, with a vestry on one side balanced by an organ chamber on the other. We had a nice altar, with the legal ornaments, and an altar rail. We had a lectern, and the proper number of benches for the congregation. We even had a font, which was carved out of chalk by the C. R. E.'s batman and given as an offering to the church. The C. R. E., a most devout and staunch Presbyterian, was proud of his architectural achievement and told me that now he had handed over to me a complete church he wished every service which the Church of England could hold to be celebrated in it. He said, "In addition to your usual services, I want men to be baptised, to be married, and to be ordained in that church." When I protested that possibly no men could be found desiring these offices, he replied, "The matter is perfectly simple. Like the centurion in the Bible, I am a man under authority. All I have to do is to call up ten men and say 'Go and be baptised tomorrow morning in Canon Scott's Church', and they will go. If they don't, they will be put in the guard room. Then I will call up ten more men and say, 'Go and be married in Canon Scott's church.' If they don't, I will put them in the guardroom. Then I will call up ten more men and say, 'Go and be ordained in Canon Scott's church'. If they don't, I will put them in the guard room." All this was said with perfect solemnity. As a matter of fact, when another division was occupying Chateau d'Acq, a man really was baptised in the little church. It was used daily for a time by the Roman Catholic Chaplain.

A photograph of the building is preserved in the Canadian War Records Office. The first morning I rang the chime of bells for the

184

early service, our A. D. M. S. avowed that he, mistaking the character of the sound, and supposing that it was a warning of a gas attack, sat up in his bed in the sweltering heat and put on his gas helmet.

From Chateau d'Acq I used to go and take services for the siege artillery on the Lens-Arras road, and also at the charmingly situated rest camp at Fresnicourt. We knew however that a bombing raid might occur at Chateau d'Acq on any clear night. Whenever we heard German planes in the air we always felt how unprotected we were, and it gave us a sense of relief when the buzzing sound grew fainter and fainter and died off in the distance.

The cool green shade of the trees made a pleasant roof over our heads on the hot days of early summer, and at dawn in the woods opposite we could hear the nightingales. Later on, the owner of the Chateau sold some of the bigger trees, and we found on our return to it in the following year that the beauty of the place had been destroyed, and the hillside looked like the scene of a Canadian lumber camp. However, the rose-trees in the garden with their breath of sweetest odour were a continual joy and delight to the soul.

CHAPTER XIX.

Paris Leave

June 1917

MY time for leave was due again, and as we were allowed to spend it in France without interfering with the number of those who desired to see their friends in England, I determined to go to Chamounix. I thought that the sight of a great natural wonder like Mont Blanc would have an uplifting effect upon the mind, at a time when everything human seemed to be going to rack and ruin. The white peaks of the Alps in their changeless purity against the blue of the infinite sky seemed to me a vision which the soul needed. So I started off one lovely morning on my way to Paris. I went by side-car to Amiens, where I took the train. It was a delightful expedition, and I left with a good conscience, because our men were not expected to attack, and were in a quiet sector of the line. The driver of the car, with the prospect of a good meal at Amiens and a good tip, was in the best of humours. The air was sweet and fresh and the grass wore its brightest green. The sunshine beat down from a cloudless sky, and when we paused for repairs, as we had to do from time to time, birds' songs furnished us with a most enjoyable concert. An expedition of this kind was made doubly charming by having in it a touch of adventure. When we came to a village, at once the map had to be studied and the turns in the road noted. A conversation with some of the villagers as we journeyed, always broke the sense of loneliness, and gave us an insight into the feelings of the people. However, on this particular occasion, I was not able to complete the journey to Amiens in the side-car. Either the car broke down, or the driver preferred to go on by himself, for the thing came to a dead stop just as a car from the Corps was about to pass us. The occupants kindly invited me to go on to Amiens with them. It was a swifter way of continuing the journey and much more comfortable, so I said good-bye to my original driver and started off with my new friends.

Amiens was a bustling place then and very unlike the Amiens I saw a little over a year later. I started by train at six-thirty p. m., and at eight-thirty, after a pleasant journey, arrived at Paris, where

PARIS LEAVE

I went to the Hotel Westminster. On the next evening, I started off with some friends for Evians-les-Bains. The train was very full, and there were no berths in the wagon-lit, so we had to stay up all night in a crowded first-class carriage. There was an old French Curé at one end of the compartment, who, quite early in the evening, drew out a silk handkerchief and covered his head and face therewith, leading us to suppose that he had sunk into oblivion. We therefore carried on a very pleasant and vivacious conversation, as the night was warm and we were not inclined to sleep. Suddenly the old Curé pulled off the handkerchief and said in a gruff voice, "It is the time for sleeps and not for talks." and, having uttered this stinging rebuke, re-covered his head and left us in penitent silence. We arrived at Evians-les-Bains in good time, and went to a very charming hotel with a lovely view of the Lake of Geneva in front. Unfortunately, I had hurt my foot some time before and it looked as if it had got infected. Not wishing to be laid up so far from medical assistance, I decided to return the same evening, which I did, and once more found myself at the Hotel Westminster. I now determined to spend my leave in Paris. There were many of our men in the city at that time. They were all in a very impecunious condition, for there was some difficulty in getting their pay and, in Paris, money did not last long. I did my best to try and help them, and later our system of payment was improved. It was perhaps just as well for some of them that their money was short.

Poor old Paris looked very shabby to one who remembered her in former days with her clean streets and many-fountained parks. She wore the air of shabby gentility. The streets were not clean; the people were not well-dressed, the fountains no longer played. France had been hard hit by the war, and the ruin and desolation of her eastern borders were reflected in the metropolis. I spent most of my time in Paris trying to keep men straight, with more or less success. I can imagine nothing worse for a lonely young fellow, who had taken his leave after weary months in the front line, than to find himself in the midst of the heartless gaiety of the French capital. On all sides the minions of vice, diseased in mind and body, lay in waiting for their prey. To one who loved Canada and longed for the uplifting of the pure life of Canadian homes, it was a spectacle which filled the heart with anxiety. Before I left Paris, I wrote a letter to the Continental Daily Mail advocating the taking over of some hotels which could be turned into hostels or clubs for soldiers while on leave. This, I am happy to say was afterwards done.

I met many of our men at the soldiers' tea-rooms called "A corner of Blighty" in the Place Vendome, and I organized several dinner and theatre parties which went off very pleasantly. When the men had companionship, they did not feel the lure of vice which came to them in moments of loneliness. I met some interesting people in Paris, and at a Sunday luncheon in the charming house of the Duchess de la M— I met Madame—, the writer of a series of novels of rather lurid reputation. The authoress was a large person with rich orange-coloured hair, powdered cheeks, and darkened eyelashes. She wore a large black hat, enormous solitaire pearl ear-rings, and, as a symbol of her personal purity, was arrayed in white. She lamented the fact that women writers were not allowed to visit the front. When I told her that Mrs. Humphrey Ward had been there, she said, "Oh yes, they allowed her to go because they said she could write good English, but she cannot get the ear of the American people in the way *I* can."

There were two or three French officers present, one of whom was an attaché at the Embassy in Madrid. I was much impressed by their quiet dignified bearing, so typical of the chivalrous heroism of France, and so unlike anything which we could look for in the officers of the German Army. I could not help observing that the French were much depressed and filled with anxiety as to the issue of the war. A French lady said to me "How can we go on much longer; our man-power is nearly exhausted?" It is a supreme delight to me to think that that wonderful nation, which suffered and bled so deeply and bore its wrongs so nobly, has now been avenged on the ruthless enemy, and that the tricolour once more floats over Alsace and Lorraine. Profoundly patriotic though we of the British Empire are, there is something in the patriotism of the French which goes down into the deepest roots of the human soul. I remember once in the private burying place of a noble family who owned a chateau not far from our front line, seeing a little child's grave. The child had died in Canada at the age of two years, and its body had been brought back to its ancestral resting place. On the tombstone, under the inscription were the words:—

"Petit ange
Priez pour
la France."

PARIS LEAVE

I was very much struck by the prayer. That the sorrow for a child's death should be coupled with the love of country seemed most strange and pathetic. I venture to say that it would be impossible to find a parallel instance of such a blending of emotions in any English churchyard. The present owner of the Chateau, which was at least two or three hundred years old, was away fighting for his country, and long grass and weeds filled the uncared for corner by the side of the old church. In past history, we have fought with the French again and again, but we always felt that we were fighting with gentlemen, and were sure that every courteous deed done by us would meet with an equally courteous response. One of the saddest things in the war was that, while we often admired the military efficiency of the Germans, we had absolutely no respect for their officers or men, nor could we regard them as anything but well-trained brutes. The ties which bind us to France now are very intimate and personal, and it is a matter of thankfulness to all who love human idealism and true culture, that the reproach of the defeat of 1870 has been washed away in blood, and that France will emerge from her fiery trial a purer and a loftier nation.

I was not sorry when my Paris leave was over and I returned to my Headquarters at Chateau d'Acq. It was always delightful to get back to my war home and settle down again in the midst of those on whose shoulders the fate of civilization rested. I arrived back on June 29th, just in time to prepare for the special services which were to be held throughout the Corps on Sunday, July 1st, it being the jubilee of the Dominion. I made arrangements with the band of the Royal Canadian Regiment, as our Divisional band was away, to march over from Villers au Bois and play for us at the service. We had special hymns and prayers neatly printed on cards, which the men were to retain as souvenirs. The parade was held just outside St. George's Church, our new Divisional Commander, General Macdonell, and his staff attending. The occasion was particularly interesting to me, because I was the only man in the whole Canadian Corps at the front who could remember the first Dominion Day. I could remember as a child being taken by my father on the 1st of July, 1867, to hear the guns firing a salute on the grounds of McGill College, Montreal. Canada had travelled a long distance on the path of nationhood since that far-off time, and now, after fifty years, I had the satisfaction of being

189

with the great Canadian Army Corps on European soil, engaged in the biggest war of history. Such an experience is not often the privilege of a human life, and the splendid body of men before me gave promise of Canada's progress and national glory in the future. Everyone felt the peculiar significance of the celebration.

Owing to the fact that my foot was still troubling me, I was sent down to the rest-camp at Fresnicourt, where I met many of the officers and men in that delightful old Chateau. The country round about was very pretty, and the views from the hills were charming. Every night I used to have either a service, or a talk with the men, on the grass beside a little stream. They were all enjoying the rest and refreshment that came from being able to live in pleasant surroundings and away from shells and work in the trenches. On July 18th, I went by sidecar to St. Omer where the Senior Chaplains of the Army were summoned to a conference. We were billeted in the large building used as the Chaplains' Rest Home, and there enjoyed the great privilege, not only of meeting one another, but of listening to some splendid addresses and lectures by those in charge. It was pleasant to revisit St. Omer. The quaint old French town, with its rambling streets and polite inhabitants, took one away from the thoughts of war and gave one almost a feeling of home. In the smoking-room at night, we had the opportunity of discussing with one another the various moral and religious problems with which the chaplain had to contend, and many were the interesting experiences of those chaplains. On the last day of our meetings, at the early Eucharist, we had an address from the Archbishop of York, who had just come over to France. Later on, he gave an address at a general meeting of the chaplains at Bethune.

While at St. Omer I paid a visit to the Second Army School in their magnificent buildings in Wisques, where I saw the room that my son had occupied, and met some of the people who remembered him. The place was used as a training school for officers and was most wonderfully equipped. The building was a modern convent, and the large unfinished chapel, with its high vaulted roof, was used as a dining-room. It was inspiring at dinner to see the hundreds of young officers, all so keen and cheery, sitting round the tables, while a good band played during the meal. It was hard to realize that they were only having a momentary respite from the war, and, in a week or two, would be once more up in the line facing wounds and death. The Commandant took great pride in the institution, and told me of the splendid records of the men who had passed through his hands.

Our Divisional Headquarters now moved to a place called Bracquemont, near Noeux les Mines. Here I had a very fine room in the house of the manager of one of the Mines, the offices of which were on the other side of the road. The house was well built, and had a most charming garden at the back. It was large and commodious, and I always feared that my billet would attract the covetous desires of some high staff officer and that I should be thrown out to make way for him. My room was on the ground floor with two large windows opening on the street, enabling me to get the Daily Mail from the newsboy in the morning. The ceiling was high and the furniture most sumptuous. A large mirror stood upon the marble mantel-piece. I had linen sheets on the bed and an electric light at my side. It did not seem at all like war, but the end of the mahogany bed and some of the chairs, also one corner of the ceiling, had been perforated by bits of shrapnel. So in the midst of luxury, there was the constant reminder that the war was still going on— a death's head at the feast.

CHAPTER XX.

WE TAKE HILL 70.

July and August, 1917.

BRACQUEMONT was a very charming home. There were many men about us, the artillery horse lines were there as well as two battalions in rest, and various other units. Behind the British C. C. S. there was a large hall with a stage at one end. Here our concert party gave a performance every night. Between us and the front line, were the villages of Maroc, Le Brebis, Mazingarbe, and Bully-Grenay, which were our billeting area while we occupied the trenches in advance of Loos. I was thus in easy reach of all the units in the Division and could do a great deal of parish visiting.

In the country behind us, there were many Chinese Labour Companies and one of Zulus. When not at work, they were encamped in large compounds surrounded by barbed wire. Our band used to play occasionally for the entertainment of the Chinese, who very much enjoyed both the music and the compliment that was paid to them by its being provided. On one occasion, I went with General Thacker to visit one of the Chinese Labour Companies. The officer in charge wished us to see some of their sports, and so we sat on chairs at the top of the field and the Chinamen came up and gave us an exhibition of their skill in something that looked like fencing. They used sticks for foils. We could not quite see who won in the encounter, or what constituted the finishing stroke, but, as soon as each pair of performers retired they turned and bowed solemnly to the General and made way for two other combatants. They were great powerful men, very different from the type of Chinese one sees in this country. One of the performers we were told by the O. C., could carry a weight of five hundred pounds on his shoulders. After the gymnastic performance, we had a concert, and a man sang, or rather made a hideous nasal sound, to the accompaniment of something that looked like a three stringed fiddle. The song, which greatly delighted the Chinese listeners, consisted of an interminable number of verses; in fact we never heard the end of it, for the O. C. stopped it and told the musicians that the officers had to leave. He told us that the men were well behaved, and that only once had he had occasion to hold a court-martial.

The Zulus were encamped near Ranchicourt. They too were a stalwart lot of men, but felt the cold of the winter very much. I was riding past them in the road one day and spoke to the British sergeant in charge of them. He pointed out one young man who, he said, was the son of a chief, and, in his own country, was entitled to a body-guard of fifteen men. In recognition, therefore, of his aristocratic birth, he was allowed to wear three stripes. While we were talking, the boy looked round and saw that we were speaking about him. The sergeant called out something to him in Zulu language, and the boy smiled and nodded to me. I asked the sergeant what he had said to him. He replied: "I told him that you thought you had met him before, and it pleased him." This accounted for the boy's smiling at me and the nod of recognition. I suppose he thought that on some occasion in my rambles through Africa we had met in the jungle. At any rate, I admired the sergeant's tact and savoir faire. There was a great mixture of races among the allied forces in France, and I always felt sorry for the poor heathen that they should be dragged into the war of the Christian nations.

Our front trenches were not comfortable places. To reach them one had to pass through Maroc and along a road on the outskirts of Loos. Beside the road, in the cellars of a broken building, called Fort Glatz, was a dressing station. The neighborhood was frequenty shelled, for the road from Maroc to Loos was under observation from the two mysterious iron towers in Wingles. Beyound Fort Glatz, the enginneers had a store of trench materials. The place was called "Crucifix Dump," on account of the large crucifix which stood there on a mound of earth. The figure on the crucifix was made of metal and it had been struck by shrapnel. It looked so pathetic standing there amid the ruin and desolation around, mutely saying to those who had ears to hear, "Is it nothing to you, all ye who pass by; behold and see if there was ever sorrow like unto my sorrow?" From a shrapnel hole near the heart of the figure, birds could be seen flying in and out, getting food for their young. At the foot, there was the grave of a German officer who had been killed when the Germans occupied Loos.

I often used to go to Bully-Grenay to visit some of the siege batteries. They had comfortable billets but the Germans soon found out their location and sent over some very big shells. One large shell had a curious experience. It fell in the road to the south of Bully-Grenay, burrowing under the ground without exploding. Then it rose and went through the side of a brick house, and finally reposed on the floor of an upper room. We all went to see it lying there, like some gigantic sea monster dead and stranded on the shore. The potential force of the huge shell was enormous, but it lay there perfectly harmless after its strange pilgrimage.

I was passing one of the siege batteries one day, when I saw a number of men working round a damaged gun-pit. I went over to it and found that a shell had landed there that morning, just as they were changing shifts on the guns. It had killed and buried a number of the men, at the same time setting fire to our ammunition. The bodies of those who were buried were burnt almost to ashes by the terrific heat, and only charred bits of them were recovered.

South of Loos there was the famous Double Crassier. It was a large slag heap on which once ran a line of railway. The top, of course, was in sight of the Germans, but down in the hollow on our side of it we had a great number of battery positions. That little corner where our guns were concentrated was an easy target for the German artillery, and many were the high explosives and gas-shells which they dropped. In the town of Maroc itself there was a large fosse or mine-head. The buildings round it were capacious, and well made. They were of course now much damaged, but the cellars were extraordinarily commodious and extensive. They were lined with white tiles, and the largest one was fitted up as a place of rest and amusement with a canteen where the men could get coffee, cakes and cigarettes. I stationed one of our chaplains there to look after the work and hold services in one of the cellars which was fitted up as a chapel. In the large room there were benches, and a stage afforded a good floor for boxing. I determined to start boxing there as a sport for the artillerymen, who had few opportunities of enjoying the entertainments which were given behind the line. I had a great friend in one of the Highland battalions, who had been wounded three times in the war, and was heavy-weight champion of the 1st Division. I got his O. C. to attach him to r ~, and I placed him in the cellar at Maroc where he began to instruct the men in the noble art of self defence. People used to wonder why I had a prize-fighter attached to me, and I told them that if the Junior Chaplains were insubordinate, I wanted to be able to call in some one in an emergency to adminster discipline.

I always said, with perfect truth, that since my prize-fighter was attached to me I had had no trouble with any of the chaplains. It is wonderful what things one can do in the Army which are not according to the King's Regulations. By right, as Senior Chaplain of a Division, I was entitled only to one man who was to act in the dual capacity of batman and groom, but later on I managed to get a man to act as secretary, who was given sergeant's stripes and looked after the office when I went on my wanderings through the Division. Then I got a man who knew something about music to be appointed as my organist. He used to travel with me in the staff car with my portable organ when I went to take church parades on Sunday. He was afterwards gassed and I lost him, but he did useful work while he was with me in helping the singing. The prize-fighter made another addition to what I called the Senior Chaplain's battalion. Then, as time went on, I was able to get a man to take over the duties of a batman, and I finally obtained a chauffeur to run my side-car. This large army of assistants was a sore puzzle to our Camp Commandant, who had to arrange for their rations and discipline. I was always being asked how many men I had on my staff. However, to use a soldier's expression "I got away with it."

The road through Maroc was not a pleasant one to travel. It was liable to be shelled at any moment. On one side of the street was a large brick wall which had been perforated by a shell and the place was called "The Hole in the Wall." The Germans knew that we had many batteries concealed in the ruined town, so they never left it alone for very long. I was going up to the front one day, when I met in the street an artillery officer coming back. We had not seen each other for some time, and he gave me such a warm greeting that I at once determined to reward him by reciting to him one of my poems. I got about half way through when the enemy, not knowing, of course, what was going on, began to shell the place, and some bits of mud and brick fell in the road not far off. In spite of the beauty of the poem, my friend began to get restless, and I was faced with the problem of either hurrying the recitation and thereby spoiling the effect of the rhythm, or of trusting to his artistic temperament and going on as if nothing was happening. I did the latter, and went on unmoved by the exploding shells. I thought the Major would see that the climax of the poem had not yet been reached and was worth waiting for. I was mistaken.

He became more and more restless, till at last he said, "Excuse me, Canon, but I think I must be hurrying on." He left me standing in the road with the last part of the poem and its magnificent climax still in my throat. I looked after him for a moment or two, then turned sorrowfully, lamenting the depravity of human nature, and pursued my journey. I had not gone far in the street before I came to a large pool of blood, where a man had just been killed. There was some excuse, therefore, for my friend's conduct, for he must have passed that pool of blood before he met me, and his nerves were probably not in their normal condition. He went back to his battery and told his friends there that I had actually buttonholed him in Maroc and insisted upon his listening to a miserable poem of mine while shells were falling in the place.

In order to avoid the danger of passing through the town, we generally used a path across the fields. I was returning from the trenches with some men one night along this path, when we saw from Maroc flashes of a light which was apparently being used as a signal. At once we were seized with an attack of spy-fever, and I said to the men, "There is someone signalling to the Germans." The night was so dark that signalling could have been seen at a considerable distance. Immediately we started off towards the light, which went out when we approached, but we discovered an officer in a mackintosh, and I at once asked him who he was. Tired as our men were, for they were coming out after being several days in the trenches, they followed me and were so keen on the adventure that one of them had drawn his revolver. The officer became very rude and he used some blasphemous words towards me in the dark, which naturally provoked a stern rebuke. I told him I was a Lieut.-Colonel, and that I should report him to his commanding officer. Then we asked him to give proof of his identity. I could see by his manner that he was becoming exceedingly uncomfortable, so I insisted upon his leading us to his headquarters. He did, and we stumbled on over telephone wires and piles of bricks till he brought us into the yard of a broken down house, in the cellars of which we found the officers of his battery. The O. C. was very polite and, when I pointed out to him the danger of flashing a light in the neighborhood of the track which was used by our infantry battalions at night when going to or coming from the trenches, he said his unit would be more careful in the future. After a little conversation we left. A day or two afterwards I met one of the officers of the battery, and we had a good laugh over the incident, but he told me that it was even more amusing than I had thought, for the young officer had a dug-out in the field and was making his way thither with nothing on but his pyjamas and his mackintosh. When we asked him for some proofs of his identity, he was terrified lest we should search him and find him in this peculiarly unmilitary costume, which might have made us still more suspicious.

Ever since our moving to Bracquemont, we had been preparing to complete the work of our advance towards Lens by an attack on Hill 70, the high ground to the north-west of that city. Compared with the taking of Vimy Ridge, the exploit was of course a minor one, but, for many reasons, it was felt to be an exceedingly dangerous task and one which would cost us dearly. The Germans had had time to concentrate their forces in front of us, and they knew the value of the commanding position which they held. Everyone felt anxious as to the result of the enterprise, and we had learnt from recent experiences on the Ridge and at Fresnoy how powerful the enemy was. Although, of course, I did not let the men see it, I was always worried when we had an attack in view. When I held sevices for them on parade, or addressed them at their entertainments, or met them by the roadside, I used to look into their eyes and wonder if those eyes would soon be viewing the eternal mysteries "in the land that is very far off." I tried to make it a point never to pass anyone without a handshake or a word of cheer and encouragement. How their faces used to brighten up at some trifling kindness or some funny story!

I was fond of visiting the men who acted as the road control on the east side of Maroc. One of their number was of course on guard day and night, so I was always sure of meeting a friend whenever I passed. I never went down to their cellar without being offered a cup of tea and other dainties. They used to sleep on shelves, and often invited me to rest my weary limbs there. I would thank them for their kindness, but thought it prudent, for reasons of personal cleanliness, not to accept it. It always gave me great pleasure to come upon friends in out of the way places. I remember meeting an officer late one night near the front at Loos. It was very dark, and, as soon as he recognized me, he exclaimed, "Here's old Canon Scott, I'll be d—d!" "My friend," I said solemnly,

"I hope you will not allow that sad truth to get abroad. The Canadian Government is paying me a large salary to try and keep you from that awful fate, and if they hear that your meeting me has had such a result, I shall lose my job." He apologized for the expression, and said it was only meant as an exclamation of surprise.

By the beginning of August, everything was ready for the attack, and on the 14th, carrying my rations with me, I made my way to the 7th Siege Battery; for I had arranged to go to their observation post and watch the barrage from there. I started off in the evening, with one of the gunners. We skirted Maroc and reached the O.P., which was called St. Pat's. It was a long walk over the open and through the trenches before we got into the place. From it we looked down the slope towards our front line, and beyond this we saw the rise in the ground called Hill 70, held by the Germans. The barrage was to begin at four twenty-five in the morning; so the gunner and I went down into a dugout and tried to get a little rest. Before we got to sleep, however, we became aware of the smell of gas, and, hearing the tramping of feet in the trench at the top of the stairs, I went up and found the men of the 14th Battalion with their helmets on going forward in preparation for the advance. They recognized me because I did not put on my mask, and as they passed they shook hands with me and I wished them "good luck in the name of the Lord." Such cheery souls they were, going forth in their stifling helmets to the unknown dangers which awaited them.

I found that sleep was impossible, so I went up to the O.P. and waited for the barrage. It was a lovely night; the stars were shining beautifully, and the constellation of Orion hung on the horizon in the eastern sky, with the pale moon above. A great silence, stirred only by the morning breeze, brooded over the wide expanse of darkness. Then, at four-twenty-five, the guns burst forth in all their fury, and all along the German line I saw not only exploding shells, but the bursting oil drums with their pillars of liquid fire, whose smoke rose high in the air with a peculiar turn at the top which looked like the neck of a huge giraffe. At once the Germans sent up rockets of various colours, signalling for aid from their guns, and the artillery duel of the two great armies waxed loud and furious. I stood on the hill with some of our men, and watched the magnificent scene. Nothing but the thought of what it meant to human beings took away from our enjoyment of the mighty spectacle. When day dawned, we could see, silhouetted against the morning sky, men walking over the hill-top, and now and then jumping down into the captured trenches. Once again our Division had got its objective. At various points difficulties had been encountered, and in a place called the "Chalk Pit", which afterwards became our front line, the Germans had made a determined stand. They had a wonderful dugout there, like a rabbit-warren, with many passages and entrances, from which they were bombed out with great difficulty. One of our western battalions suffered heavily in taking the stronghold.

I went on to Fort Glatz and to some of the other advanced aid-posts. We had many casualties, but we felt that the worst was not yet over, for we knew that, although we had taken the hill, the Germans would make a desperate fight to get it back again. All day long our artillery pounded away and our infantry consolidated the line. Our Pioneer Battalion did splendid work in digging trenches under heavy fire, in order to connect our advanced positions. When the sun set and the night once more cast its shade over the earth, there was no cessation in the sound of battle.

The next morning I visited the wounded in the C. C. S., and in the afternoon went by car once more to the 7th Siege Battery and thence made my way through Maroc to the front, as I had heard from the General that the artillery were having a hard time. Their guns had been firing incessantly since the barrage started. I met many men on the journey who gave me accounts of their experiences during the battle, and, by the time I reached the Y. M. C. A. coffee-stall in a ruined building on the Maroc-Loos road it was quite late. Here in a cellar I found some men making coffee for the walking wounded, who were coming back very tired and glad of a shelter and a hot drink. I went on down the road to the well concealed trenches which led to the 1st and 2nd Artillery Brigade Headquarters. In the deep dugout, I found the O. C.s of the two brigades and their staffs hard at work. It was an anxious time, because ammunition was short, and every available man was employed in carrying it up to the guns. The Senior Colonel asked me if I would go round to some of the gun pits and talk to the men. They were tired out, he said, with the constant firing, and there was still no prospect of a rest. I told him that if he would give me a runner to act as guide, I would visit all the gun-pits of the two Brigades. Accordingly a runner was sent for, and he and I started off at midnight. It was very dark, and when we emerged from the trench and turned to the right on the Lens-Bethune road we met parties of wounded men coming back, and the batteries in the fields beside us were firing over our heads. We visited first the cellar of a building by the way, where there was an aid post. Here were many men being attended to by the doctors. They were all worn out, and did not look forward with much pleasure to their journey back to Maroc along the dark and dangerous road.

From the dressing station, my guide and I went into a trench and along this to the gun positions. As we came to each, we visited the officers and men. We got a glad welcome from the faithful, true-hearted fellows who were working with might and main to save the lives of their comrades in the front line. Some of the guns were fearfully heated and were hard to handle. Yet the S. O. S. signals from the front trenches would go up every now and then, telling our gunners that the Germans were making another counter-attack, and asking for artillery support to save the situation. We made our way through the trench towards the batteries at the foot of the Loos Crassier. In doing so, we had to pass under the road. I was going on ahead, and when I stooped down to pass under the bridge, to my surprise I could dimly descry in the darkness a row of silent men sitting on each side of the passage facing one another. I said, "Good-night, boys," but there was no answer. The figures in the darkness remained motionless and still. I could not quite make out what the matter was, for our men always responded to my greeting. Suddenly, an enemy flarelight went up in the distance, and I saw, to my horror, that the two rows of men sitting so silently were Germans. I was wondering if I had run my neck into a noose, when a voice from the other end of the passage called out, "They are prisoners, Sir. I am taking them back with me and giving them a few minutes rest." I must say that I was greatly relieved. I went on to the gun-pits just in front of the crassier, and here the men were working hard. It was splendid to see their absolute disregard of everything but their duty. I felt myself to be such a slacker beside them, but I told them how gloriously they were carrying on, and how their work was appreciated by the infantry. The night began to wear away, and when I reached the gun-pits that were further back it was broad daylight. In fact, I visited the last one at six a. m. Some of the batteries had by this time ceased firing, and the men had fallen asleep in all sorts of curious positions, ready to be roused in an instant. Altogether, my guide and I visited forty-eight gun-pits that night, and it was about seven o'clock when we returned to Brigade Headquarters.

The next night the Germans sent over a rain of gas-shells on the batteries, and the men at the guns found it impossible to see the sights through the eye-pieces of their gas-helmets, and so chose to face the poison unprotected rather than run the risk of injuring our infantry by bad firing. There were of course heavy casualties among the gunners as a result of this. Some died and many were badly gassed, but the line was held.

As I was returning after spending the night at the gun-pits, I felt terribly tired. The morning sun rose higher and higher, and beat down with summer heat on my steel helmet as I made my way along the path which skirted the town of Maroc. I sat down by the side of a trench to have some breakfast, and opened a tin of milk and my tin of bully beef and was just preparing to have a meal, when I must have fallen asleep instantaneously. How long I slumbered I do not know, but when I woke up I found, standing in front of me, three amused and puzzled Australian tunnellers. When I fell asleep, I must have upset my breakfast, which was lying at my feet, and the tunnellers were evidently enjoying what they considered to be the discovery of a padré a little the worse for wear. They were somewhat surprised, not to say disappointed, when I woke up, and they said, "You seem to be very tired, Sir." I told them that I had had very little sleep for several nights, and had been walking all night long, winding up my story (for the honour of the cloth) with the statement that I was a teetotaller. Whether they believed it or not I do not know, but we had a long talk together and they told me of the work they were doing in digging a tunnel from Loos to the front line.

The next day I went to the advanced dressing station and saw the men that were gassed being brought in. So strongly were their clothes saturated with the poison that, as they were being cut off, in order that the bodies of the men might be washed with the liquid used for counteracting the burning effects of the gas, our eyes and throats smarted from the fumes. There was nothing more horrible than to see men dying from gas. Nothing could be done to relieve their suffering. The body, as well as the throat and lungs, was burned and blistered by the poison.

THE WAR AS I SAW IT

The German counter-attack had now spent itself, and Hill 70 was ours. One more splendid deed had been achieved by the Canadian Corps, and we now held in our hands the commanding position which threatened the town of Lens.

CHAPTER XXI

Every Day Life

August to October 1917

HILL 70 being now in our grip the Division came out of the line on August 21st, and moved back to our old billets in Bruay.

Every night, as usual, our concert party gave a performance in the theatre. We were very proud of them. The men's costumes were well made and very taseteful. "Babs," our leading lady, was most charming and engaging, in spite of the fact that her hands looked decidedly masculine. The townspeople enjoyed the entertainments as much as we did, and the battalions were given their own special nights. Occasionally, some of the jokes appeared to me a trifle too broad. At such times I would pay a visit to the Greenroom, as Senior Chaplain, and mildly suggest their withdrawal. I must say that the men took my interference in good part and kept their exuberance of spirits well in check. Our Divisional band was up to high-water mark, and their rendering of the hymns and chants on Sundays made our services in the theatre extraordinarily hearty.

One afternoon I motored over to Quatre Vents to take a funeral service in the cemetery there. Instead of returning, I went down to Cambligneul to see the men of the 7th Battalion. They were enjoying a rest in the quaint old town. In the evening, I went down to the Y.M.C.A. hut which was in charge of the British. Here I found our men crowded into the building, not knowing what to do with themselves. The officer in charge of the hut was a quiet man, who was doing his best in superintending the work at the counter. It struck me, however, that he felt a little embarassed by the situation, and did not know how to provide amusement for the wild Canadians. I asked him if he would object to our having a stag-dance. He said, "Certainly not, you may do anything you like." At once we got several dozen candles and illuminated the place. Then we sent out for a pianist and some violinists, and got up a scratch orchestra. We then cleared away the tables and benches and turned the place into a dance-hall. The orchestra struck up a lively two-step, and great burly chaps chose their equally

burly partners, and started off in the dance with such gusto that
the place was filled with the sounds of dissipation. This attracted
more men from outside, and finally we had the liveliest scene imaginable. I actually found myself joining in the mazes of the waltz,
and amid roars of laughter the dancing went on fast and furious.
So delighted was the Y.M.C.A. officer, that he mounted the platform at the end of a dance, and in spite of my protest, called for
three cheers for the man who had suggested the entertainment.
At the close of the evening, we had cups of hot coffee and biscuits,
and parted in the best of humours. I was then confronted by a problem that had not presented itself to me before, and that was, how
I was to get back to my home in Bruay, which was about ten miles
off. Once more my favourite text came to my mind, "The Lord
will provide." So I bid good-bye to my friends in the hut and went
off, trusting that a car or lorry would pick me up on the road. This
time I found that the Lord did not provide, so I started at about
half-past ten on my homeward journey on foot. As I passed
through the sleeping village of Estrée-Cauchie, I came upon some
men of another Division who had been imbibing very freely in an
estaminet, and who were about to wind up a heated argument with
a free fight. It was very dark, and it was hard for me to convince
them that I was a chaplain with the rank of Lieut.-Colonel, until I
turned my flashlight upon my white collar. Happily, my efforts as
peacemaker were not in vain. I poured oil on the troubled waters
till I saw them subside, and the men went off to their billets. One
young fellow, however, was experiencing that interest in spiritual
problems, which was sometimes aroused in the most unexpected
quarters by free libations of spirituous liquors. He caught hold
of my arm and implored me to enlighten him on the theological
differences which separated Anglicans and Presbyterians. I forget
which he was himself, but at the time the problem was a matter of
extraordinary interest to him. While I always considered it my
duty to impart enlightenment to darkened souls whenever I could,
the recollection that I had about seven miles to walk to my home that
night rather tempered my missionary zeal, and by a promise to discuss the whole matter on our next meeting I managed to tear myself away and proceed on my journey.

It was a long tramp down the silent road in the darkness. The
houses in the little villages through which I passed were tightly
shut. Not a light could be seen, and Providence supplied no car or

lorry for my conveyance. On a hill in the distance, I saw the revolving light which acted as a signal to the aeroplanes. It would shine out for a few seconds and then die away. The air was fresh and cool, and I had time to meditate on the curious events of the intense life which I lived. It was still day in Canada, and the sun was shining over our cities, the great lakes, the prairies, and the jagged peaks in the mountain province on the Pacific coast. When was this life going to end? Were we really making any progress? Overhead, my beloved friends the stars, kept up their silent twinkling, which gave them an appearance of life. In the valley lay the old medieval Chateau of Ohlain. I thought of the historical figures from the pages of French history who had walked along that road centuries before, filled with the anxieties and problems of their own age. Now and then, some bird of the night would break the silence with its cry or twitter, and still I plodded on. At last, long after midnight, I reached the outskirts of Bruay, and entering the High Street, made my way to my billet, where Alberta was waiting to give me a warm welcome.

It was the privilege of the British Army to have as its commanders, good and devout men. One always felt that, in any appeal, the cause of religion would be upheld. General Horne, who commanded the First Army, of which we formed a part, was a man of sincere religious life, and never failed to show his appreciation of the chaplains and their work. One day he invited all the Chaplains of the First Army to have tea with him at his headquarters in the beautiful Chateau of Ranchicourt. It was a lovely afternoon, and we motored over to the meeting in busses. Tables were set for tea and refreshments on the lawn, and the Count and his charming daughter were there, giving a touch of home life to the gathering. All the chaplains who could be off duty were present. After tea, while we sat on the grass, the General gave us a very helpful talk on religious work among the men from a soldier's point of view. The old Chateau, with its beautiful gardens in front of the huge elms gave a fine setting to the scene.

On August 31st I was driven over to a field at the back of Villers-Chatel, where the 2nd Brigade was to hold a memorial service for those who had been killed at the taking of Hill 70. I had been asked to give the address. The place chosen was a wide and green field which sloped gradually towards the line of rich forest trees. On the highest part of the ground facing the woods, a small platform had been erected and was decorated with flags. On this the chaplains stood, the Corps Commander and the Brigadier and staff being at one side. Before us, forming three sides of a square, were the four battalions of the Brigade. The scene when viewed from the platform was magnificent. The sky was blue, the sun was shining, and the glorious trees guarded the green mysteries of the forest behind. The troops were in splendid form, and the bright red patches on their arms gave a touch of colour which set off the khaki uniforms. Every one of the men had been through the battle and was a hero. The service went well, and the hymns, to the accompaniment of the band, were sung heartily. At the close, the Corps Commander and staff went round to each battalion, and those who had won honours came forward to receive them. As the officers and men stood in turn before the General, the A.D. C. read out a short account of what each had done to win the decoration. It was deeply moving to hear the acts of gallantry that had been performed. Fixed and motionless each man would stand, while we were told how his courage had saved his company or platoon at some critical moment. I remember particularly hearing how one sergeant who got the D.C.M., had carried his Lewis gun, after all the other members of the crew had been wounded or killed, and, placing it at a point of vantage, had, by his steady fire, covered the advance of a company going forward to attack. Little do people at home know by what supreme self-sacrifice and dauntless courage those strips of bright-coloured ribbon on the breasts of soldiers have been won. After the decorations had been presented, the men fell back to their battalions. The band struck up the strains of "D'ye ken John Peel?", and the whole Brigade marched past the General, the masses of men moving with machine-like precision. Even the rain which had begun to fall did not mar the fine effect.

Our stay at Bruay was not to be of long duration. In the early hours of September 5th a bomb dropped in the garden behind the administration building where our Headquarters were, waking us from sleep with a sudden start. It did no harm, but on the next day we were informed that we were all to move back to our old quarters in Barlin. I always said that I regarded a bomb dropped on Headquarters as a portent sent from heaven, telling us we were going to move. Accordingly on September 6th we all made our way to Barlin, where I was given a billet in an upper room in an estaminet. The propriety of housing a Senior Chaplain in an estaminet might be questioned, but this particular one was called the estaminet of St. Joseph. An estaminet with such a title, and carried on under such high patronage, was one in which I could make myself at home. So on the door was hung my sign, "Canon Scott, Senior Chaplain," which provoked many smiles and much comment from the men of the battalions as they passed by. I was looking out of my window in the upper storey one day when the 2nd Battalion was marching past, and, to the breach of all good discipline, I called out to the men and asked them if they did not envy me my billet. A roar of laughter went up, and they asked me how I got there and if I could take them in as well. I told them that it was the reward of virtue, and only those who could be trusted were allowed to be housed in estaminets.

Near me, at Barlin, the motor machine-gun brigade was encamped. It had been there for some time, and I was glad to meet old friends and renew acquaintance with the unit that had such a distinguished career at the front. I had not seen them much since the old days at Poperinghe, but wherever they went they covered themselves with glory. To spend an evening in the hut used as the sergeants' mess was a delight. The rollicking good humour that prevailed was most contagious, and I shall always treasure the memory of it which has now been made sacred through the death of so many whom I met there. I used to visit the tents, too, and sitting on a box in their midst have a smoke and talk with the men. Heavy indeed has been the toll of casualties which that noble brigade has suffered since those happy days.

Word was sent to the Division one day by the British troops holding our trenches on Hill 70, that some bodies of our men were lying unburied in No Man's Land. One of our battalions was ordered to provide a burial party and I decided to accompany them. I was to meet the men at a certain place near Loos on the Lens-Arras road in the evening, and go with them. The burial officer turned up on time, but the party did not. At last the men arrived and we went through the well-known trenches till we came to the front line. Here I had to go down and see some officers of the British battalions, and try to find out where the bodies were. Apparently the officers could give us little information, so we decided to divide up into small parties and go into No Man's Land and search for the dead ourselves. As we were in sight of

the enemy, we could not use our electric torches, and only by the
assistance of German flarelights were we able to pick our steps
over the broken ground. We found a few bodies which had
not been buried, but it was impossible to do more than cover them
with earth, for the position was an exposed one. We did the best
we could under the circumstances, and were glad to find that the
number of unburied had been greatly exaggerated. On another
occasion I took a burial party out one night, and found that the officers and men sent were a new draft that had never been in the
line before. They were much interested in the novel and somewhat
hazardous nature of the expedition. On this occasion when we returned to Bully-Grenay, the morning sun was shining brightly overhead, and it began to get quite warm. The men were very tired
with their night's work, and when we halted they lay down on the
pavement by the road and went to sleep. One poor fellow actually
collapsed, and we had to send off to a dressing station for a stretcher on which he was taken away for medical treatment. A burial
party, from the nature of the case, was not a pleasant expedition,
and Canada ought to be grateful for the way in which our Corps
burial officers and the men under them carried out their gruesome
and often dangerous duty. One of our burial officers, a fine young
fellow, told me how much he disliked the work. He said, "There
is no glory in it, and people think that we have an easy time, but
two of my predecessors have been killed and I expect to get knocked
out myself some day." A year later he was killed near Cambrai,
after he had faithfully done his duty in caring for the bodies of
the slain.

Our front trenches were now to the right of Hill 70, in advance
of Liéven, and it seemed as if we were going to be stationed in
the neighborhood for some time, for the rumour was that the Canadians had to complete their work at Vimy by the capture of Lens.
Barlin, therefore, and the area around it was a great centre of Canadian life and activity. We had our large Canadian tent-hospitals,
our brigade schools, and various Y. M. C. A. places of entertainment, besides our officers' clubs.

In an open field near my billet were stationed the horse lines of
our Divisional Train, and it used to give me great pleasure to pass
the long rows of wagons which by the constant labour of the men
were kept in prime condition. The paint was always fresh, and
all the chains were polished as if they were merely for show.

It would be hard for people at home to realize that the wagons which had been used for years under such rough conditions always looked as if they had just come out of the shop, but that was the case. The constant attention to detail in the army, the smartness of the men, and the good turn-out of the horses and limbers, have a great moral effect upon every department of the service. The men were always grumbling about polishing buttons and chains, but I told them that the impression of efficiency it gave one made it quite worth while. A Division that could turn out such a fine looking Train as we had could always be depended upon to do its duty.

14

CHAPTER XXII.

A Tragedy of War

THERE is nothing which brings home to the heart with such force the iron discipline of war as the execution of men who desert from the front line. It was my painful duty on one occasion to have to witness the carrying out of the death sentence. One evening I was informed by the A. P. M. that a man in one of our brigades was to be shot the next morning, and I was asked to go and see him and prepare him for death. The sentence had already been read to him at six o'clock, and the brigade chaplain was present, but the A. P. M., wished me to take the case in hand. We motored over to the village where the prisoner was and stopped at a brick building which was entered through a courtyard. There were men on guard in the outer room and also in a second room from which a door led into a large brick chamber used as the condemned cell. Here I found the man who was to pay the penalty of his cowardice. He had a table before him and on it a glass of brandy and water and writing materials. He was sitting back in his chair and his face wore a dazed expression. The guards kindly left us alone. He rose and shook hands with me, and we began to talk about his sentence. He was evidently steeling himself and trying to fortify his mind by the sense of great injustice done to him. I allowed him to talk freely and say just what he pleased. Gradually, I succeeded in getting at the heart of the true man which I knew was hidden under the hard exterior, and the poor fellow began to tell me about his life. From the age of eleven, when he became an orphan, he had to get his own living and make his way in a world that is often cold and cruel to those who have no friends. Then by degrees he began to talk about religion and his whole manner changed. All the time I kept feeling that every moment the dreaded event was coming nearer and nearer and that no time was to be lost. He had never been baptised, but wished now to try and make up for the past and begin to prepare in a real way to meet his God.

I had brought my bag with the communion vessels in it, and so he and I arranged the table together, taking away the glass of brandy and water and the books and papers, and putting in their place the white linen altar cloth. When everything was prepared, he knelt down and I baptised him and gave him his first communion. The man's mind was completely changed. The hard, steely indifference and the sense of wrong and injustice had passed away, and he was perfectly natural. I was so much impressed by it that while I was talking to him, I kept wondering if I could not even then, at that late hour, do something to avert the carrying out of the sentence. Making some excuse and saying I would be back in a little while, I left him, and the guard went into the room accompanied by one of the officers of the man's company. When I got outside, I told the brigade chaplain that I was going to walk over to Army Headquarters and ask the Army Commander to have the death sentence commuted to imprisonment.

It was then about one a. m. and I started off in the rain down the dark road. The Chateau in which the General lived was two miles off, and when I came to it, I found it wrapped in darkness. I went to the sentry on guard, and told him that I wished to see the General on important business. Turning my flashlight upon my face, I showed who I was. He told me that the General's room was in the second storey at the head of a flight of stairs in a tower at the end of the building. I went over there, and finding the door unlocked, I mounted the wooden steps, my flashlight lighting up the place. I knocked at a door on the right and a voice asked me who I was. When I told my name, I was invited to enter, and an electric light was turned on and I found I was in the room of the A. D. C., who was sitting up in bed. Luckily, I had met him before and he was most sympathetic. I apologized for disturbing him but told him my mission and asked if I might see the General. He got up and went into the General's room. In a few moments he returned, and told me that the General would see me. Instead of being angry at my extraordinary intrusion, he discussed the matter with me. Before a death sentence could be passed on any man, his case had to come up first in his Battalion orderly room, and, if he was found guilty there, it would be sent to the Brigade. From the Brigade it was sent to the Division, from the Division to Corps, from Corps to Army, and from Army to General Headquarters. If each of these courts confirmed the sentence, and the British Commander-in-Chief signed the warrant, there was no appeal, unless some new facts came to light. Of all the men found guilty of desertion from the front trenches, only a small percentage were executed. It was considered absolutely necessary for the safety of the Army that the death sentence should not be entirely abolished. The failure of one man to do his duty might spoil the morale of his platoon, and spread the contagion of fear from the platoon to the company and from the company to the battalion, endangering the fate of the whole line. The General told me, however, that if any new facts came to light, suggesting mental weakness or insanity in the prisoner, it might be possible for the execution to be stayed, and a new trial instituted. This seemed to give hope that something might yet be done, so I thanked the General for his kindness and left.

When I got back to the prison, I made my way to the cell, not of course, letting the condemned man know anything that had happened. By degrees, in our conversation, I found that on both sides of his family there were cases of mental weakness. When I had all the information that was possible, I went out and accompanied by the brigade chaplain, made my way once again to Army Headquarters. The chances of averting the doom seemed to be faint, but still a human life was at stake, and we could not rest till every effort had been made. I went to the room of the A. D. C., and was again admitted to the presence of the Army Commander. He told me now that the only person who could stop the execution was the Divisional Commander, if he thought it right to do so. At the same time, he held out very little hope that anything could be done to commute the sentence. Once more I thanked him and went off. The brigade chaplain was waiting for me outside and we talked the matter over, and decided that, although the case seemed very hopeless and it was now half-past three, one last effort should be made. We walked back through the rain to the village, and there awoke the A. P. M. and the Colonel of the battalion. Each of them was most sympathetic and most anxious, if possible, that the man's life should be spared. The A. P. M. warned me that if we had to go to Divisional Headquarters, some seven miles away, and return, we had no time to lose, because the hour fixed for the execution was in the early dawn.

The question now was to find a car. The only person in the place who had one was the Town Major. So the Colonel and I started off to find him, which we did with a great deal of difficulty, as no one knew where he lived. He too, was most anxious to help us. Then we had to find the chauffeur. We managed to get him roused up, and told him that he had to go to Divisional Headquarters on a matter of life and death. It was not long before we were in the car and speeding down the dark, muddy roads at a tremendous rate, whirling round corners in a way that seemed likely to end in disaster. We got to the Divisional Commander's Headquarters and then made our way to his room and laid the matter before him. He talked over the question very kindly, but told us that the courts had gone into the case so carefully that he considered it quite impossible to alter the final decision. If the action of the prisoner had given any indication of his desertion being the result of insanity, something might be done, but there was nothing to suggest such was the case. To delay the execution for twenty-four hours and then to have to carry it out would mean subjecting a human being to unspeakable torture. He felt he could not take it upon himself to run the chance of inflicting such misery upon the man. The Colonel and I saw at once that the case was utterly hopeless and that we could do no more. The question then was to get back in time for the carrying out of the sentence. Once more the car dashed along the roads. The night was passing away, and through the drizzling rain the gray dawn was struggling.

By the time we arrived at the prison, we could see objects quite distinctly. I went in to the prisoner, who was walking up and down in his cell. He stopped and turned to me and said, "I know what you have been trying to do for me, Sir, is there any hope?" I said, "No, I am afraid there is not. Everyone is longing just as much as I am to save you, but the matter has been gone into so carefully and has gone so far, and so much depends upon every man doing his duty to the uttermost, that the sentence must be carried out." He took the matter very quietly, and I told him to try to look beyond the present to the great hope which lay before us in another life. I pointed out that he had just one chance left to prove his courage and set himself right before the world. I urged him to go out and meet death bravely with senses unclouded, and advised him not to take any brandy. He shook hands with me and said, "I will do it." Then he called the guard and asked him to bring me a cup of tea. While I was drinking it, he looked at his watch, which was lying on the table and asked me if I knew what time "IT" was to take place. I told him I did not. He said, "I think my watch is a little bit fast." The big hand was pointing to ten minutes to six. A few moments later the guards entered and put a gas helmet over his head with the two eye-pieces behind so that he was completely blindfolded. Then they hand-cuffed him behind his back, and we started off in an ambulance to a crossroad which went up the side of a hill. There we got out, and the prisoner was led over to a box behind which a post had been driven into the ground. Beyond this a piece of canvas was stretched as a screen. The firing party stood at a little distance in front with their backs towards us. It was just daylight. A drizzling rain was falling and the country looked chilly and drear. The prisoner was seated on the box and his hands were handcuffed be-hind the post. He asked the A. P. M. if the helmet could be taken off, but this was mercifully refused him. A round piece of white paper was pinned over his heart by the doctor as a guide for the men's aim. I went over and pronounced the Benediction. He ad-ded, "And may God have mercy upon my soul." The doctor and I then went into the road on the other side of the hedge and blocked up our ears, but of course we heard the shots fired. It was sick-ening. We went back to the prisoner who was leaning forward and the doctor felt his pulse and pronounced him dead. The spirit had left the dreary hillside and, I trust, had entered the ranks of his heroic comrades in Paradise.

The effect of the scene was something quite unutterable. The firing party marched off and drew up in the courtyard of the pris-on. I told them how deeply all ranks felt the occasion, and that nothing but the dire necessity of guarding the lives of the men in the front line from the panic and rout that might result, through the failure of one individual, compelled the taking of such measures of punishment. A young lad in the firing party utterly broke down, but, as one rifle on such occasions is always loaded with a blank cartridge, no man can be absolutely sure that he has had a part in the shoot-ing. The body was then placed in a coffin and taken in the ambu-lance to the military cemetery, where I held the service. The us-ual cross was erected with no mention upon it of the manner of the death. That was now forgotten. The man had mastered himself and had died bravely.

I have seen many ghastly sights in the war, and hideous forms of death. I have heard heart-rending tales of what men have suf-fered, but nothing ever brought home to me so deeply, and with such cutting force, the hideous nature of war and the iron hand of discipline, as did that lonely death on the misty hillside in the early morning. Even now, as I write this brief account of it, a dark nightmare seems to rise out of the past and almost makes me shrink from facing once again memories that were so painful. It is well, however, that people should know what our men had to endure. Before them were the German shells, the machine-guns and the floods of gas. Behind them, if their courage failed, was the court-martial, always administered with great compassion and strict justice, but still bound by inexorable laws of war to put into execution, when duty compelled, a grim and hideous sentence of death.

If this book should fall into the hands of any man who, from cowardice, shirked his duty in the war, and stayed at home, let him reflect that, but for the frustration of justice, he ought to have been sitting that morning, blindfolded and handcuffed, beside the prisoner on the box. HE was one of the originals and a volunteer.

CHAPTER XXIII.

VISITS TO ROME AND PASCHENDAELE

October and November, 1917

IT was a good thing, after the bitter experience which I had just passed through, that permission was granted me at this time to take some men on a leave trip to Rome. My visit to Paris had convinced me that it was no proper place for men to spend their leave in, so when my next leave was nearly due I wrote to Division and asked permission to take a party to Italy in order that some of our men might have the benefit of seeing the great monuments of European history and art. Weeks passed away and I heard nothing about the matter, until at last a telegram came through granting my request. I had only asked permission to take twelve men with me whose names had to be sent in beforehand. But the telegram which granted permission was couched in such vague terms, merely referring to a certain file-number, that I, knowing that nobody would take the trouble to turn up the original document, said nothing about it, and by a stroke of good luck succeeded in taking with me forty-six men, including two chaplains, two young officers and one of the staff of the Y. M. C. A. Two of the men, alas, became casualties in the Paris barrage on the first night, and were reported "missing, believed dead," but were found two days afterwards by the police and sent back. The rest of us had a glorious time and travelled to Rome via Marseilles, Nice—which included a visit to Monte Carlo—Genoa and Pisa. I shall never forget the delightful trip across France by daylight, and the moonlight night at Marseilles, where we put up at the Hotel Regina. The men were in fine form and presented a splendid soldier-like appearance. Their new uniforms were set off by the bright red patch upon their sleeves, and their buttons were kept well polished. I told them, before we started, that I did not wish to be either a detective or a nursery-maid, but I asked them to play the game and they did. We were going into the country of an ally and I knew that such a large party would be under very critical observation wherever we went. I had really no authority over the men beyond that which they were willing that I should exercise. The individuals of the party were not specially selected, but I felt perfect confidence that we should have no trouble,

216

although I was naturally very much teased by members of "C" mess who prophesied that I should lose some men in Paris, some in Marseilles and some in Rome, and my friends even went so far as to declare that they doubted whether I should ever come back myself. We were favoured with glorious weather, and travelled by daylight the whole length of the Riviera. The utmost good humour prevailed, and the glorious view of the blue Mediterranean on one side, with that of the romantic mountains on the other, drove from our minds all uncomfortable memories of the war. In fact we seemed to get into another world.

The train arrived at Pisa at about nine o'clock p. m. and was to wait there for three hours, so we all got out and had some supper and started off to see the famous leaning tower by moonlight. The sudden appearance of British troops in the quaint old town caused quite a sensation, and the people came out of the cafes to see us and a mob followed us wherever we went. We were of course pounced upon by the vendors of souvenirs, and a number of the men came back to the station carrying alabaster leaning towers under their arms. I warned the party about the danger of loading themselves with such heavy and brittle mementos, for we had still a long journey before us. The wisdom of my warning was apparent later on, for on leaving Rome the alabaster towers had begun to lean so much that they could no longer stand up. A shelf full of leaning towers propped up one against another, looking as if they had just partaken of an issue of rum, was left in the hotel. We journeyed all night, some of the men sleeping on the seats, some on the floor, and some in the hatracks overhead, and in the morning amid intense excitement we arrived at the station in Rome. I had been able to get a shave and clean up in the train, so on arrival was ready to go and hunt for a hotel. I told the men, however, to find their way to the Leave Club and make themselves presentable and that I would return for them as soon as possible. After securing billets in the Hotel Bristol, I went back for the party. Although I knew the men would want to go about the city by themselves, I felt it would be a good thing for our esprit-de-corps, that we should march to the hotel in a body. So, not knowing how to give military orders myself, and remembering what real colonels always did in similar predicaments, I turned to the senior sergeant and said, "Sergeant, make the men fall in, and when they are ready I will take over the parade." When the sergeant came up to me and saluting said the parade was ready, I found to my dismay that the men were facing the wrong way and if I said "Quick march", they would walk into the brick wall opposite. I went up close to the sergeant and whispered to him, "Turn the men round." This he did, and placing myself at their head I shouted, "Quick March." I think that moment, as I started off to march through Rome at the head of that fine body of men who followed two abreast, was the proudest of my life. I had always been interested in history, and have read Gibbon from cover to cover, so the thought suddenly flashed upon me, "Julius Caesar once led his forces through Rome. Later on, Augustus Caesar led his forces through Rome. In the middle ages, Rienzi led his forces through Rome, and now, (here my head began to swell till it grew too big for my cap) Canon Scott is leading his forces through Rome." We marched through the streets at "attention" and looked not to the right nor to the left, in spite of the fact that we passed many groups of admiring onlookers. When we arrived at the hotel, I called out, "Halt", in proper military tones and the men halted, but I did not know the usual formula for telling them to disperse, and I did not want such a proper beginning to have a miserable end. I thought of saying, "Now I will dismiss the congregation," but that sounded too religious. I knew that if I said, "Now we will take up the collection," my army would fly off quickly enough. However, while I was debating with myself, the men took the law into their own hands and, breaking off, went into the hotel.

We happened to arrive in Rome just at the time of the great Italian disaster in the North, and we found the populace plunged into great anxiety. English and French newspapers were banned by the censor, so it was difficult to find out what was happening, but I was told privately that matters were very critical, and there might be a revolution in Rome at any moment. I was also advised to see that our men behaved with great circumspection, for German agents were secretly trying to make trouble between the British and Italians. I told our men to remember we had to help on the cause of the Allies and to be very careful about details, such as saluting every Italian officer. I think they saluted every Italian private as well. I also told them, in case they were questioned on the subject, to say they were quite pleased with the war, in fact that they rather enjoyed it and were not a bit afraid of the Germans, and were determined to fight until a decisive victory gave us a chance of lasting peace.

VISITS TO ROME AND PASCHENDAELE

Wherever we went on the journey, we stayed at the best hotels, for I had told each man to bring with him a thousand francs. It was a great puzzle to the Italians that Canadian soldiers were able to stay at the most select hotel in Rome, and also that the officers and men were able to mix together in real comradeship. The Highlanders in our party of course attracted the greatest attention, and were frequently followed by an admiring crowd as they passed through the streets. Colonel Lamb, the military attaché at the Embassy, was very kind to us and secured us many privileges, not the least acceptable of which was free transportation. We split up into small parties, and visited the sights of the Eternal City as we pleased. On the first night after dinner, we paid a visit to the Coliseum by moonlight, which is something to remember. Wherever we went we met with the kindest treatment. The ladies of the Leave Club gave us an entertainment one evening, which was attended by the military and naval attachés at the British and American Embassies, and by some of the English residents. I was proud of the appearance of the men. Before we left the hotel at Nice, an English lady, the wife of a British General at the front, came up and congratulated me upon the men, and said they were the most gentlemanly young fellows she had ever seen. I think it was a help to them to feel that their appearance in Rome at that critical time was something which gave our party a kind of political significance, and the phrase, "to help on the cause of the Allies," became a watchword among us.

One night an Italian Colonel asked some of our men to dine with him at his hotel and took them to the theatre afterwards. On another occasion, five of our men were sitting in the front row of one of the theatres when an actor gave an impersonation of the different sovereigns of Europe. When he appeared as King George, the orchestra struck up our National Anthem, and at once our men rose up and stood to attention. One of them told me afterwards that he felt cold shivers going down his back as he did so, because he was in full view of everybody. For a moment there was a pause, then the audience, understanding what the action meant, rose en masse and stood till the music was over and then clapped their hands and shouted "Viva l'Inghilterra!"

Many of our men were very anxious to see the Pope, and so it was arranged that we should have an audience. Colonel Lamb informed the 1st Italian Division that we would march in a body through their district. We started off in the morning, our young Highland officer being in command. As we passed through the streets, the people greeted us very cordially. Many of them raised their hats. The traffic, too, would stop to let us pass. We went over the bridge of Hadrian and arrived at the entrance of the Vatican beside St. Peter's in good time. There we were met by an Irish priest, who remembered me from my previous visit. I asked him if the men should break ranks but he told me to let them come in in formation. So, two by two, we mounted the glorious Royal Staircase, the splendid surroundings being a good setting for the fine looking soldiers. At the various landings, the Swiss Guards in their picturesque uniforms presented arms, and we found ourselves at last in a wonderful hall with richly frescoed walls and ceiling. Here the men were halted and passed in single file into the audience chamber. We had to wait for quite a long time, and at last the Pope entered, clothed in white and looking much older and more worn than when I had seen him only a year and a half before. He was very guarded in what he said to us, because we were the first soldiers whom he had received in a body, and any expression he might make with reference to the war would be liable to various interpretations. He spoke to some of our men in French and then wished us health and protection and a safe return to Canada. Then, giving his blessing he left us, and we made our way to the outer room where we reformed and marched off as we had come.

That afternoon we were photographed in the Coliseum, and I visited the interesting old church of St. Clement afterwards. Every evening, after a day spent in rambling among antiquities, we used to attend the opera in the Grand Opera House. It acted as a sort of relaxation after the serious business of sight-seeing. Rumours now reached us of the attack that our Division was making up in the Salient, and one night when I was having tea in the Grand Hotel I went over and asked a young British staff officer whom I saw there, if he had any news. He said to me that the Canadian Corps were making an attack at Passchendaele under the most appalling conditions of mud and rain and had covered themselves with glory. I asked him if it were true that Sir William Robertson had come to Rome. "Yes," he said, "I am his son. He has brought me with him and we are all very proud of the Canadians." At another table I saw M. Venezelos. It was understood now that Britain and France were to come to the assistance of Italy, but still Venice was in imminent peril, and the Italians were heart-broken at the way the 3rd Italian Army had behaved. Refugees from the North began to pour into Rome and affairs were very serious. I told our men of the gravity of the situation and the increased importance of helping on the cause of the Allies in every possible way.

It is the custom at Rome on All Soul's day, November 2nd, to place flowers and wreaths on the marble steps in front of the equestrian statue of Victor Emmanuel. This year, I was told, the people were going to make a special demonstration. It occured to me that it might not be a bad idea if we, too, placed a wreath to the memory of our comrades. I put the matter before Colonel Lamb and he said it was a very good idea indeed, but asked us to put on the card which would be attached to our wreath, the words, "To the brave Italian dead, from their comrades in the British Empire," rather than, "To the brave Italian dead from their Canadian comrades." He said he was anxious to emphasize the connection between the British and the Italians. An Italian major made the arrangements with me for carrying out the project. Poor man, he was so moved at the thought of the disgraceful surrender of the 3rd Italian Army that his eyes filled with tears as he talked about it, and he said, "What will our Allies think of Italy when her men behave like that?" I told him it was only a small part of their army that had failed and that the rest had behaved very gallantly. That afternoon, preceded by two of our sergeants carrying a large wreath of laurel tied with purple ribbon, to which we attached two cards with the inscription, one in English and one in Italian, we marched through the crowds of onlookers, who took off their hats as we passed, until we reached the great marble steps which lead up to the gilded statue of the late King. Here there was a magnificent display of flowers made up in all sorts of designs. The crowd gave away before us, and one of the officials, who had been directed by the Italian major, took the wreath from us and gave it a place of honour in front of the statue. We stood in a long line on the marble steps and saluted and then turned and left. The people clapped their hands and shouted, "Viva l'Inghilterra!" We were pleased at the impression the simple act of courtesy made, and felt that it was helping on the cause of the Allies.

Our men were always very much amused by the moving picture shows, the characters of these entertainments being so different from that of similar exhibitions at the front. They were so tragic and so sentimental that they did not appeal strongly to the wholesome minds of Canadian soldiers. It was always very interesting to hear their criticisms of the customs and outlook of the people with whom we were sojourning. There is no doubt that the army mind is the sanest and most wholesome in the whole community. It may not express itself in the most artistic terms or the most religious language, but its judgments are absolutely sound and worthy of the most careful consideration. I am sure that Canadian political life, unless other influences nullify it, will be immeasurably bettered by the soldiers' vote.

I had the great privilege of a visit to Cardinal Gasquet in the home of the Dominicans not far from St. Peter's. The interview had been arranged for me by an English priest whom I met at the hospital of the Blue Nuns, where I had taken two of our men who were ill with pneumonia. The Cardinal is engaged in the stupendous task of revising the text of the Latin Vulgate. He showed me photographs of the ancient manuscripts with the various readings noted. It will be years before the great task is completed, but when it is, it will remain untouched for centuries to come. He told me that news had just been received of the consecration of the first Roman Catholic Bishop in Russia. This had been made possible by the overthrow of the reigning dynasty. He was most kind, and told me many interesting things about life in Rome during the war, and before I left asked me to write my name in his visitor's book, pointing out to me on the upper part of the page the recent signature of the Cardinal Archbishop of Cologne.

Altogether we had been absent by this time for nearly two weeks, and had still a long return journey ahead of us. I thought, however, that the valuable service our men were rendering the great cause justified our over-staying our leave. In fact, when I went to say good-bye to Colonel Lamb, he and his staff told me that the presence of our men in the City at that time had been worth any amount of printed propaganda. I hinted that some statement of that kind to General Currie might be a good thing. To my great delight, soon after we had returned, General Currie received the following letter, which has an official stamp which I never expected :—

VISITS TO ROME AND PASCHENDAELE

BRITISH EMBASSY,
ROME.

9th November, 1917.

"Dear General,

"With reference to the recent visit to Rome of a party of Cana-
"dian officers and soldiers, I am requested by H. E. Sir Rennel
"Rodd to inform you of the excellent impression produced among
"the inhabitants of this city, by the soldierlike turnout, and excellent
"and courteous behaviour of all ranks belonging to the party.

"Their visit has helped to inspire Italians with a feeling of con-
"fidence in their allies at a time of great anxiety and trial.

Believe me,

"Yours very truly,

"(Sgd.) CHARLES A. LAMB,

Colonel,

Military Attaché.

Rome."

We left for Florence on Saturday November 3rd. The ladies of
the Leave Club came to see us off, and after a delightful trip in
brilliant sunshine, we arrived at our destination at seven in the
evening. On our journey we passed many trains filled with
refugees, who were crowded together in third-class carriages. As
the Austrian and German armies advanced in the North the people
in the villages were given a quarter of an hour in which to decide
whether they would stay or go. They were warned, however,
that if they stayed and the Italians ever tried to retake the towns
they would all be put to death. I was told by some officers of a
British hospital in Turin, who had had to leave the Italian front
in a hurry, that it was a sad sight to see the inhabitants of the towns
fleeing down the roads from the advancing enemy. Old and infirm
people dragged themselves along. Parents lost their children and
children lost their parents in the crowd, and the people took with
them only the things which they could carry on their persons.
Florence was crowded with these unfortunates, who were lying out
at night in the squares and being tended by the citizens. There was
a great crowd at the station when we arrived, and a number of
Italian soldiers who spoke English gathered round our party and
told us that the war was over and that the soldiers would not fight
any more. Our men, however, were equal to the occasion, and told

them that *we* were going to keep on fighting no matter what the Italians did, and that there could be no peace until we had a decisive victory. The whole city was astir, and many Italian regiments were quartered there. I told the men before we sought for accommodation in the crowded town, how important it was that we should show a determined face at this time.

On the following afternoon, which was Sunday, I had a curious experience. The Y.M.C.A. officer and I were going off to see the great church of Santa Croce, which is the Italian Westminster Abbey, many great Italians having been buried there. As we passed down the street my friend went into a shop to buy some chocolates. While I was waiting, I heard the stirring notes of the Marseillaise, and looking round saw a band coming up the street followed by three Italian flags, a number of soldiers, and a rabble of men, women and children. I called to my companion to come out quickly and salute the Italian colours. As they passed, we stood on the curb and saluted with strict military precision. In fact we saluted so well that the delighted members of the procession grabbed us by the hand and finally dragged us into their midst, others clapping their hands and shouting "Viva l'Inghilterra!" I was separated from my companion in the rabble and called over to him and asked him what it was. He said, "I think it is a Socialist demonstration." This rather dismayed me, but I turned to one of the people by my side and asked him in French what the crowd was. He told me it was the society for finishing the war, so I called out to my friend, "It's all right Captain, it is the society for finishing the war. I have wanted to join that society for some time." I saw at once that the procession was an attempt to pull the Italians together and rouse them to a supreme effort to resist the enemy and save Italy. The crowd was so enthusiastic about the presence of representatives of the British Army, that they finally caught us by our legs and carried us on their shoulders through the streets. It was a most amusing incident. I could not help thinking that the crowd were the descendants of the men who had burnt Savonarola at the stake. My friend, whose sense of humour had failed him, shouted over to me, "I hate being made a fool of like this." I told him not to be rude as we were helping on the cause of the Allies. Finally, overcome by our struggles, the men let us down, and we were pushed along in the crowd to the square in front of the Hotel Minerva. Here the leaders of the procession invited us into the hotel and we were taken upstairs to the front room, out of which opened a balcony overlooking the square. A young Italian officer, who had been a lawyer before the war and had lost both his eyes, went on to the balcony and made a most impassioned appeal to his countrymen. The crowd in the square was now very dense, and received his speech with great enthusiasm. When it was over, one of the officers of "The society for finishing the war," came and urged me to address the crowd. I was so pleased to find that my French was better understood in Italy than in any place except England, that I asked my friend if I should speak to them in French. He looked at me very sourly, for he had not quite got back his equanimity, and said curtly, "You had better not." Then I said, "I will talk to them in Italian." I shall never forget the look of dismay which passed over his countenance, but I told him it was helping on the cause of the Allies. I went out on the balcony, and the people seeing the British uniform and probably mistaking me for a general, at once began to cheer. I took off my cap, waved it in the air and shouted at the top of my voice "Viva l'Italia." It was the only speech they wanted. It was neither too long nor too short. The crowd repeated the words, and then shouted, "Viva l'Inghilterra!" and the band actually struck up "God save the King" and followed it by "Rule Britannia, Britannia rules the waves" (I wished at the time she had ruled under the waves as well.) I went back to the room and the Italians were so delighted with my short and pithy speech, that they invited me to dine with them that night and bring two officers with me. When we got down to the square, the mob crowded round us and shook hands with us, and I was afraid that some of the ladies were going to embrace us. I think people thought we were part of the advance guard that had been sent from France to the assistance of Italy.

That night three of us attended the dinner given by the officers of "The society for finishing the war," in a very fine restaurant. The Deputy for Florence, who had been one of the members of the government which had declared war on Austria, was present and I sat by the side of an alderman of the city. Opposite to me was an English lady who acted as an interpreter. At the close of the dinner the Deputy rose and made a very eloquent speech, welcoming us to Italy and saying how much Italians appreciated the fact that England was one of her Allies. I replied in English, which was translated by our fair interpreter, and told them how glad we were to be with them and that we had come, some of our

15

men seven thousand miles, as a voluntary army to fight not only for the British Empire, but for something even bigger than that, for our common civilization, and that the war had made the Allies one family. I said that our men were determined to fight to the bitter end, for we could have no true peace until we had a decisive victory. Then I added that, if our Division were sent to Italy, we should all come with great pleasure, knowing that the Italians were our comrades and warm friends. I thought too, during my speech, that a dugout in Florence would be worth two in Bully-Grenay. The party seemed very pleased with my remarks and we all exchanged visiting cards and separated good friends. The whole affair was very amusing, and when the Italians pushed back the enemy in 1918, I used to tell the men, amid roars of laughter, that nothing but my modesty prevented my saying who it was that had saved Italy, that no one would ever hear from my lips the name of the man who, when Italy was lying prostrate at the feet of the advancing foe, shouted into her dying ear the startling words "Viva l' Italia" and set her on her feet.

Two days afterwards, accompanied to the station by an admiring crowd and three ladies carrying Italian flags, we bade farewell to Florence and started on our return journey. We spent the afternoon in Pisa, and, after a night's journey, arrived at Turin in the morning. Our men got out of the train and were making their way to the station when they were met by the British R.T.O. a very large officer who wore an eyeglass. He brought them quickly to attention by calling out, "Who are you?" They told him they were Canadians on leave, and I, fearing bloodshed, went up to the officer and explained who they were and why they had come. He told me that there had been a mutiny in Turin that summer and relations between the British and Italians were very much strained, owing to the action of German agents. He said he had been living on the top of a volcano for the past three months, and was afraid to allow any large body of troops to go about the town lest there might be trouble. I assured him that our men would behave with great circumspection. He then told me that they would have to be back in rest-billets, near the station, not later than ten o'clock. I asked if he could not make it eleven, because I knew that the men wanted to go to the theatre. He agreed to this and asked me to tell them that roll would be called in the rest-billets at eleven o'clock. I halted the men and said, "Boys, roll will be called in the rest-billets tonight at eleven o'clock sharp." Whether it was or not we never knew, for none of us was there to hear. The men went to the theatres and to the various hotels afterwards. No trouble ensued, and when we left on the following afternoon the R.T.O. was most friendly and gave us a hearty send-off, no doubt feeling too relieved at our departure to make any inquiries.

Although we had had a most delightful trip I was really thankful we were at last setting our faces towards the North. We arrived in Paris the next morning, and before we left the station I told the men that every one of them had to be at the train that evening. I had taken it upon myself to extend their leave, as I thought their presence in Italy was beneficial to the cause, but I asked them to show their gratitude by not failing to return all together. That night, to my intense satisfaction, they all turned up at the station at seven o'clock, and we started for Calais. We arrived there the next morning, and in the afternoon left for the front.

We arrived at Poperinghe that night at six o'clock. It was dark, a drizzling rain was falling, and the mud was thick. We could hear the big guns firing, and the men were coming and going in all directions. We took a hasty farewell of one another and then parted. No one we met cared whether we had come from Italy or were going to Jericho. The men did not know where their headquarters were, and I was particularly anxious not to find mine. I went over to the Officer's Club and secured a shake-down in the garret, but, as I heard that our Division had made an attack that day, I determined to go up to the line. I started off after dinner in an ambulance to the old mill at Vlamertinghe, where there was a repetition of the sights and sounds which I had experienced there on two previous occasions. Later on, I went forward in another ambulance through Ypres to an advanced dressing station. Then I started to walk up the terrible, muddy roads till I came to the different German pill-boxes which had been converted into head-quarters for the battalions. Finally, after wading through water and mud nearly up to my knees, I found myself the next afternoon wandering through the mud and by the shell holes and miserable trenches near Goudberg Copse, with a clear view of the ruins of Paschendaele, which was held by another division on our right. The whole region was unspeakably horrible. Rain was falling, the dreary waste of shell-ploughed mud, yellow and clinging, stretched off into the distance as far as the eye could see. Bearer parties, tired and pale, were carrying out the wounded on stretchers, making a journey of several miles in doing so. The bodies of dead men lay here and there where they had fallen in the advance. I came across one poor boy who had been killed that morning. His body was covered with a shiny coating of yellow mud, and looked like a statue made of bronze. He had a beautiful face, with finely shaped head covered with close curling hair, and looked more like some work of art than a human being. The huge shell holes were half full of water often reddened with human blood and many of the wounded had rolled down into the pools and been drowned. As I went on, some one I met told me that there was a wounded man in the trenches ahead of me. I made my way in the direction indicated and shouted out asking if anybody was there. Suddenly I heard a faint voice replying, and I hurried to the place from which the sound came. There I found sitting up in the mud of the trench, his legs almost covered with water, a lad who told me that he had been there for many hours. I never saw anything like the wonderful expression on his face. He was smiling most cheerfully, and made no complaint about what he had suffered. I told him I would get a stretcher, so I went to some trenches not far away and got a bearer party and a stretcher and went over to rescue him. The men jumped down into the trench and moved him very gently, but his legs were so numb that although they were hit he felt no pain. One of the men asked him if he was only hit in the legs. He said, "Yes," but the man looked up at me and pulling up the boy's tunic showed me a hideous wound in his back. They carried him off happy and cheerful. Whether he ever recovered or not I do not know. If he did and ever sees this book, I wish he would write and tell me how he is.

That was our last attack at Paschendaele. Our Division had taken its final objective. The next morning, the infantry were to come out of the line, so in the late afternoon I returned with some stretcher bearers. Several times shells came near enough to splatter us with mud, and here and there I turned aside to bury those for whom graves had just been prepared.

At the front that day, a runner and I had joined in a brief burial service over the body of a gallant young officer lying where he fell on the side of a large shell-hole. As I uttered the words—"I am the Resurrection and the Life, saith the Lord," it seemed to me that the lonely wind bore them over that region of gloom and death as if it longed to carry the message of hope far away to the many sad hearts in Canada whose loved ones will lie, until the end, in unknown graves at Paschendaele.

CHAPTER XXIV.

OUR LAST WAR CHRISTMAS.

OUR Division moved back to Barlin and I was once more established in my old billet. As our artillery were still at Ypres, I determined to go back on the following day to the Salient. I started in a car the next morning at six, and arrived at Talbot House, Poperinghe, in time to have breakfast with Padré Clayton, who was in charge of that splendid institution. Then I made my way to Ypres and found my son at his battery headquarters under the Cloth Hall Tower. It was a most romantic billet, for the debris of the ruins made a splendid protection from shells, and the stone-vaulted chambers were airy and commodious, much better than the underground cellars in which most of the men were quartered. The guns of the battery were forward in a very "unhealthy'" neighbourhood. The officers and men used to take turns in going on duty there for twenty-four hours at a time. They found that quite long enough, as the forward area was continually exposed to shells and aeroplane attacks. I went on to visit our own field batteries, and found them distributed in a most desolate region. The mud was so deep that to step off the bath-mats meant sinking almost to the knees. In order to move the guns, planks had to be laid in front of them for a track, and the guns were roped and dragged along by the men. It was hard physical labour but they bore it, as they did other difficulties and dangers, with the utmost good humour. It was tiring enough merely to walk out to see them, without having anything else to do. What those men went through at that time no one can imagine. Just to watch them laying the planks and hauling on the ropes which drew the heavy mud-covered guns made me weary. When I meet some of my gunner friends in Montreal and Toronto looking so clean and happy, I think of what they did behind Passchendaele Ridge, and I take off my hat to them.

I spent three days at Ypres, and then, by jumping lorries, made my way back to St. Venant and Robecq, where I spent the night. The next morning I left for Bethune, and thence by the assistance of lorries and a car continued my journey to our new Divisional Headquarters, which had found a home at Château de la Haie.

OUR LAST WAR CHRISTMAS

Here I had a billet in an upstairs room over what had been part of a stable. The room was neither beautiful nor clean, but served as an abode for me and Alberta and her newly-arrived family. The Chateau was a large house of no distinction, but it stood in delightful grounds, and at the back of it was a pond whose clear waters reflected the tall, leafless trees which bordered it. One fact made the Château popular and that was, that, up to that time, no shell or bomb had fallen in the neighborhood. It was said that the location of the Château was not to be found on the enemy's maps. Round about were huts with accomodation sufficient to house a whole brigade. The charm of the place was completed by our 4th Division having erected there a large and most artistic theatre, which would seat on benches nearly one thousand men. It had a good stage and a pit for the orchestra in front. This theatre, when our concert party was in full swing, was a source of infinite delight to us all. It was built on the slope of a hill, the stage being at the lower end and a good view of the play therefore, could be had from all parts. The scenery was beautifully painted and the electric lights and foot-lights well arranged.

Near us was the village of Gouy-Servins, where many men were billeted, and in huts at Souchez and other places along the valley the various units found their homes. The year's campaign was now over and we could look foward to a quiet time during the winter. "C" mess had a very comfortable hut, with an open fireplace. We were supposed to have the liveliest entertainments of any mess at Headquarters, and had therefore many visitors. I shall never forget the jolly face of our president, the D.A.D.M.S., nor the irrepressible spirit of our A.P.M., son of a distinguished father who commanded an Army, nor the dry common-sense humour of our Field Cashier. What delight they took in ragging the Senior Chaplain, whose automatic ears, as he averred, prevented his hearing the things he should not. Nor must we forget the Camp Commandant, often perplexed like Martha with much serving. It was a goodly company and one much addicted to bridge and other diversions. I shall not forget the continual appeals of a gallant staff officer with two or three ribbons, who asked me penitently every morning for a moral uplift, which I noticed completely evaporated before evening. There was a freedom about our gatherings that was quite unique and has left pleasant memories in the mind, in spite of the fact that I told my fellow members they were the most godless crowd in Christendom. One day when we were at Ecoivres, a shell fell by the house, while we were having dinner. Someone asked me afterwards if it had "put my wind up?" "Not a bit", I replied, "I knew that the Devil was not going to destroy one of his favourite machine-gun emplacements."

There was much excitement at this time over the question of conscription. The soldiers were to have votes and much depended upon their being given in the right way. It was a critical time, as our man-power was being exhausted. Recruiting under the voluntary system had become inadequate to meet our needs. Beyond this, however, one felt that the moral effect of Canada's refusing conscription would be very harmful. The Germans would at once see in it an indication that Canada was growing weary of fighting and they would consequently take heart. It was most essential then that our men should cast a solid vote for the coalition government. I felt it my duty therefore to do as much electioneering work as I could. At night I used to address the men in the theatre between the acts of the play, and tell them that if we threw out the conscription bill, it would go a long way to undo the good of all they had done and destroy the value of the sacrifice our dead comrades had made. Once I was invited to speak to a battalion of the 4th Division during an entertainment which they were holding. When I closed my address I told them that the last thing I wanted to do was to influence their vote. All I asked of them when they went to the polls was to make a cross in front of Borden's name. From the laughter and cheers with which this statement was received, I think they probably did. A few of the men told me that the thing which made them hesitate about voting for conscription was that they could not bring themselves to do anything which would force others to come and endure the hellish life at the front. The great unionist victory at the polls in Canada, which we heard of on December 18th, showed us that the heart of the young country was sound, and this no doubt was noted by the Germans. ·

One more, (and this was the last,) St. George's church was built for me near the Château. Thus I was enabled to have a daily celebration of the Holy Communion.   . .

The arrival of one of the battalions of the 4th Division gave us the first indication that we were to move. On December 20th we left once more for Bruay. Here I found that my old billet was no longer available, but I managed to find a home in a clean little cottage in the same street, where I had a room down-stairs for an office, cheered by an open fire, and a large bare room up-stairs in which I put my bed. On the garden-gate I hung out my sign "St. George's Rectory." Once again I found myself in the familiar neighborhood with all the beloved battalions round us as before. The theatre was filled night after night, and there were the old gatherings of officers in the hotel. We regarded it as a great stroke of luck that once more we were going to spend Christmas out of the line.

On Christmas Eve, when I was preparing to go up to the midnight Communion Service in the theatre, a new C. of E. Chaplain arrived and came with me to assist. On the stage the altar was set as before, and the dear old flag which now for three long years had been devoted to the sacred purpose shone out as the frontal. The band played the Christmas hymns and a large number of men attended. Some of them, but not many, had been there the year before. It was very beautiful and solemn. At midnight on New Year's Eve we repeated the service. Again there was a large congregation, and to me as I looked back to the gathering held in that place just one year ago it was quite overpowering. How many of those who had been with us at the dawn of 1917 had passed away? The seats where they had sat were filled with other men. The hymns they had joined in were sung by other lips. In my heart went up the cry, "How long, O Lord, how long?" Once more the hands of the weary world clock had passed over the weeks and months of another year, and still the end was not in sight. As we stood in silence, while the buglers sounded the Last Post for the dying year, a wild and strange vision swept before me: I saw again the weary waste of mud and the shell ploughed ridge at Vimy; the fierce attacks at Arleux and Fresnoy; the grim assault on Hill 70 and the hellish agony of Paschendaele. Surely the ceaseless chiselling of pain and death had graven deeply into the inmost heart of Canada, the figures 1917.

CHAPTER XXV.

Victory Year Opens.

January and February, 1918.

VICTORY Year, though we did not know it by that name then, opened with fine bracing weather, and there was the usual round of dinners and entertainments with which we always greeted the birth of a new twelve-month. We had several Canadian-like snow storms. In the midst of one, I met a forlorn despatch rider coming up the main street on his wheel with the blinding snow in his face. I stopped him and asked him if he wouldn't like to have some dinner, and I took him into the hotel. He had been to Bethune to buy some V.C. ribbon for one of the men of his battalion who was going to be presented with it on the following day, and was so proud of his mission that he made no complaint about the long and tiring journey through the snowstorm. The country behind Bruay is broken up into pleasant valleys, and there are plenty of trees on the hills, so the winter aspect of the district made us feel quite at home. I used to give many talks to the men on what I called "The war outlook", I thought it helped to encourage them, and I was perfectly sincere in my belief, which grew stronger as time went on, in spite of notable set-backs, that we should have victory before the end of the year.

We had a visit at this time from Bishop du Pencier, who came to hold a confirmation for us at Divion. There were forty candidates, nearly all of them being presented by chaplains of the 1st Brigade. It was a solemn service and made a deep impression upon the men. The hymns were sung very heartily, and the Bishop gave a most helpful address. I remember specially one young fellow called Vaughan Groves, who came to me for the preparation. He was a small, rather delicate young lad about nineteen years of age, and was a runner for the 2nd Brigade. He had a fine open face and had the distinction of having won the M.M. and bar. To have won these honours as a Brigade runner was a mark of rare courage. I felt the deepest admiration for the boy, who was the only son of a widowed mother in Canada. He never touched liquor and had lived a perfectly straight life, and his was just the type of character which found scope for great deeds in the war. After the confirmation I lost sight of him, until some months afterwards when, as I was going through Arras one night, I looked into a cellar near the 2nd Brigade Headquarters, and seeing a number of men in there, went down to have a talk. I found they were the Brigade runners, and so I at once asked for my young friend. They told me that he had been wounded in the arm and when he came to the dressing station, finding there a man who was dying from loss of blood, had at once offered his own blood for transfusion into the veins of the sufferer. So much had to be taken from him that the boy got very weak and had to be sent back to England to recuperate. The men added that it was just the thing that little Vaughan would do. He was the finest, cleanest little chap, they said, that they had ever met. It was always delightful to hear such testimony from men to the innate power of human goodness. I have never seen or heard of Vaughan Groves since, but I hope that some one may read this book who will be able to tell me how and where he is.

I was not sorry when our rest was over. There was more time to get home-sick when we were out of the line. If we had to be in the war at all, the happiest place was at the front. So when on January 23rd I left Bruay for Bracquemont, I did so with little regret. My billet at Bracquemont was the same which I had occupied in the previous September, and it seemed quite like home. Once more our men held the trenches on Hill 70 and the battalions in the back area were billeted in Mazingarbe, Le Brebris, and Sains-en-Gohelle.

The day after I arrived, I determined to do some parish visiting in the slums—as I called the front line. I started off in my old trench uniform and long habitant boots, carrying with me a supply of bully-beef, tinned milk and hardtack. I went through Bully-Grenay and then out through Maroc to Loos. Here once again the dressing station at Fort Glatz was occupied by a doctor and staff from one of our ambulances. I spent a little while there and then continued my journey up the road past Crucifix Corner to the trenches. The 7th and 8th Battalions were in the line. The day was fine and the warm sunshine was hardening the mud, so things did not look too unpleasant. I went to the 7th Battalion first and found the gallant men carrying on in the usual way. Hugo Trench was very quiet, and from it one could obtain a good view of the German lines and of Lens beyond. It was great fun to go into the saps and surprise the two or three men who were on guard in them. The dugouts were curious places. The entrance steps were steep, and protected by blankets to keep out gas. At the bottom would be a long timber-lined passage, dark and smelly, out of which two or three little rooms would open. The men off duty would be lying about on the floor sound asleep, and it was often hard to make one's way among the prostrate bodies. The officers' mess would have a table in it and boxes for seats. On a shelf were generally some old newspapers or magazines and a pack of cards. In the passage, making it narrower than ever, were a few shelves used as bunks. At the end of the passage would be the kitchen, supplied with a rude stove which sent its smoke up a narrow pipe through a small opening. In the trenches the cooks were always busy, and how they served up the meals they did was a mystery to me. Water was brought in tins from a tap in one of the trenches to the rear, and therefore was not very abundant. I have occasionally, and against my will, seen the process of dish-washing in the trenches. I could never make out from the appearance of the water whether the cook and his assistant were washing the plates or making the soup, the liquid in the tin dish was so thick with grease. However, it was part of the war, and the men were doing their best under most unpropitious circumstances.

I had come prepared to spend a night in the trenches, and had decided to do so in the large German-made dugout in the chalk-pit which was held by "D" Company of the 8th Battalion. The officer on duty with the 7th Battalion kindly acted as my guide. The day had worn away, and the bright moon was lighting up the maze of yellow trenches. We passed along, exchanging many greetings at different places, until we came to the outpost of the 8th Battalion at the top of the path which leads down to the chalk-pit. Here four men were sitting keeping guard. They gave me a warm greeting, and I told them that if I were not in a hurry to let my guide go back to his lines, I would stop and recite some of my poems in the moonlight. It struck me that they seemed more amused than disappointed. So wishing them good-luck, we started onward down the slippery path which led into the pit, where many shells had torn up the ground and where were remains not only of uniforms and mess-tins and rifles but also of German bodies. We had hardly reached the entrance to the dugout when two or three of those shells which the men called "pineapples" arrived in quick succession. They sounded so close that we dived into the place of refuge. We found the O.C. of the company inside, and he kindly arranged to give me a large bed all to myself in one of the chambers of the dugout. Suddenly a runner appeared and told us that the pineapples had hit the outpost, killing not only some of the men to whom I had just been talking but also the Adjutant of the battalion. I at once got up and went back to the place. The line was quiet now, and the whole scene was brightly lighted by the moon and looked so peaceful that one could hardly imagine that we were in the midst of war, but, lying in the deep shadow at the bottom of the trench, with its face downwards, was the body of the Adjutant. He had been killed instantly. In the outpost beside the trench, were the bodies of the men who had been on duty when I passed a few minutes before.

I stayed with the sentry guarding the bodies until a stretcher party arrived and carried them away. Then I went back to the dugout and visited the men who were crowded into its most extraordinary labyrinth of passages and recesses. In the very centre of the place, which must have been deep underground, there was a kitchen, and the cooks were preparing a hot meal for the men to eat before "stand to" at dawn. The men of course were excessively crowded and many were heating their own food in mess-tins over smoking wicks steeped in melted candle grease. All were bright and cheerful as ever, in spite of the stifling atmosphere, which must have been breathed by human lungs over and over again. It was quite late when I stretched myself on my wire mattress with my steel helmet for a pillow. Only a piece of canvas separated me from the room where a lot of men were supposed to be sleeping. They were not only not asleep but kept me awake by the roars of laughter which greeted the stories they were telling. However, I managed to doze off in time, and was rudely wakened early in the morning by the metallic thud of pineapples on the ground overhead. I was wondering what it meant when a man came down to the O.C.'s room, next to mine, and aroused him with the somewhat exciting news, "Major, the Germans are making an attack." It was not long before the Major was hurrying up the steps to the passage above, and it was not long before I followed, because I always had a horror of being bombed in a dugout. In the passage upstairs all the men were "standing to" with fixed bayonets, and plenty of Mills bombs in their pockets. They were a most cheerful crowd, and really I think that we all felt quite pleased at the excitement. A man came up to me and asked me what weapon I had. I told him I had a fixed bayonet on the end of my walking stick. This did not seem to satisfy him, so he went over to a cupboard and brought me two bombs. I told him to take them away because they might be prematures. He laughed at this and said, "How will you protect yourself, Sir, if the enemy should get into the trench?" I told him I would recite one of my poems. They always put my friends to flight and would probably have the same effect upon my foes.

By this time the rain of pineapples overhead was very heavy, and I went to the door of the dugout where the Major was looking out. It was a curious scene. Day had just dawned, and we could see the heaps of broken rubbish and ripped up ground in front of us, while directly opposite at the top of the chalk-pit was our front line. Pacing up and down this was a corporal, his form silhouetted against the gray morning sky. He had his rifle with fixed bayonet on his shoulder, and as he walked to and fro he sang at the top of his voice the old song, "Oh my, I don't want to die, I want to go home." The accompaniment to the song was the "swish" of the shells overhead and the bursting of them in the trenches behind. I told the Major that if we could only get a moving picture of the corporal and a gramaphone record of his song with its accompaniment we could make thousands of dollars by an exhibition of it in Canada.

The next night I stayed at Cité St. Pierre. Who will ever forget the road up to it, and the corner near the ruined fosse, which was always liable to be shelled unexpectedly? In cellars beneath the unwholesome and dilapidated town our men found billets. They were really quite comfortable, but at night when the place was as black as pitch, and one had to grope one's way in the darkness along debris-covered streets, shaken every now and then by the German missiles from the sky, one longed for Canada and the well-lighted pavements of Montreal and Toronto.

On February 14th, at the officers' club at Corps Headquarters in Camblain l'Abbe, we had a great gathering of all the officers who had landed in France three years before. The one hundred and fifty who sat down to dinner were only a small part of the original number, and, before the anniversary came round again, many of those present were called to join the unseen host to whose memory that night we drank in silence. It was strange to look back over three years and think that the war, which in

VICTORY YEAR OPENS

February 1915 we thought was going to be a matter of months, had now been protracted for three years and was still going on. What experiences each of those present had had! What a strange unnatural life we had been called upon to live, and how extraordinarily efficient in the great war game had each become! It was a most interesting gathering of strong and resolute men filled with sublime ideals of duty and patriotism, who nevertheless were absolutely free from all posing and self-consciousness. They had learnt how to play the game; they had learnt both how to command and how to obey; they had learnt how to sink selfish interests and aims, and to work only and unitedly for the great cause.

On February 19th I held the dedication service at the unveiling of the artillery monument at Les Tilleuls. Owing to its exposed position no concourse of men was allowed, but there was a large gathering of the Staff, including the Army Commander, and of course a number of officers from the artillery. The lines of the monument are very severe. A plain white cross surmounts a large mass of solid masonry on which is the tablet, which General Currie unveiled. It stands in a commanding position on Vimy Ridge, and can be seen for miles around. Many generations of Canadians in future ages will visit that lonely tribute to the heroism of those, who, leaving home and loved ones, voluntarily came and laid down their lives in order that our country might be free.

CHAPTER XXVI.

The German Offensive.

March, 1918.

OVER four months had passed away since my return from Rome, so leave was again due. Immediately after the unveiling of the Artillery monument I started off in a car for Boulogne, and the next afternoon arrived in London. Conditions there were worse than they had been the year before. The streets were darker and food was scarcer. I went as for north as Edinburgh, but when I arrived at that city I found it cold and wintry and wrapped in mists. There were many naval men there, and I paid an interesting visit to a damaged submarine which was being repaired in the dry-dock. It was of course nice to meet friends again, but, beyond that, my last leave was not a pleasant one. It was a time of great anxiety. The Americans had come into the war, but they were not yet ready. Another campaign was before us, and the issue of it none could foresee. I was haunted perpetually by the dread of meeting with some accident, and so being sent back from the front. Several times I had a vivid dream, that I had got back to Canada and found that the war was still going on and I could not return to it. I shall never forget the joy of waking on such occasions and looking with dawning consciousness upon my surroundings and feeling that I was still at the front. It was a happy day for me, therefore, when on March 8th I arrived once more at Bracquemont, in the midst of my beloved war-family, and able to revisit Liévin, Loos, and Hill 70.

My favorite home in the trenches was the dugout in the chalk-pit, which I have just described, and I often wish I could be suddenly transported there and revive old memories. We were planning at this time to make a big gas-attack along the Canadian Corps front. Three thousand gas-cylinders were to be fired by electricity upon the enemy. As I wanted to see this, I made my way to the chalk-pit. The time fixed for the event was five minutes to eleven at night. If the attack was to come off, the word "Japan" was to come through on the wires; if, owing to the wind being in the wrong direction, the attack had to be postponed, the word "Russia" would be sent. At 10.45 I climbed up the steps to the observation post at the back of the chalk-pit and waited. From this point I had a good view of the line towards Lens. I watched the luminous hands of my watch, and they passed the hour of eleven without anything occuring, as the breeze came from the East. I knew the word "Russia," the name of the country that failed us, must have been sent over the wires. It was a queer sensation to sit up there in the dark with no sound but the soft murmer of the night wind in our ears, and the crash of an occasional shell. In those long dark stretches of waste land around me, thousands of human beings on both sides of the line were awake and active, either burrowing like ants in the ground or bringing up rations and war material along the communication trenches.

I spent four nights that week in the chalk-pit waiting for the attack, and on March 21st, the night of the day on which the Germans launched their fierce attack against our Fifth Army, my patience was rewarded and the wind was propitious. I mounted the observation post and once more peered over the black stretches of country under the starlit sky. Suddenly, at five minutes to eleven, there was a burst of artillery fire, and over our heads with the usual swishing sound the gas-cylinders sped forth. The German lines were lit with bursting shells. Up went their rockets calling to their artillery for retaliation. I could hear their gas bells ringing to warn their men of the poison that was being poured upon them. It must have been a drenching rain of death. I heard gruesome tales afterwards of desolate enemy trenches and batteries denuded of men. The display of fireworks was magnificent, and the German artillery in the rear were not slow in replying. A great artillery duel like that in the darkness of the night over a waste of ground on which no human habitation could be seen had a very weird effect, and was wonderful to behold. I climbed down into the dug-out and made my way through it to the chalk-pit, and then up to an outpost beyond. Here were four men, and I found that three of them had just come up from the base and that this was their first night in the line. They did not seem to be enjoying it as much as I thought they should, so I remarked that it was a beautiful night and pointed out to them the extraordinary romance of being actually out in the front line during such a bombardment. They seemed to get more enthusiastic later on, but the next morning I was wakened in my room by the laughter of men on the other side of the canvas wall, and I heard one old soldier telling, to the amusement of his fellows, of my visit on the previous evening. He said "We were out there with the shells falling round us, and who should come up but the Canon, and the first thing the old beggar said was, 'Boys, what a lovely night it is.'" The men roared at the idea. It was always illuminating to get a chance of seeing yourself as others saw you.

That day, before I had gone to the chalk-pit, I heard from a staff officer at Corps of the German attack in the South, and I gathered from his manner that things were not going well. On March 29th we suddenly shifted our headquarters to Château de la Haie. Here we were told that we had to be ready to move again at a moment's notice. Very bad news had come from the South, for the Germans were advancing, and our Fifth Army had been pushed back. The enemy had now got the initiative into his hands, and things were exceedingly serious. The Americans would not be ready for some time, and the question was how to stay the onrush of the fresh divisions which the Germans were hurling against us. An order from General Currie, couched in beautiful language, told us that there was to be no retreat for Canadians, and that, if need be, we should fall where we stood. There was no panic, only firmer resolve and greater activity in every department. Though I made it a point of never questioning our staff about war secrets, I soon became aware that our Division was to be sent South to try and stem the oncoming tide.

Every night the 4th Divisional concert party gave an entertainment in the theatre, which was crowded with men. A stranger could not have told from the roars of laughter that shook the audience from time to time that we were about to face the fiercest ordeal of the war. The 2nd Brigade was quartered round us first, and one night in the theatre an officer appeared in front of the stage between the acts and ordered all the officers and men of the 5th Battalion, who were present, to report at once to their headquarters. Instantly the men got up and left, the rows of vacant seats looking quite tragic. The play went on. Again, another battalion, and another, was called off. The audience dwindled. It reminded one of the description in the "Tale of Two Cities" of the condemned men in prison waiting for the call of the executioner. Before the close of the performance the theatre was almost empty. The 2nd Brigade moved away that night and the 3rd took their places the next day. I knew that they, too, would have to move suddenly, so I arranged that at night we should have a service followed by a Celebration of the Holy Communion in the theatre after the play was over. Once again the building was crowded with an enthusiastic audience, and, after the play was ended, I announced the service. To my astonishment, most of the men stayed and others crowded in, so we must have had nearly a thousand men present. The concert party had received orders to pack up their scenery immediately and move off. While I was on the stage getting the altar ready the scene shifters were hard at work behind me. In spite of this disturbance, we had a wonderful service. I gave them a short address, and spoke about the high call which had come to Canadians to do big things, and how the eyes of the world were upon us. We were the champions of right, and I asked them to go forth in the power of God and do their duty. Then I began the Communion Service. The colours of the flag which hung over the altar glowed like an inspiration. The two altar lights shone like stars above it. At the back of the stage (but we heeded them not) were the busy men packing up the scenery. We sang the hymn "O God our help in ages past," and at the time of communion about two hundred officers and men mounted the stage in turn and knelt in rows to receive the Bread of Life. It was a thrilling moment, and it showed how, underlying the superficial thoughtlessness of the soldier's life, there was the deep and abiding sense of the reality and need of God. The service ended about eleven P.M.

After shaking hands with some of the men I went back to my billet and there found that we had to start that night for parts unknown. All our surplus baggage had been sent off and only what was absolutely necessary was retained. The members of "C" mess were sitting round the table having a little liquid refreshment and waiting for the bus which was to take them off. Our A.D.M.S., who was starting at once, kindly offered to take me with him in an ambulance. Alberta and I, with two or three men, got into the vehicle, and I bid farewell for the last time to Château de laHaie. It was a bright moonlight night and the air was cold, but the roads were dry and dusty. The A.D.M.S., who was the only person who knew our destination, sat in front with the driver and told him the various turns to take. Clouds of dust blew back into the ambulance as we sped onward. It was a curious expedition. The war seemed to be more real than ever. One felt that a new page in its history was being turned. I wondered what was in store for us and what our experiences were going to be. I was also surprised that one was able to go forth without any emotion upon an adventure of such magnitude. On and on we rattled down the moonlit roads, past sleeping villages, and round sharp curves which jolted us in the car, until at last, at half-past two, we pulled up suddenly in front of some large iron gates which gave entrance to the grounds of a château standing back some distance from the road. The A.D.M.S. and his staff got out and hunted for a cottage which they could use as an office.

I thought I had better go off and find a place where I could spend the rest of the night. With my haversack over my shoulder and followed by Alberta, I entered the gate, and made my way up the avenue till I came to the Château. It was a large and picturesque building, and stood out nobly against the outline of the trees in the park. The moon lit up the gray stone front, which was made all the richer by the variegated light and shade. The mansion, however, showed no inclination to be hospitable. All the windows were tightly closed with shutters, and there was no appearance of life anywhere. I knew we were not far from the advancing Germans, and I supposed that the inhabitants had all fled. I was so cold and tired that I determined to force an entrance and spend the night inside. I walked round to the back, where I saw a great park richly wooded. A large door in the centre of the building, reached by a broad flight of stone steps, seemed to offer me a chance of getting inside. I went up and tried the handle, when, to my surprise, the door opened and I found myself in a beautiful hall richly furnished and lighted by a lamp. Antlers hung on the wall, and the place had the appearance of an English country-house. After my long ride, and at that hour of the night, I felt as if I were in a dream. I saw a door to the right, and opening it was admitted to a modern drawing-room luxuriously furnished. A grate fire was burning on the hearth, and on a centre-table stood silver candelabra with lighted candles. There were also pi. 's of bread and butter, some very nice cups and saucers, and a silver coffee-pot. At once I said to myself, "I am evidently expected." It was like a story from the Arabian Nights. I looked about the place and not a soul appeared, Alberta tucked herself up on a rug and was soon fast asleep. I was just preparing to partake of the refreshments which, it seemed, some fairy godmother had provided, when in came one of our A.D.Cs. He was as much surprised to see me as I was to see him. He told me that our Divisional Commander had arrived there about an hour or two before and had gone to bed, and that we were in the home of a certain count whose servants had all fled. He also told me that there was a bedroom that I could have upstairs, and which would not be occupied by our staff until the next evening. I had a cup of coffee, and then, calling Alberta and taking a candle, I climbed a very rambling staircase till I reached the top storey, where I found an empty room with a very dirty bed in it. However, I was glad to get a place in which to rest, and so, with my rain-coat for a covering, I went to sleep. The next morning, having foraged for some water in which I had a good wash, I went off to the village to get some food. I met many of our units coming up in busses. Some were halted by the wayside, and nobody knew what we were going to do or why we were there. The Imperial transport officer in charge had either acted under wrong orders or else the drivers did not know the roads. Some of our battalions had lost their way, one even entered a village at the other end of which were the Germans, and two of our Engineer Companies disappeared completely for two days.

The country people were hurrying off in carts, taking their household goods with them. I found a primitive farmhouse where I was able to buy some eggs and bread, and I invited a number of stragglers in to have something to eat. By noon, however, we got orders from the Army to move back to a place called Fosseaux. There we occupied an empty château which before the war must have been a very fine place. A wide grassy road nearly a mile in length, bordered on each side by fine old trees, stretched off into the distance in front of the central door. The entrance to the road was guarded by an exquisitely wrought iron gate, flanked on each side by stone pillars surmounted by carved heraldic figures. It was now cold and rainy, and our two Artillery Brigades were halted in a field opposite and were awaiting orders. Before nightfall they had left, and the forward section of our Division made their headquarters in a hut at Warlus; the members of "C" mess remaining at Fosseaux.

March the 29th was Good Friday, and a strange one it was. There was much stir and commotion everywhere, and we were so unsettled, that all I could do was to have a service in the cinema in the evening, and on Easter Day two Celebrations of Holy Communion at which I had only twenty-eight communicants. Our men had gone in to the line to the southeast of Arras, round Telegraph Hill, where an attack by the Germans was expected, as their advance to the south had been checked. I made my way to Arras, and spent the night in one of the mysterious caves which lie under that city. It was called St. Sauveur Cave, and was entered from a street behind the station. The 1st Brigade was quartered there. In the morning I walked down the long dark passage till I came to an opening which led me to some high ground where there had evidently been a good deal of fighting. From there I made my way over to the front line, where the 1st Battalion was entrenched. I passed numbers of wooden huts broken by shells. Many men must have been quartered there at one time. It was sad to go into them and see the waste and desolation, and the lost war material scattered in all directions. On my way I came to a deep trench which some Imperial machine-gunners were holding. They had had an anxious time, and were glad to have a visitor. Several of them regretted that they had not been able to attend any Easter service. I told them we would have one there and then, as I was carrying the Blessed Sacrament with me. So we cleaned a corner of the trench, and there I had a short service and gave the men communion.

Our trenches were not satisfactory, as we did not know accurately where those of the Germans were. That night, instead of going back to the 1st Brigade I made my way to the huge Rouville Caves under Arras, where the whole of the 3rd Brigade were quartered. It was a most curious abode. No one knows when the caves were dug. They were probably extended from time to time as the chalk was quarried for the purpose of building the town. Long passages stretched in different directions, and from them opened out huge vaulted chambers where the battalions were billeted. I spent the night with the 14th Battalion, and the next day held services in turn for each of the four units of the Brigade. The 16th Battalion occupied a huge cavern with others branching off from it. I could hardly imagine more picturesque surroundings for a military service. The candle flames twinkled like stars in all directions in the murky atmosphere, and the singing of the men resounded through the cave. Overhead was the town which the enemy was shelling. In one of the caves we found the foundation of what had been an old prison, with a date upon it of the 18th century. It was very pleasant wandering down the passages, with a candle stuck on the top of my steel helmet, and meeting everywhere old friends who were glad of the temporary rest. Life there, however, was very strange. One could not tell whether outside it was day or night. I made my way back that afternoon by a passage which led out to one of the Arras sewers, by the side of which there was a stone pavement enabling one with a good flashlight to walk safely. The exit from the sewer, which now consisted of a shallow stream of perfectly clear water, led me up to a house in one of the streets, and thence by a car I made my way to Warlus, and home to Fosseaux.

A few days afterwards our headquarters were moved up to Etrun, and there we found ourselves crowded into the quaint little town. The Chateau was our headquarters, and a tar-paper house which the Engineers built for me under a spreading hawthorn tree became my home. Etrun was a most interesting place historically. It had been the site of a Roman camp where Valentinian had his headquarters in the 4th century. The large mound, or vallum, which the Romans had thrown up to protect themselves from the attacks of the German tribes, is now a thickly wooded hill, pierced by the road which connects the village with the Arras highway. The grounds of the Château were most delightful, and before the French Revolution the house had been a convent. In the garden was the recumbent stone effigy, overgrown with moss, of one of the sisters. The most beautiful thing about the place is the clear stream, wide and deep, which comes from underground and flows over sparkling white pebbles through the green meadows to the river Scarpe. This stream was evidently the source of attraction to the Romans, who always made their camps where there was a plentiful supply of running water. The garden on one side was built up in stone terraces along which were gravel walks, where, no doubt, the nuns of old enjoyed their holy meditations. In the stream, as it wandered through the meadows, there was a plentiful supply of water-cress, which looked exquisitely green against the pebbles at the bottom. How one did long for the war to end, so that we might be able to lie down in the grass, free from anxiety, and enjoy the drenching sunlight and the spring song of the birds.

CHAPTER XXVII.

In Front of Arras

April, 1918

ETRUN was a convenient place for a headquarters. My hut was comfortable, and the tree that grew beside it stretched its thickly-leaved boughs over it, as though wishing to protect it from the sight of enemy planes. Visitors were always welcome. In the garden were many other huts, and a path led to the churchyard in which stood the old church. It was strongly ' built, but very crudely furnished, and spoke of many generations of humble worshippers to whom it was the gate of heaven. On one side of the garden was a stream, which turned a quaint mill-wheel, and an island in the stream, connected with the banks by a bridge, made a pleasant resort. A little nest of beauty, such as Etrun was, in the midst of the war, most restful to the soul, especially after a visit to the line. Of course, we had to be careful about screening all lights, for a shell landed one night in a hut opposite mine. Luckily the shell was a "dud". Had it not been, my sergeant, groom, and batman would have been no more, for it burrowed its way into the ground under the floor of their abode, as they were having supper.

On one occasion about one in the morning, we were awakened from sleep by three terrific explosions. They sounded close, so I thought that some of our men might have been hit. I got up and went off to see where the shells had landed. The quaint old hamlet lay silent in the moonlight, and not a soul was stirring. I went down one of the narrow streets, and met a tall figure in black coming towards me. It was the Curé, who was bent on a similar mission, fearing that some of his people had been wounded. We went round the place together until we met a man coming up the road, who told us that a bomb had struck the railway bridge and exploded two mines which we had in readiness in case the Germans were to make an advance. The bridge had been completely shattered, but luckily our sentries there had escaped. The Curé and I then parted and went back to our beds.

It was a great treat for our men who were billeted in vil-

248

lages in the Scarpe Valley to have plenty of water, and in the various mill-ponds they found swimming-places. Our front line at this time extended for quite a long distance north and south of the Scarpe. In fact the river acted for a short distance as No Man's Land. On the north of the Scarpe were the ruins of the village of Fampoux, and on the south those of Feuchy. How well our men will remember the towns of Maroeil, Anzin, St. Nicholas and St. Aubin. I used to go off across the meadow lands, now bright and fresh with spring verdure, till I got to the St. Eloi road, and then by jumping lorries would make my way to St. Nicholas and on to Cam Valley. On the east side of the valley were quaint dugouts which were occupied by the battalion in reserve. A path up the valley led to the communication trench, and finally down Pudding Lane to Pudding Trench. The ground was elevated, so that from one of the trenches which led down towards Fampoux I was able to see with my glasses the country behind the German lines. I saw quite distinctly one day the spires of Douai, and in another direction on a hillside I could make out a railway train which must have been carrying German troops. I had many interesting walks through the trenches, and slept there several times. On one occasion I took Alberta with me, but she would persist in going off into No Man's Land hunting for rats. The arrival of a minnenwerfer, however, gave her a great fright and made her jump back into the trench with alacrity, much to the amusement of the men, who said that she knew the use of trenches.

One day I went down the trench which led into Fampoux. Whizzbangs were falling every now and then, so the men were keeping low. At one place there was a good view of the German lines. An officer and a sergeant stood there looking through their glasses and pointed out to me a spot in the hillside opposite where we could see a number of the enemy. They came out of one trench, crossed the road, and went down into another. The officer told me that he had counted over a hundred that day. I asked him why he did not telephone to Battalion Headquarters to inform the artillery. He told me he had no telephone. Then I said, "Why don't you send a runner?" He explained that Fampoux was occupied as an outpost, and that no runners were allowed to be sent from there during the daytime; orders to this effect being very strict. "I am not a runner," I said, "and I am not in your Battalion. If you will give me the map-location of the place where you think the Germans are congregating, I will take it back with me to the liason officer at Battalion Headquarters." He was very pleased with my offer, because at this time we were daily expecting a big attack upon our lines. To get back we had to crawl down a steep place in the trench, which was in view of the Germans, until at last we reached the cellar of a ruined house which the O. C. of the company used as a billet. He got out his maps and gave me the exact location of the road and trenches where the Germans had been seen to pass, and where apparently they were massing. I got him to write down the map-location carefully on a piece of paper, and then, armed with this and feeling very important, I started back, this time avoiding the trench and going up the Fampoux road on the side of which there was some torn and broken camouflage. I came across a steel helmet by the wayside with part of a man's head in it, and the road had been pretty well battered by shells, but I felt exceedingly proud at being able to do something which might possibly avert an attack upon our men. I went on till at last I saw in the hillside the beginning of a trench, and made my way up this to Pudding lane and found Battalion Headquarters. The Artillery officer had been having a quiet time and was delighted at the prospect of ordering a "shoot." At once he telephoned back to the brigade, and not long after, when the quiet sun was setting in the West, a most terrific bombardment of artillery, both field and heavy, smashed the German trenches on the hill opposite. The headquarters men and I looked over the valley and saw the line of bursting shells. Much to their amusement, I told them that this was my music, that I had ordered the shoot. I felt like the fly on the axle of a cart, who said to his companion fly, "Look at the dust we are making."

On another occasion, I was filled with almost equal pride, when, meeting on the roadside a company of men who were going into the trenches for the first time and were waiting for a guide, I offered my services and actually led the company of young heroes into the trenches myself. The humour of the situation was so palpable that the men felt as if they were going to a picnic.

The trenches on the Feuchy side of the Scarpe were well made, and led up to the higher ground to the east of Arras, where they joined the lines of a Scots Division. At one point we saw in No Man's Land a lonely tent, which I was told had been occupied by a British chaplain before we had been driven back. I paid a most enjoyable visit to the engineers in Arras and stayed at Battalion Headquarters. They were in a large and comfortable house in the Place St. Croix. In the dining room we had a grate fire, a rug on the floor, and several easy chairs. A most sumptuous dinner was served, and one could scarcely believe that we were in a war.

The men of the battalion were billeted in the deep cellars under a row of houses at the end of the Grande Place. Some of these houses dated back to the time of the Spanish occupation, so the cellars must have been very ancient. They were vaulted in stone and were connected together by passages, so they were not only quite safe from shells but were exceedingly interesting and picturesque. We had several services for the men and one for a field ambulance which made its home in the Deaf and Dumb Asylum. In a large room in the Asylum there was a good piano, so it enabled us to use the place at one time as a church and at another as a ballroom. There was a strange charm about dear old Arras which is quite indescribable. In spite of the ruined buildings and the damaged grass-grown streets, there was the haunting beauty of a quiet medievalism about the city. The narrow streets, the pleasant gardens hidden behind the houses, spoke of an age that had passed. Arras has been the centre of interest in many wars, and Julius Caesar made his headquarters there in B. C. 65. The river Scarpe has carried to the sea many memories of hostile hosts that have fought along its banks. To walk back from the dressing station in the small hours of the morning, when the moon was shining on the silent and half-ruined streets and squares, was a weird experience. Surely, if ghosts ever haunt the scenes of their earthly life, I must have had many unseen companions with me on such occasions. There were still two or three shops in the place where souvenirs and other small articles were sold to the men, and there were hoards of champagne and other wines in some of the cellars, but only a few of the inhabitants remained and they lived hidden lives in the underground retreats.

Our Division, however, was soon moved from Etrun to Château d'Acq, where I arrived at four one morning after a visit to the trenches. I found my billet in an Armstrong hut. The people who had occupied the Château since we were there must have experienced an air raid, because extraordinary precautions had been taken to guard against bombs. I lit my lamp and found that the bed was surrounded on all sides by a wall composed of two thicknesses of sandbags. When I got down into it I felt as if I were in a grave. In the morning I got my batman to remove the fortification, as I thought there was no occasion to anticipate the sensations of being buried. However, at night I often heard German aeroplanes overhead, and it was a relief when their intermittent buzzing died off into the distance.

We were now a long way from the front line, but by jumping lorries I was still able to go forward and visit the slums. On returning from such a visit one afternoon I suffered a great loss. The order had gone out some time before that all stray dogs were to be shot, and many poor little four-footed souls were sent into whatever happy land is reserved for the race which has been the earliest and best friend of man. I had kept a sharp lookout on Alberta, but I never dreamt that anyone would shoot her. However, that evening while I was getting ready to go off to Ecoivres, and Alberta was playing in front of my hut, the sergeant of the police, carried her off, unknown to me, and ordered a man to shoot her. When I came out from my hut, and whistled for my faithful friend, I was told that she had been condemned to death. I could hardly believe it; but to my dismay I found that it was only too true, and the poor little dog, who was known all over the Division and had paid many visits to the trenches, was not only shot but buried. Filled with righteous anger, I had the body disinterred and a proper grave dug for it in front of a high tree which stands on a hill at the back of the grounds. There, surrounded by stones, is the turf-covered mound, and on the tree is nailed a white board with this epitaph neatly painted in black:—

HERE LIES ALBERTA
of Albert
Shot April 24th, 1918.

The dog that by a cruel end
Now sleeps beneath this tree,
Was just the little dog and friend
God wanted her to be.

Alberta, much respected in life, was honoured in death, for nearly all the men at Headquarters were present when she was buried, and one of them told me that at a word from me they would lay out the police. I should have liked to have given the word, but I told them that we had a war on with the Germans, and that we had better not start another till it was finished. On the following day the board with the epitaph was placed in position in the presence of a Brigadier-General and our kind-hearted and sympathetic C. R. E. I was so filled with indignation at the loss of my companion, who, wherever I tied up Dandy, would always mount guard over him and allow no one to approach him, that I determined to seek a billet away from Headquarters, and near the front. However, this intention was frustrated a day or two later by an order which came through for our Division to go into rest at a place called Le Cauroy, not far from the town of Frevent, and about 15 kilometres to the southwest of Chateau d'Acq.

CHAPTER XXVIII.

Sports and Pastimes

May and June, 1918

IT was late in the evening when I reached the Château at Le Cauroy, and I found that I was to be billeted in the house of the Curé, on one side of the fine avenue of lime trees. Ross was waiting for me and took the horse, and I went inside to my room. A curious sensation came over me of having seen the place before. It seemed as if I had been there in one of my dreams, but the mystery was cleared up on the following day by my finding out from the Vicaire that this was the place where I had spent such a gloomy Sunday on the 22nd of October, 1916, during our return from the Somme. The count who owned the Château was naval attaché to the French Embassy in London, but his wife and children, with the servants, occupied apartments on the right wing of the building. The presence of a lady gave a special charm to the place, and tennis on a good court under the trees in the park was most enjoyable. On several occasions some of our Canadian Sisters from the C. C. S. at Frevent honoured us with their presence at dinner, which was followed by a dance. Under the trees in the avenue, a most picturesque open theatre was erected by the engineers, and here our concert party gave us nightly performances of their new play, which was called "The Marriage Market." Hundreds of men from the battalions around would sit on the soft grass under the overhanging trees through which we could see the stars, and on the brightly lighted stage, with the orchestra in front, we had an exhibition of real talent. The weather was delightful and the men enjoyed a holiday in the country. At a little distance behind the Château there was a clear stream blocked by an ancient mill-dam. Here we could get a swim and bask in the sun in the long cool grass. Altogether we were very happy at Le Cauroy.

A great change had come over the war at this time, for Foch had assumed the supreme command. While we had had excellent leaders all through the campaign, one always felt that there was a need for some electrifying personality at the head of things. In a mysterious way the knowledge that Foch had taken the conduct of the war in hand gave us just that touch of magnetism which we needed. As matters stood, the German attacks had been successful up to a certain point, but we were still waiting for their main offensive. When or where this was to begin we did not know, but we were convinced that it would be, for us, a life or death struggle. The fact that Foch was in command and that he was keeping his head gave us confidence. He seemed like a surgeon who shows his greatness by the very coolness with which he performs some critical operation. The men were always asking if we were losing the war, and I always told them that it was like this—the Germans were advancing and losing and we were retreating and winning. We practised daily the art of open warfare for which the country round us offered splendid opportunities. We knew that we had been taken out of the line in order to prepare to become "shock troops", and the knowledge of this gave our life a great inspiration.

It was the right policy, in view of what was before us, to give the men all the amusement possible, so football and baseball were indulged in freely by officers and men. We were too well trained now to worry much about the future. In fact, although I had often preached on the text, "Sufficient unto the day is the evil thereof," I never fully acted upon the principle until I had been in the war for three years. It is certainly the true secret of happiness and I hope that the softer life of peace time will not rob one of it. When Mrs. Carlyle was asked what caused her most suffering in life, she replied, "The things which never happened." It would have surprised the people at home if they could have seen the cheeriness and lightheartedness of men who were being trained day by day to deliver the hammer strokes which were to smash the huge war machine of Imperial Germany.

The 2nd Brigade one day gave us a most successful circus in a large field near our Headquarters. The arrangements and weather were perfect, and the spectators were delighted with a performance that surpassed Buffalo Bill's Wild West show. Afternoon tea and dancing followed at a chateau, and aeroplanes gave us a fine exhibition of the skill of the new branch of the service by flying low and dropping messages and red smoke bombs. I met one of the young airmen, and in a fit of enthusiasm asked him if he would take me up with him some day. He was quite keen about it, and asked me to let him know when to send for me. Our plans, however, were upset a day or two afterwards by the Headquarters of the Division moving off to the beautiful Château at Villers Chatel. They left in the morning, and as usual I followed leisurely on Dandy. I went through some pretty villages. No soldiers were to be seen, and the quiet ordinary life of the people was undisturbed by the war. The world was bathed in sunshine and the fields were brilliant with new crops. Every little hamlet was embowered in trees, and the small white houses with their red tiled roofs spoke of peace. In the solemn light of evening I came to the entrance gate of my new home.

The Château of Villers Chatel was a fine modern building with an old round tower at one end. This tower is all that remains of the original structure, but it was kept in good condition and the interior was most artistically arranged. My room was in the garret and was approached by a spiral staircase, very narrow and steep. The Château was enlivened by the presence of two Countesses; both very pleasant ladies who had their own apartments and who kindly entertained us at night in their cheery drawing-room. On the wide lawn in front of the Château a huge chestnut tree stood, rich in leaves, with low boughs branching in all directions and covering a wide radius, and with their tips almost touching the grass. The tree furnished a green shelter for a large number of persons. The sun could not penetrate the foliage, and the giant trunk was covered with rugged bark beautifully coloured. Here, on Sunday mornings, I placed my flag-covered altar, and Church Parade was held under the tree. The men, over a hundred in number, stood in a semi-circle in front of me, and the bright sunlight beyond the rim of overhanging boughs lit up the green grass around. It was one of the most beautiful places imaginable for a church service, and the branches made a vaulted roof overhead. On one side of the garden was a large and elaborate cement grotto, and a statue of the Blessed Virgin stood in a niche at the back. Seats for worshippers were placed in front. The Countesses were moved by piety to keep a number of candles blazing in the grotto all night, invoking thereby the protection of Our Lady. Our staff, who walked not by faith but by sight, were much worried by the strong light which could easily be seen from a German aeroplane. However, no one could muster up courage enough to interfere with the devotion of our hostesses, and as a matter of fact we never had any bombing raids at Villers Chatel. It was a question among the officers as to whether our immunity should be attributed to the power of prayer or to extraordinary good-luck.

At the end of the lawn facing the Château was a forest of magnificent trees. It was in the fields at the back of this wood that we had held the memorial service for the 2nd Brigade, which I have already described. One of the forest paths was in the form of a pergola. The trees had been trimmed so that the boughs overhead were interlaced and it went for about half a mile into the forest, like the vaulted aisle of a church. The sunlight through the green leaves overhead cast on the pathway a mysterious light sugestive of fairyland.

Our battalions were once more in their old billets in the neighbourhood, and as we were still at rest I had many opportunities of visiting them. How well I remember going about and delivering my lecture on our leave trip to Rome. As I look back upon my war-memories, I think that those talks were the most delightful experiences I have ever had. I really had nothing to say, but I knew that anything which could occupy and amuse the minds of those brave lads, who were daily preparing to hurl themselves against the enemy, was worth while. I would go to the C.O. of a battalion and say, "Colonel, I would like to come and give your men a talk on our leave trip to Rome." He would always take the matter very seriously, thinking I had some learned discourse on architecture, or some other absolutely futile subject to give the men. But being too polite to tell me to go to Jericho, or somewhere else, he would say, "Yes, I am sure it would be very interesting. How long will the lecture last?" On my replying, "About two hours and a half," his countenance would fall. He was struggling between his fear of offending me and his fear of doing something which would bore the men. Sometimes colonels would say, "That's a long lecture." But I urged them to take my word for it and to let the thing go ahead, and if I saw I was boring the men I would stop. So the lecture would be announced. I suppose I must have given it to something like twenty thousand men. I would arrive at the battalion headquarters in the afternoon, have dinner with the C.O. and Adjutant in their billet, and then walk over to some pleasant field on which a thousand men were drawn up in line, presenting a most proper military appearance. The sun would be setting behind the trees which skirted the parade ground, and, after telling the Colonel and other officers to keep in the background, I would go over in front of the battalion and tell them that the Colonel had handed the parade over to me, and that they were to break ranks and sit on the ground as close as possible. At once military stiffness was dispelled, and amid much laughter the men would crowd around and squat on the ground tightly packed together. Imagine what a picture that was. Splendid stalwart young men they were, hundreds and hundreds of them, with healthy merry faces, and behind them in the distance the green trees and the sunset. Of course smoking was allowed, and I generally had some boxes of cigarettes to pass round. Then I would tell them of our trip to Rome and of my following out the injunction of making the most of a fortnight's leave by turning it into three weeks; of my puzzling the R.T.O. in Paris by asking for transportation to Rome via Marseilles, as we had abandoned the idea of travelling via Calcutta on account of the submarine menace; of my being unable to enter the Casino at Monte Carlo because officers were not admitted in uniform, and the only mufti I had brought with me was my pyjamas which I had left at the hotel; of the two casualties in the Paris barrage; of the time I gave C.B. to "Yorky" when I saw he had partaken too freely of coffee, and of the delightful memories of Italy which we had brought back with us. The talk was not all humorous. I managed to get in many little sermons between the lines, or as I put it, "the lecture was impregnated with the poison of morality." Men assimilated that poison more readily when handed out to them in such doses. Then the sun would set and the evening shadows lengthen, and finally the stars would come out over the scene and the mass of men before me would merge into one great blur, which sent up, nevertheless, roars of merry laughter. What appealed to them most was the way a padré and forty-four wild Canadians, in the biggest war the world has ever known, were able to break through the Hindenburg line of army red tape.

Our machine gun battalion was quartered south of the St. Pol road at a place called Averdoignt. It was a lovely little village, very quiet and well away from the line, with pretty orchards and a stream at the back. When it was only possible to have a voluntary service in the evening, I would get a group of men as a body-guard and start off down the village to the quaint old church, halting at every farmyard on the way and calling out to those billeted there, "Come on, you ..athen, come to the voluntary church parade." In the most good-natured way, dragging their reluctant pals with them, men would come out and swell our ranks until, by the time we reached the church, there was a good congregation. There against the wall of the building I would plant a table borrowed from the Curé's house, make it into an altar, distribute hymn books, and start the service, while the evening lights in the sky tinged the scene with a soft beauty.

When we were in the line the machine-gunners were always split up into small sections over the front, their guns of course being very carefully concealed. In consequence, just when I thought I had reached an area which was quite uninhabited, I would stumble on some queer little hole, and, on calling down it to see if there were any men there, the answer would be, "The machine-gun battalion," and I would find myself among friends. At Averdoigt they had one of the best rest billets they ever had, and they enjoyed it thoroughly.

Owing to the great distance which I had to cover in doing my parish visiting among the battalions, the difficulty of transportation, which had been serious from the beginning, became even more pressing, and some good friend suggested to me on the quiet that I should try to get a Clino, (that is a machine-gun side-car) from the Motor Machine-Gun Brigade. With great trepidation, I made an excursion one day to their headquarters at Verdrel. The O.C. was most kind and sympathetic. I shall never cease to invoke blessings upon his head. He took me over to the machine-shop and there presented to me, for my use until it should be recalled, a new Clino which had just come up from the base. The officer in charge uttered a protest by saying that they only had six Clinos for the Brigade, but the major remarked dryly, "And after Canon Scott has got his we shall only have five." Surely once again the Lord had provided for me. I was driven back to the Château in the new machine, but then had to find a driver. One was provided by the signallers. He was a graduate in science of McGill, so I used to lay stress upon my personal greatness from the fact that I had a university graduate for my chauffeur. Many and varied were the drives which Lyons and I had together, and many and varied were our adventures. Had the Clino not been both exceedingly strong and very new it would have come to grief long before it did. To go rattling down the St. Pol road at forty-five kilometres an hour was a frequent occurence. All I had to sit upon was a seat without arms, while my foot rested on a bar in front. People asked me how it was I did not tumble off. I told them that I tied myself to the back of the seat with my spinal cord. I got the sappers to make me a large box which fitted on the back of the vehicle and had a padlock. In it I used to carry my bag of a thousand hymn books and other necessaries for church parades, and on the top of the box, as a protection to my car, I had the words "Canon Scott" painted in large white letters. The dust as we threaded our way through the streams of lorries almost choked us, but we could cover the ground in a short space of time which was a great thing. Lyons never managed the lights very successfully, and one rainy night after midnight, when I was returning from saying good-bye to the artillery who were moving South, in a lonely part of the road he ran the machine into some bushes on a bank by the wayside, and we found ourselves sitting in the mud without our hats. We did not know where we were and the rain was heavy, but we managed to disentangle the car and finally got home, resolving that further night excursions were out of the question. About a fortnight afterwards I received an order to return the Clino, but before I did so I journeyed to Corps Headquarters and made a passionate appeal to General Currie for its retention. As a result I received a private intimation to keep the car and say nothing about it. Ot course I was the envy of everyone, and when they asked me how I got the Clino I said I did not exactly know. Whether it was sent to me from heaven with the assistance of General Currie, or whether it was sent to me from General Currie with the assistance of heaven, was a theological question which I had no time to go into during the war. When our Division was marching into Germany, after I was knocked out of the campaign, the dear old signallers used to patch up the Clino, even making new parts for it, in order that Canon Scott's car might get into Germany. Alas! the poor thing, like the one-horse shay, went to pieces finally one day and had to be left at Mons. During those last busy months, I do not know how I could have got on without it.

As I was a bit under the weather at this time my friend, General Thacker, invited me to go and stay with him at his headquarters in the Château at Berles, where I was given a charming room looking out on the garden. I found myself in the midst of the artillery brigades who were now at rest, and very pleasant it was to see them away from the unwholesome gun-pits where they were usually to be found. I could lie on the grass in the garden, read one of Trollope's novels and listen to the birds overhead. A walk through the wood led to a huge field of scarlet poppies, which, when the sun shone upon it, made a blaze of colour which I have never seen equalled. As one approached it, one could see the red glow light up the stems of the trees as though they were aflame.

We had many boxing and baseball contests, which roused great excitement, but the crowning glory of the time was the Divisional sports which were held in a large field at a place called Tincques on the St. Pol road. A grandstand and many marquees had been erected, and the various events gave great delight to the thousands of spectators. In the evening our concert party gave a performance on the stage in the open air, which was witnessed by a large and enthusiastic audience. After it was all over, I unexpectedly met my airman friend, Johnny Johnson, who told me that he had been waiting a long time to take me up in his machine. I explained to him that, owing to our headquarters having moved away to Le Cauroy, I thought it was too far off to get in touch with him. In my secret heart, I had looked upon my removal as a special intervention of Providence on my behalf, but Johnny was not disposed, however, to allow any difficulty to stand in the way, so it was arranged that he should send for me at Berles the following day and take me to the headquarters of the 13th Squadron at Izel-les-Hameaux. There was nothing for it but to jump with alacrity at such a noble offer, so on the following morning I started off in the Squadron's car for their headquarters.

My pilot had gone off to bring up the new machine which was to take me on my first aerial voyage. The Squadron had most comfortable billets in huts, and were a most charming lot of young men. A Canadian amongst them, taking pity upon a fellow-countryman, gave me a kind introduction to his fellow officers. Johnny Johnson returned in the afternoon, and during tea I heard him explaining to the other men that he had had his choice of two machines, an old machine with a new engine and the other a new machine with an old engine. Although I was engaged in conversation at the other end of the table, I listened with great interest to this discussion, and felt much relieved when I heard that Johnny's choice of an old machine with a new engine was approved of by his hearers. He told me that the air was very bumpy and that he would not take me up until the sun was lower in the sky. Having arrived

at that happy state of inward peace which a man experiences when
he goes off to the dentist to have a tooth pulled, I did not mind when
I was to be taken up. At six o'clock, however, Johnny said we must
get ready, so I was provided with a fur-lined leather coat, leather
helmet, goggles and a large pair of fur gauntlets. We went over to
the aerodrome where our fiery steed was champing its bit as though
longing to spring into the "vast inane." Two or three attendants
were getting it ready. It was an R.E.8 plane and a machine gun was
fixed on one side. Johnny climbed into his position and I took a seat
behind him. An attendant came up and asked my name and address.
It sounded as if I were making my last will and testament. I had a
letter with me addressed to my son which I was to drop over his
battery lines in Liévin, and also a red smoke bomb but declined an invitation to take any more formidable weapon. Then I told my pilot
not to be anxious about me whatever happened. I always expected
to be killed at the front so never worried how or when the event
was to occur. The engine was then started. For a time the machine
meandered about the field without showing any disposition to
mount into the air and I was beginning to think, like the Irishman
who was taken for a ride one day in a sedan chair that had no
bottom in it, that, "If it were not for the honour and glory of the
thing I might as lief walk," when, all of a sudden, we began to
plunge, left the ground, and, mid a fearful buzzing, mounted
higher and higher. We rose over the huts and above the village
trees and then by a corkscrew motion which necessitated the machine going almost on its edge, we made our way heavenwards.
I did not feel the least bit seasick but it was a curious sensation
to look down and see absolutely nothing between me and the
church of Izel-les-Hameaux crowned by its sharp pointed spire
with no cork on it. I looked at my young friend in front of me,
who was busy with the handles and cranks of his machine. He
was only a boy of nineteen and my fate was literally in his
hands, but his head was well set on his shoulders and he seemed
completely self-possessed and confident. After we had mounted to
six thousand feet, we struck out in the direction of the front.

It was a lovely afternoon and a most wonderful panorama spread
below us. The great plain beneath us was marked off like a chess-
board in squares of various shades of yellow and green, dotted
here and there with little villages surrounded by the billowy crests
of trees. We saw straight white roads going off in all directions,

and beyond, towards the east, low murky clouds behind the German
lines. We flew on and on till we reached the war zone and here
the fields were marked by horse-tracks and the villages had been hit
with shells. Before us in the distance I saw the line of our observation balloons and thought, if anything happened to the machine, I
would get out into one of them, but when we passed over them they
looked like specks on the ground below. I could see the blue ribbon
of the Scarpe winding off into the great mists to the east, and then
beneath us lay the old city of Arras. I could see the ruined Cathedral, the mass of crooked streets and the tiny, dusty roads. Further
on was the railway triangle, where one night later on I got a good
dose of gas, and then I saw the trenches at Fampoux and Feuchy.
Still onward we sailed, till at last Johnny Johnson shouted back,
at the same time pointing downwards, "The German trenches."
I saw the enemy lines beneath us, and then Johnny shouted, "Now
I am going to dip." It was not the thing I specially wanted to do
at that particular moment, but I supposed it was all right. The
plane took a dive, and then Johnny leaned over and fired off some
rounds of the machine gun into the German lines. We turned to
come back and rose in the air, when, in the roar of the wind I
heard a bang behind me, and looking round saw, hanging in the air,
a ball of thick black smoke. Then there was another beneath us and
some more at one side. In all, the Germans followed us with six
shells. Johnny turned round and shouted, asking me how I felt.
"Splendid", I said, for I really did enjoy the novelty of the experience. Many times have I looked up into the clouds and seen a
machine followed by "Archies" and wondered what it felt like to be
up there, and now I knew. One phrase however, which I had often
read in the newspapers kept ringing in my ears—"Struck the petrol
tank and the machine came down in flames." And the last verse of
"Nearer my God to Thee," also ran through my head, "Or if on joyful wing upwards I fly." We turned now to the right and flew over
Vimy Ridge, and then made two or three turns round Liévin where,
above his battery, I dropped the letter for my son. It was delivered
to him two weeks afterwards in a hospital in London. We flew
out over Lens and crossed the German lines again, skirting the
district which the Germans had flooded and then turned our faces
homewards. Above the Château at Villers Chatel, I dropped the
red smoke bomb. We circled round in the air at a great height
while I wrote on a piece of paper, "Canon Scott drops his blessing

from the clouds on 1st Canadian Divisional Headquarters," and put it in the little pocket of leaded streamers. Alas, it was lost in a wheat field and so did not do them any more good than the other blessings I have dropped upon them. We then turned to Berles where I could see beneath me the old house and the tiny beings in white playing tennis on the court. We reached the aerodrome at Izel-les-Hameaux and landed safely after being in the air for fifty-five minutes. It was a most delightful experience for a non-combatant. The next day the engine of the machine gave out and Johnny Johnson was compelled to make a forced landing. Luckily it was behind our lines. I went several times again to try to have another flight, but from the excuses made I inferred that joy-rides of this description had been banned. The following year in London I heard by accident that poor Johnny Johnson had been killed a few weeks after our trip. He was a splendid young fellow and absolutely without fear. May his brave soul rest in peace.

Nearly two months had passed since we had been in the line, and the Germans had made no attack. We wondered what had happened to them. I thought that perhaps influenza had laid them low. At any rate we were not anxious to end the happy time we were having. The climax of our glory was reached on the 1st of July when we celebrated the birthday of the Dominion by Corps sports on the field at Tincques. It was a most wonderful occasion.

Dominion Day fell on a Monday, and on the previous afternoon, knowing that large bodies of men, including the contestants, were congregated at Tincques, I determined to go over and pay them a visit. I found the village full of troops and all very keen about the next day's show. In a little lane, were some 1st Division men, and they were enjoying the excitement of a game which was very popular at the front, called "Crown and Anchor." It is played with special dice on a board or square of green canvas. On the canvas were painted an anchor and crown and I think a heart and spade. The game was banned by the army on account of its unfairness. The banker had, I think, sixty-four chances to one in his favour. The consequence of this was that very soon he became possessed of all the money which green youths, unsuspecting their disadvantage, chose to lay on the board. This game, in the hands of a sharper, was often the means of robbing a battalion of very large sums of money; sometimes forty thousand francs were made by the banker. The police had orders to arrest anyone playing it, and I used to do my best to stamp it out. Though I do not play for money myself, I never could see any great harm in those poor boys out there getting a little relaxation from their terrible nervous strain by a game of bridge or poker for a few francs. But a game which was founded wholly on dishonesty was something which I felt was unworthy of our men. Whenever I saw them crowding round a little spot on the grass I knew there was a game of crown and anchor going on, and I would shout, "Look out, boys, I am going to put the horse on the old mud hook"—a phrase I had heard the men use—and then canter Dandy into their midst scattering them in all directions. Over and over again I have gone into a ring of men and given the banker five minutes to decide whether he would hand over his board and dice to me or have his name reported to the police. He never failed to do the former, although sometimes he looked rather surly at losing a very fruitful source of revenue. I have brought home with me enough crown and anchor dice to make the mouth of an old soldier water. On this occasion I became possessed of the crown and anchor board and the dice in the usual way. But, as the men said they wanted to have some amusement, I went to an officer's billet and got a pack of cards for them, and they settled down to a game of poker.

Some pious souls proposed that I should have a service that evening in the field where the sports were to be held. I thought that it would be a good idea, but was not sure how large a congregation I should have. I got together a little body-guard in the village and we went off collecting stragglers by the way. When we came to the corner of the field where I proposed to hold my service, we found to my dismay that it was full of masses of men crowding around what I knew were crown and anchor boards on the ground. I did not mind doing police work in my own Division, where I was known by the men, but I did not feel called upon to act as A. P. M. for the Corps, so I had to start another line of campaign. I marched on at the head of my congregation straight into the midst of the gamblers. The men on the outskirts saw me coming and I could see them warning the players. Those sitting on the ground stood up and wondered what was going to happen. Looking very serious, I went right through the crowd, without saying anything, to a distance on the other side, and then the curiosity of the men was aroused and they all followed. When I stood still I found myself surrounded by hundreds of men who were waiting to see what I was going to do. Without a smile, I pulled out the crown and anchor board from my pocket and, to the astonishment of all, laid it on the ground and called out, in the gamblers' language, "Who is for the old sergeant-major?" Never before have I seen such an expression of surprise on people's faces. Among the crowd were some Imperial soldiers and they could not make out what sort of padré I was. For a moment, in spite of the grinning countenances of the 1st Division men, there was a pause of silent horror. Then they all burst into a roar of laughter, and I told them I had come out there that evening, as it was Sunday, to hold a service and did not know what text to take for a sermon. Now they had given me one. I held up the crown and anchor board and said I was going to preach about that, and I delivered a discourse on honesty. When it was over, they asked me to give my lecture on our leave trip to Rome. I thought it might be a good diversion for the time. My side-car was brought up, and sitting on it, in the midst of the men, who crowded about me on the ground, I gave them a long talk which lasted until it was too dark for any more crown and anchor.

The next day brought us glorious weather, and from early in the morning battalions were pouring into Tincques. The grounds were splendidly laid out and bordered with many stands and marquees. There must have been nearly forty-thousand spectators present. The Duke of Connaught, Sir Robert Borden, and all sorts of great people attended, and the playing of "O Canada" by the massed bands was something which, as a British General told me, made a big lump come in one's throat. It was the last Dominion Day we were to spend in France. We were on the eve of tremendous events, and it was a splendid manifestation of Canada's glory at the front. There was such a gathering of old friends who had not met for years, that one really could not attend to the various events and sports that were taking place. We met for a moment, and the old days would be talked over, and then we parted, some, alas, never to meet again in this world. That vast crowd which fringed the huge expanse of ground was quite the most thrilling spectacle that Canadians had ever seen. Tincques must be a quiet place now, and perhaps only a few marks in the great field still remain to show where the sports were held. But there were gathered there that day the vast host of noble gentlemen who saved the honour and freedom of our young country.

CHAPTER XXIX.

THE BEGINNING OF THE END.

July to August 7th, 1918.

THE possession of a side-car gave me the opportunity of getting much further afield in my visits. Our 1st Divisional wing, where the new drafts were received and trained for the front line, was at this time back in a place called Loison, in the quiet and beautiful country between St. Pol and General Headquarters. I had done a great deal of parish visiting among our battalions in rest and given the story of my leave trip to Rome many times, so I thought I would make an excursion to the Base. We had a delightful trip down the St. Pol road through little villages and towns which looked as they did in pre-war days. The country where the Divisional wing was stationed was very charming. It was well watered by many pretty rivers, and hills covered with trees gave diversity to the landscape. I told the men they were living in a land flowing with milk and honey. I stayed at the headquarters of the wing in a delightful old house on a hill surrounded with fine trees. Each Brigade had its own reserve, so there were many men in the village, and an old mill pond enabled me to have two or three good swims. In a Y. M. C. A. tent, courses of lectures in connection with the Khaki University were being given on various subjects. One evening, naturally I gave them a talk on our leave trip to Rome. On another, in a corner of the field, I gave them an informal lecture on English literature. Having got so far from home, I determined to go a little further, and so we made a trip to Boulogne, where my son who had been gassed was still in a C. C. S., and that afternoon on our return we went to Montreuil to see what G. H. Q. looked like. I was told that Montreuil was a very picturesque old walled city, but that we should not be allowed to enter. However, I had been able to do so many forbidden things in the war that I thought it would be worth trying, so the old Clino sped over the hard macadamized roads from Boulogne till we came to the valley on the opposite side of which the town is situated. We saw many cars coming and going, and many troops by the way, and finally we sped up the hill which leads to the entrance gate. A sentry was standing there, who saluted most properly, and we passed into the sacred city without molestation. It was a delightful old French town, full of historical interest. The narrow streets and quaint old buildings carried one back in thought to the days of chivalry and battles waged by knights in shining armour. We saw some of the churches, and then went to the officers' club for tea. The waitresses at the club were English girls who had taken the place of the men needed at the front. I got them to provide for my friend Lyons in their sitting-room, and I went in to have tea with the officers. A great many were there sitting at small tables. It was interesting to see the badges of so many different regiments. Most of the officers had a good supply of ribbons, and a few of them had lost an eye or a limb, or bore other marks of wounds. I think that almost all of them were staff officers and that some of them were generals. It struck me that the atmosphere to a stranger was rather chilly. The demeanour of the people was much less free than that which we had been accustomed to at the front. Of course Montreuil held the brains of the army, and it was quite right that the directing intelligences there should feel the loftiness of their position. I made up two lines as I was having tea, which I thought hit off the mental attitude of some of the officers present, when they saw a stranger and looked him up and down through their monocles,

> "I'm on the staff of the G. H. Q.,
> And I'd like to know who the devil are you?"

There had been such a democratic upsetting of traditions and customs in the Service, owing to the obliteration of the original British Army, that it was quite refreshing to find that a remnant of Israel had been saved.

I paid two visits to the Divisional wing within a few days of each other, and on one occasion, on a baking July day, addressed a battalion of draftees who were about to be sent up to the front. They were a fine looking lot of men and knew their drill. Poor boys, they little knew what was in store for them in those last hundred days of the war.

Rumours were current now that the time for our great attack had come, so there were no more joy-rides for me to the pleasant fields and society of Loison. On my return on July 14th I found our Headquarters once again at Etrun, and our Division were holding their old trenches to the north and south of the Scarpe. Once more I had the pleasure of sleeping in Pudding trench and doing what I called "consolidating the line." I did a good deal of parish visiting in the trenches at this time. I felt that big changes might occur at any moment, and I wanted to be with the men in any ordeal through which they might have to pass. Very strange scenes come before me as I look back upon those days before our great attack. One night I stayed with the gallant Colonel of the Canadian Scottish at Tilloy. His headquarters were in No Man's Land, and the front trench ran in a semi-circle to the rear. The Colonel, having found a good German dug-out in the cellars of the ruined château, preferred to make his headquarters there. We did not know where the enemy's front line was, and our men were doing outpost duty in shell-holes further forward. They had to be visited every two hours when it was dark, to see that all was well. That night I asked the Colonel if I might go out with the patrol. He demurred at first, and then gave his consent only on condition that I should take off my white collar, and promise not to make any jokes with the men on duty for fear they should laugh and give away our position. I made my promise and started with the patrol officer and his runner. It was a curious sensation wandering off in the darkness as silently as possible, tripping now and then on bits of wire and almost slipping into the trenches. We came to the different shell-holes and whispered conversations were held. The sentries seemed surprised when I spoke to them, as they could not recognize me in the darkness. I whispered that I had promised the Colonel not to tell any funny stories for fear they should laugh, so I merely gave them the benediction, in return for which spiritual function I got a very warm handshake. To do outpost duty in a place like that must have been more interesting than pleasant, for at all times the sentries had to keep straining their eyes in the darkness to see if a patrol of the enemy was coming to surprise them. On our return we saw some shells falling to the right in the shadowy desolation of what was called Bully-beef Wood.

On another occasion, I was coming out near Feuchy along the railway triangle when the Germans dropped some gas shells in the cutting. Two of the men and I were talking together, and we had just time to dive into Battalion Headquarters and pull down the gas blankets. We put on our helmets, but not before we had got a dose of the poison. As I sat there with my throat burning, I was filled with alarm lest I should lose my voice and be unable in the future to recite my poems. It was hard enough, as it was, to keep my friends long enough to hear my verses, but I thought that if I had to spell them out in deaf-and-dumb language no one would ever have patience to wait till the end. However, after a few days my throat got better, and my friends were once again forced to lend me their ears.

The railway triangle was a well-known place, and any men who may have lived in some of the dug-outs along the banks are not likely to forget it. In the valley there was a large artificial lake in which I had some of the most pleasant swims I have ever enjoyed, although the waters were sometimes stirred up by the advent of a shell.

It was part of our strategy to let our men get the impression that we were going to stay in the trenches before Arras for a long time. We had several raiding parties with a view to finding out the position and strength of the enemy, and our C. C. S's were well equipped and looked as if they were going to remain there forever. Our Corps Headquarters, too, were not far from Etrun, and the concentration of Canadians in the neighborhood gave us the impression that we had found a more than temporary resting place. An American Chaplain was sent up to stay with me for a visit in order to see what conditions were like at the front. He was a Lutheran, although not of German extraction. I took him up to Arras one night, where we had dinner with the engineers, and afterwards saw the 10th Battalion start off for the trenches. He was much impressed with the spirit and appearance of the men. It was late when we got back to my quarters, and to my surprise on the next morning an order came through that the American Chaplain had to return immediately. Neither he nor I could understand it. I began to think he must have got into some scrape, as no explanation was given. The real reason came out afterwards.

On August 1st our Divison suddenly packed up and started once more for Le Cauroy. We knew now that big things were in store for us and that the Canadian Corps were going to attack. We heard rumours of the preparations the French and Americans had made in the South, and we felt that at last the Allies were going to get the initiative into their hands. Whither we were gonig, however, we did not know, but we all devoutly hoped that it would not be the Salient. The secret of our destination was kept most profoundly. We

270

were told that everything depended upon our holding our tongues and exciting as little curiosity as possible among the inhabitants. Once again, as before Vimy, but to even a greater extent, we felt the electric thrill which kindles the imagination of an army going into battle. The rapid move which the Canadian Corps now made was the most sporting thing we ever did, and it appealed strongly to the hearts of young men who were keen on games and had been inured to a hardy life in Canada. Swiftly and secretly the battalions entrained at various points and left for parts unknown. I went in my side-car to the machine-gun headquarters at Liencourt, and on the next day to the Curé's house at Le Cauroy. I found out from Headquarters that our Division was going south within a day or so, but that I was not to tell the men. The brigades were billeted in the neighboring villages, but were soon to move. I was only one day at Le Cauroy, and on the 3rd of August, after a rainy morning, started off in my sidecar for Hornoy, a little village not far from Amiens. We left Le Cauroy in the afternoon, and soon the sun came out making the freshly washed country more beautiful than ever. It was very interesting finding our way by the map, and as we neared our destination I met many friends in the other divisions who were stationed in the villages through which we passed. By the time we reached Hornoy, the sun had set. My billet was to be with the Curé. I went over to the neat white Presbytère which was approached by a large gate leading into the garden. The old man came to meet me at the door of his house, and put me through a lot of questions in what I thought was a needlessly gruff manner. I found out afterwards that he was very kind, and that his gruffness was only assumed. He gave me a room upstairs comfortably furnished, and invited me to come into his office whenever I pleased. The church, which could be entered from the garden, was in good order, and parts of it were very old. The day after we arrived at Hornoy was Sunday, August 4th. It was the fourth anniversary of our declaration of war, and I had hoped to hold a big service for the men. Unfortunately, we were all scattered and, as our hymn books did not turn up, having been confiscated as a reprisal by some of the crown and anchor men, my plans were frustrated. In the afternoon I went by sidecar to Amiens and found the city looking very different from its appearance on my last visit. The streets were absolutely deserted. Many of the houses had been damaged by shells. The Cathedral roof itself had been pierced in some places and the noble interior looked very dreary, the floor of the nave being covered with bits of broken stone and glass. It was sad to think that it might share the fate of Rheims. Some Canadians were wandering about the streets rather disconsolately. The empty city gave one a terrible sense of loneliness. On the following evening about midnight the 16th Battalion and the 3rd Battalion of Engineers passed through Hornoy in trains, going forward.

Our own orders to move came two days later, on August 7th, and I left for St. Feuchien. I went off in my side-car to the quaint old village. It is situated on the top of a low hill, and consists of a few streets and some large buildings standing in their own grounds. One of these was the country home of the Archbishop of Amiens, and this was to be our billet. I entered the grounds by a broken-down gate and drew up in front of a large brick building, one wing of which was a chapel and kept locked up. In front of the building was a well full of empty tins and other refuse. The interior of the place had once been quite fine, but was now absolutely filthy, having been used as billets. The billiard tables, however, could still be used. The room assigned to me was on the ground floor at the back. The dirt on the floor was thick, and a sofa and two red plush chairs were covered with dust. A bed in the corner did not look inviting, and through the broken windows innumerable swarms of blue-bottle flies came from the rubbish heaps in the yard. The weather was very hot and there was apparently no water for washing. I made an inspection of the building upstairs, but all the rooms had been assigned to different officers. The Archbishop's room was very large with a huge bed in it, but wore an air of soiled magnificence.

Everybody was in a great rush and, although I did not know when our attack was to take place, I felt that it might happen at any moment; and so, not worrying about my billet, I started off in my side-car to see General Thacker at Château Longeau. I found, as I passed through Boves and other villages, that the whole Canadian Corps was concentrated in the neighborhood. The dusty roads were crowded with lorries, tanks, whippets and limbers, besides numbers of men. When I got to Château Longeau I found, to my surprise, that the General had gone to Battle Headquarters in Genfelles Wood, and an officer whom I met on the road told me that zero hour was on the following morning. I determined therefore not to return to the archiepiscopal palace at St. Feuchien, but to go off to the attack. I returned to Boves, where, having washed and shaved, I had dinner in a damaged house with some officers of a light trench mortar battery, and after dinner started on my way to Gentelles Wood. It was a time of intense excitement. Less than a week ago we had been in the line at Arras, and now we were about to make our great attack at Amiens. The warm summer evening was well-advanced when I reached our Battle Headquarters behind the wood. All the staff officers were so busy that to ask one a question was like putting a spark to a powder magazine, so I kept out of their way and journeyed up the road to the barrier beyond which no vehicle was allowed to pass. I said good-bye to Lyons and then started off to find the trenches from which the 16th Battalion was going to lead the charge.

CHAPTER XXX

The Battle of Amiens

August 8th to 16th, 1918

IT was strange and exhilarating to go off on an expedition of that kind in the cool air and fading light of the evening. Something told us that at last the hour of victory was drawing near. The moving of the Corps had been so splendidly conducted and the preparation had been so secret that success seemed assured. This was an achievement which was completely different from all our past experience. The only question was, had we taken the Germans by surprise, or were they waiting with massed forces to resist our attack? As I left the outskirts of the wood behind me, and made my way over the green plain, now fading into the twilight, I passed a battalion of the 3rd Division manning a line of trenches. I had a talk with some of the men and told them that I had heard from a tank officer that nearly one thousand tanks were to be engaged in the attack on the following morning. Far over to the left, on a rise in the ground I saw the remains of a village, and was told that a mud road across the fields would lead me in the direction of the 1st Division front. I met as usual many men whom I knew, and finally some officers of the 15th Battalion in a dug-out. The light began to fade and I had difficulty in seeing far ahead of me, but the track at last brought me to a sunken road which turned to the right. Here on the hillside more men were waiting in dug-outs, and I was directed to a quarry, on the top of which I was to take a path that would lead me to a group of trees, where I should find the Headquarters of the 16th Battalion. When I got to the quarry I found many roads there, and whether it was that the information I had received was incorrect, or that I was more than usually stupid, I do not know. I wandered up and down for a long time, tripping over bits of wire and slipping into holes, before I was able to get to the top of the hill and look over in the direction of the German lines. At last I found a track which had evidently been used by men going up to the front. I went along it for a considerable distance and found myself on what appeared to be a plateau, but as far as I could see, no object stood out against the starry sky-line. Shells were falling in the fields to the left, and at different points on the eastern horizon the bright light of a German flare would tell us the position of the enemy's lines. I went on for some distance, straining my eyes in the darkness to see if I could discover any trees. I thought I had lost my way again. Suddenly the dim figure of a man approached, and when he came up to me, I found he belonged to one of the Imperial Battalions from whom we were taking over the line. He asked me the way to the quarry, and I was able to tell him. Then he gave me the direction I had to take to reach my destination. I resumed my walk along the narrow path and at last, to my great delight, I saw a black object in the distance. When I came up to it I found it was the group of trees for which I had been looking. The trees were growing out of a curious round hole in the ground. Here, a signaller of the 16th Battalion happened to turn up and acted as my guide. He led me down a path to the bottom of the hole where were several dugouts. In one of these I found more men of the Battalion. They were intensely keen over the prospect of a great victory on the morrow. I was told that the battalion and the companies which were going over in the first wave were in advanced trenches to the left. So, after bidding the men goodbye and good luck, I started off. At last I reached the trench, and getting down into it found the Headquarters of the Battalion had arrived there not long before. On asking where the Colonel was, I was taken to a place where a piece of canvas hung down the side of the trench. When this was lifted, I looked down into a little hole in the ground and there saw the C.O., the Adjutant and another officer studying a map by the light of a candle. The place was so tiny that I had to crawl in backwards, and finding that there was no room for a visitor, I soon took my departure. The Colonel ordered me to stay in the trench, but I had made up my mind to go forward and see the companies which were going over in the first wave. They lay along the side of a road some distance down the slope in front of us. In making my way there I passed a trench where the 5th Battalion was waiting to follow up the advance. A German machine-gun was playing freely upon the spot, but no one got hit. When I came to the advanced companies of the 16th Battalion, I passed along their line and gave them my blessing. It was splendid to meet and shake hands with those gallant lads, so soon to make the attack. They were in high spirits in spite of the seriousness of their enterprise.

The barrage was to start at 4.20, so I left them about 4.10 to go back to Battalion Headquarters in the trench, as I intended to follow up the advance with the stretcher-bearers. On my way back I met the Colonel, his orderly, and his piper, who a few minutes later was killed in the attack. I shook hands with them, and the Colonel said, "Now, Canon, if anything happens to me don't make any fuss over me; just say a few words over me in a shell-hole." I said, "You will come out all right, Colonel, there will be no shell-hole for you." Then, as my senior officer, he ordered me back to the trench. I told him I would go over the top with him if he wanted me to do so, but he would not hear of it. When I got to the trenches only a few minutes remained till the barrage was to start. I climbed up on the parapet and waited, looking off into the darkness. It was a wonderful moment. When the German flarelights went up we could see that there was a wood on the other side of the valley in front of us, and its outline began to grow more distinct against the grey of the morning sky. I could see to right and left a great stretch of country sloping gradually into the darkness. Shells still fell behind our lines at intervals. Our own guns were perfectly silent. What did the enemy's quietness portend? Were the Germans aware of our contemplated assault? Were they lying in full strength like a crouching lion ready to burst upon us in fury at the first warning of our approach? Had all our precautions been in vain? Or were we on the eve of a victory which was going to shatter the iron dominion of the feudal monster? This was one of those magnificent moments in the war which filled the soul with a strange and wild delight. For months we had been preparing for this event, and now it was upon us. The sky was growing lighter, and the constellation of the Pleiades was beginning to fade in the sky above the outline of the distant trees. I looked at my watch. Nearer and nearer the hands crept to zero hour, but they move slowly at such times. Then at 4.20 the long barrage burst in all its fury. The hissing rain of shells through the air on a twenty mile front made a continuous accompaniment to the savage roar of the thousands of guns along the line. Those guns sent their wild music round the globe, and sounded that note of victory which only ceased when the bells of the churches in all the civilized world rang out their joyful peals at the signing of the Armistice.

Up went the German rockets and coloured lights calling for

help, and ever and anon a red glow in the sky told us that we had blown up an ammunition dump. The noise was earth-shaking, and was even more exhilarating than that of the barrage at Vimy. I was so carried away by my feelings that I could not help shouting out, "Glory be to God for this barrage!" The German reply came, but, to our delight, it was feeble, and we knew we had taken them by surprise and the day was ours.

A strange sound behind us made us look around, and we saw the advancing tanks creeping down the slope like huge grey beetles. Our men were just in time to divert the course of one which threatened to cut our telephone wires. Then the 5th Battalion got out of their trenches, and the stretcher-bearers and I went off with them down the slope. The wood through which the German lines ran was called Hangard Wood and lay on the opposite side of the valley. Here and there lying in the ripe grain which covered the fields were bodies of the wounded and dead of the 13th and 16th Battalions. The stretcher-bearers set to work to carry off those who had been hit. A sergeant followed me and we skirted the wood looking for wounded, while he was able to become possessor of a machine-gun and several German revolvers. The wheat had been trampled down by the men in their charge, but was still high enough in places to conceal a prostrate form. By this time the attack had passed through the wood and the enemy were running before it. The German artillery now concentrated their fire on the valley, which soon, in the still morning air, became thick with smoke. It was impossible to see more than a few yards in front of one. We heard the crash of shells around us, but could not see where they burst. The sun had not risen and we soon lost our way in the mist. We could not tell from the direction of the sound which was the German barrage and which was ours.

I was going on ahead when I came to a large shell-hole that had been made in some previous battle. At the bottom of it lay three apparently dead Huns. I was looking down at them wondering how they had been killed, as they were not messed about. I thought that they must have died of shell-shock, until one of them moved his hand. At once I shouted, "Kamarad", and to my intense amusement the three men lying on their backs put up their hands and said, "Kamarad! mercy! mercy!" It was most humorous to think that three human beings should appeal to me to spare their lives. I told them in my best French to get up and follow me, and I called out to the sergeant, "Sergeant, I have got three prisoners." My desire to take a prisoner had been a standing joke among our men. Whenever they were going into action I used to offer them $25.00 to bring out a little German whom I might capture all by myself. I used to tell them not to bring out a big one, as it might look boastful for a chaplain. Here were three ready to hand for which I had to pay nothing. We moved on through the smoke, a most comical procession. The sergeant went ahead and I brought up the rear. Between us went the three terror-stricken prisoners, crouching every now and then when shells fell near us. At last we stumbled on a company of the 2nd Battalion coming forward, and I called out to them, "Boys, I got seventy-five dollars worth of Huns in one shell-hole." Our gallant Canadians at once took the three unfortunate men, who looked as if they expected to have their throats cut, and having relieved them of the contents of their pockets and removed their buttons and shoulder-straps, gave me one of the latter as a souvenir.

When the prisoners were disposed of and sent back with others under escort, I started forward again and seeing a tank coming down the hill got on it and so went back into the battle. We passed quite easily over some wide trenches, then when the machine came to a stop I got off and made my way to the end of the valley and climbed to the higher ground beyond. There I found myself in a wide expanse of country covered by yellow grain and rolling off in hills to the distance. Here and there I met wounded men walking back, and many German prisoners. In the fields in different directions I could see rifles stuck, bayonet downwards, in the ground, which showed that there lay wounded men. I found that these were chiefly Germans, and all of them had received hideous wounds and were clamouring for water. Poor men, I was sorry for them, for I knew it would be long before they could be carried out or receive medical attention, owing to the rapidity of our advance. I made my way to each in turn and gave him a drink from some of the water bottles which I carried round my belt. I think all the Germans I saw that morning were dying, having been wounded in the stomach. After attending, as far as it was possible, to their bodily needs, I endeavoured to minister to their spiritual. As they happened to be Roman Catholics, I took off the crucifix which I wore round my neck and gave it to them. They would put up their trembling hands and clasp it lovingly, and kiss it, while I began the Lord's Prayer in German. This happened many times that day. One man who had a hideous wound in the abdomen was most grateful, and when he handed me back the crucifix he took my hand and kissed it. It was strange to think that an hour before, had we met, we should have been deadly enemies. At a cross-road further on the Germans must have concentrated their fire when our men advanced, for many dead and wounded were lying about.

The sun was now high in the heavens and it became very hot, but the autumn fields looked beautiful, and, as there were no hedges or fences, the low rolling hills gave one the sense of great expanse, and were an ideal ground for a battle on a large scale. While I was looking after the wounded I heard the cheering of the 16th Battalion who had reached their objective and were settling down to rest and to have some food. I made my way to them and found the Colonel in high glee over what his men had done. It had been a splendid routing of the enemy. The Battalions of the 1st and 2nd Brigades followed up the attack and were now moving forward, so I followed after them. It was a delightful feeling to be walking through the golden harvest fields with the blue sky overhead, and to know that we were advancing into the enemy's land. It seemed as if by our own labours we had suddenly become possessed of a vast property and that everything we found was lawfully ours. It is no doubt that feeling which fills men with the desire to loot in a conquered country.

I had a magnificent view from the hill of the British Cavalry going into action. Thousands of little horses in the distance on the vast plain were galloping in a long line across the yellow fields, which reminded one of the great battles of old, when mounted men, and not machine-guns and gas-shells, were the determining factor. The store of water that I had brought with me was now exhausted, but I was able to get a fresh supply from the waterbottle of a dead man. The road that leads from Gentelles to Caix winds through the valley to the right of the line of our attack and follows a little stream. It is very narrow, and on that day was so crowded with cavalry, ambulances and artillery moving forward that every now and then it would become blocked. In a mill, which the Germans had used partly as artillery headquarters and partly as a depot for military stores, our men found a quantity of blankets, coats and other useful articles. Our doctors established an aid-post in the out-buildings, and made use of the materials which the enemy had left behind in his flight. A section of our machine-gunners was resting there, and it was a great refreshment to stop for a while and have a good clean-up and a shave with a borrowed razor. We were so parched with thirst that we drank out of the stream, in spite of the fact that many shells had fallen into it. Our final objective was still some miles away, so I started up the road, following after the 1st Brigade.

The Germans, finding the game was up, had left many guns behind them and blown up a large quantity of ammunition. One great heap of it lay beside the river. Very pretty hamlets lay along the valley; we passed one called Ignacourt, where there was a damaged church. We afterwards established an ambulance there. I was very tired with my long walk, not having had any sleep the night before, so was glad to get a lift on an ambulance and go forward in the afternoon to the village of Caix, which was the final objective of the 2nd Brigade. One of our ambulances had taken over a building in the Square, but was shelled out of it that night. The 10th Battalion had gone forward and taken possession of trenches beyond the village. I went out to them and there found the men in high spirits over the way the battle had gone. The old red patch Division had advanced 14,000 yards, and so had beaten the record of any division, British or enemy, during the War. It was now late in the afternoon and no further attack that day was contemplated. Before us on a slight rise in the ground lay the village of Rosières, through which the road ran parallel to the trenches which we held. Between us and the village was a slight dip in the ground, and with glasses we could see lorries full of fresh German troops, amid clouds of dust, making their way to a point in the village. There they would stop and the men would get out and hurry down the fields into the trenches. It looked as if they were going to make a counter-attack. The situation was very disquieting. I was told by one of the sergeants in our front line that we were in need of fresh ammunition, and he asked me if I would let the Colonel know. I passed through the trenches on my return and told the men how glorious it was to think that we had pushed the Germans back and were now so many miles from where we had started. I went back to Battalion Headquarters and found that they were in a cottage on the eastern extremity of the village. Across the road was a cavalry observation-post, where some officers were watching Rosières and the arrival of German troops. Luckily for us the Germans had no guns to turn upon us, although the village of Caix was shelled constantly all night. Later on, some batteries of the Royal Horse Artillery and our field guns, which had come up, sealed the fate of the Germans and prevented a counter-attack. A glorious sunset over the newly conquered territory made a fitting close to a day of great deeds and high significance. When darkness fell and the stars looked out of the quiet sky, I said good-night to my cavalry friends, whose billets were down in a hollow to the right, and started off to find some place to sleep.

The cellars of the cottage occupied by the Colonel were crowded, so I went to the village and seeing some men entering a gateway followed them. It was the courtyard of a large building, presumably a brewery. The runners of the battalion had found a deep cellar where they had taken up their abode. I asked if I might sleep with them for the night. The cellar was not particularly inviting, but it was well below the ground and vaulted in brick. The floor was simply earth and very damp. Two candles were burning in a box where a corporal was making out the ration-list for the men. I got two empty sandbags to put on the floor to keep me from getting rheumatism, and lying on them and using my steel helmet as a pillow I prepared to sleep. The runners, except those on duty, did the same. Our feet met in the centre of the room and our bodies branched off like the spokes of a wheel. When anyone turned and put his feet on one side we all had to turn and put our feet in the same direction. We heard a good many shells bursting in the Square that night, but we were safe and comparatively comfortable. Before I got to sleep, I watched with great admiration the two young non-coms who were sitting at the table arranging and discussing in a low tone the duties of the various men for the following day. The two lads could not have been more than twenty years of age, but their sense of responsibility and justice was well-developed. I thought what a fine thing it was that men were being trained like that to become useful citizens of Canada. We were up early in the morning and I made my way to Battalion Headquarters, where I heard that there was to be another attack in the forenoon.

We were now to change places with the 2nd Division. They were to shift from our right flank to our left and take over the attack on Rosières while we advanced towards Warvillers. From the cavalry observation-post, I could see with a glass the 5th Battalion going up to the front in single file along a hedge. I had breakfast with the 7th Battalion officers in their dugout by the roadside near the cavalry billets, and then started off to join the 8th Battalion which was going to attack that morning. Machine-guns from Rosières were playing on the road near the end of the wood. I determined therefore not to go round the wood but through it and so reached the other side in safety. I was sitting on a fallen tree eating some lunch and wondering whether I should be able to get up in time for the attack, when, to my great joy, over the hill to my right, I saw some troops approaching in extended order. Hardly had they appeared on the crest when the Germans at Rosières opened fire upon them and shells fell on the hill. The men kept very steady and nobody, as far as I could see, was hit. When they got down to the wood I went forward and spoke to them and found they were the 22nd Battalion, and I met several Quebecers whom I knew.

I saw the Battalion go off in the direction of Rosières and I renewed my journey to our own line. I passed the 24th Battalion who were going up on the left of the 22nd, and they told me that the 2nd Brigade were on their right. There were many trenches along the way which the Germans had abandoned on the previous day. I passed a poor horse which was badly wounded and still alive. It was attached to a broken German cart. I got one of our men to shoot the animal, and went on till I came to a railway in the hollow and followed it. There were many wooden buildings here and there which had been built by the Germans. These structures had been badly knocked about by shrapnel, and the litter of articles within showed how rapid the German flight had been. At a little distance on the east side of the track, there was a green wood, which was called, as I afterwards found out, Beaufort or Hatchet Wood. Every now and then as I walked, little puffs of dust would rise from the road in front of me, showing that machine-gun bullets were falling about. A cavalry patrol of three men, returning down the track from the direction of the wood, came towards me, and, taking me for a combatant officer, the corporal saluted and said, "That wood is very heavily held by machine-guns, Sir, we have just made a reconnaissance." "That's all right," I said, "I do not intend to take it just yet." I was going up the track, wondering where I had got to, when I saw a young officer of the 8th Battalion, followed by his men, coming towards me. I went to him and told him that I had heard the wood was very heavily held by machine-guns. He said he knew it and was going to attack from the side, so I went with them and, as they lay on the ground and got their Lewis guns in position, I pronounced the benediction over them and then continued my journey up the railroad. On the west side of the track at the top of the bank was a hedge. Here I found the 14th Battalion waiting to follow up the 8th. A young officer of the latter battalion was lying on the ground dying. He dictated a farewell letter to his wife, which I afterwards gave to the Adjutant. On the slope of ground down which the 8th had charged towards the railway I saw many bodies of dead and wounded men, so I went up to them to see what I could do. Several were dying, and I found one poor fellow who had never been baptised; so I took some water from my bottle and baptised him as he lay there. They would be carried off when the stretcher-bearers could begin their work.

While I was attending to the wounded, I looked towards the wood at the other side of the track. I was on a higher level, and so had a view of the open country beyond, and there, to my astonishment, I saw the Germans leaving their ambush and running away. I hurried down the hill to the hedge and shouted out to the 14th Battalion that the Germans were running away, and an officer came up to make sure. Then orders were given to the men to charge and they crossed the track and took possession of the wood. As soon as I had seen the wounded carried off I followed after the troops, and there once more had the joy of advancing over newly-won territory.

At a farmhouse a number of our men were gathered for a temporary rest, and there I learned that the colonel of the 8th Battalion and a large number of officers and men had been killed that morning. The battalion had to charge down the hill in the face of heavy machine-gun fire. Some tanks were standing by the farm and one of the officers offered to take me with him in the machine, but as it was to go into the 2nd Divisional area I had to decline the invitation and follow up our men on foot. I passed a number of German wounded. One of them, a young lad, was terribly alarmed when he saw me approaching, thinking I was going to murder him. He held up his hands and shouted, "Kamarad!" I think the

Germans had heard wild stories of the ferocity of Canadians. The boy then began to implore me to send him to an ambulance. He was wounded in the leg, and had bound up his wounds very neatly and skilfully. I tried to make him understand that the stretcher-bearers would come up in time, and I stuck his rifle in the ground with his helmet on the top of it, as a signal to the bearer party.

Before me at the end of the road, I saw amid trees the village of Warvillers. Many men were going towards it from all directions; and I saw our artillery brigades taking up battery positions to the left. I met two men of the 5th Battalion and we started off to the village together. The place was now in our hands, as the Germans had evacuated it some hours before. The houses were quite intact and offered prospects of pleasant billets. My companions and I, finding it was quite late in the afternoon, determined to go and have our meal in a garden near the Château. We sat down on the grass and opened our bully-beef tins, and seeing onions growing in the garden thought it would be a good thing to have that savoury vegetable as a relish. It added to the enjoyment of our simple meal to think that we were eating something which the Germans had intended for themselves. We managed to get some fresh water too from a well nearby, which looked quite clean. On the other side of a wall we could see the roof of the Château. One of the men thought he would like to go and explore and find out who was there. He came back a few minutes afterwards and said it was full of Germans. So, taking their rifles, the two men went off to attack it, thinking they had found a stronghold of the enemy. I was just having a smoke after my meal when the lads came back and said that the Germans whom they had seen were our prisoners and that the Château had been taken over by us as a dressing station. We made our way to it and found that it was a very beautiful place situated in lovely grounds. A card on a door upstairs bore the inscription, "His Excellency General," and then followed a German name. The place had been the headquarters of some enemy corps or division on the previous day. At the back of the Château was a very strong concrete dug-out divided off into rooms, which were soon filled by our officers and men. All that night the wounded were being brought to the Château, and German prisoners also found their way there. Nobody was paying much attention to the latter, and, thinking it was unwise to let them wander about, and perhaps go back to their lines with information about our location, with the permission of the C. O. of the ambulance, who was up to his eyes in work, I had them all put into one large room over which I placed a guard. They were sent back to the corps cage in the morning. The Germans evidently expected that we would use the Château because they dropped some heavy shells in the garden during the night, and we had to get the wounded down in to the cellars in quick time.

I had about three hours sleep that night, and in the morning I determined to follow up our men of the 1st Brigade who had now established themselves at a village ahead of us called Rouvroy. As I was starting off, a signaller came up to me and told me he had captured a stray horse with a saddle on it and that he would lend it to me to take me to my destination. I mounted the animal and went down the avenue in great pride and comfort, but after I got into the road a man came up and stopped me and told me, to my horror, that I was riding his horse which he had lost the night before. It requires great strength of mind and self-mastery to give up a mount to a pedestrian when you are once in the saddle. But the war had not entirely extinguished the light of conscience in my soul, so, tired as I was, I dismounted and gave up the steed. But as I saw the man ride back to the Château I began to wonder within myself whether he was the real owner or not. One thief does not like to be out-witted by another. However, there was nothing to do now but to go straight ahead. The road before me led directly to Rouvroy. Some German planes were hovering overhead, and in the fields to my left our artillery were going into action. As shells were dropping on the road I took a short cut over the fields. Here I found some of our machine-gunners, and the body of a poor fellow who had just been killed. I got to the village of Rouvroy about noon and made my way to a dug-out under the main road, where the colonel and some of the officers of the 3rd Battalion were having lunch. They gave me a cup of tea, but I told them I had taken my food on the journey, so did not want anything to eat. They looked much relieved at this, because rations were short. Their chaplain was there and gave me a warm reception. I was feeling rather used up, so lay down on a wire mattress and had an hour's sleep. When lunch was over the chaplain and I went to see the sights of the town. The ruined church was being used for a dressing station and it seemed to me it was rather a dangerous place, as the Germans would be likely to shell it. We found an old bookshop which was filled with German literature and writing paper, some of which proved very useful.

We had a good rest in a dugout, but I felt so seedy that I told him, if he heard that I had gone out of the line, not to think it was because I was suffering from "cold feet". We went back to the village, and there we found shells dropping in the main street not far from the church. In fact, one came so close that we had to dive into a cellar and wait till the "straffing" was over. Then I bid my companion good-bye and started off over the fields back to Warvillers. By this time I felt so unwell that it was hard to resist the temptation to crawl into some little hole in which I might die quietly. However, with my usual luck, I found a motor car waiting near the road for an air-officer who had gone off on a tour of inspection and was expected to return soon. The driver said I could get in and rest. When the officer came back he kindly consented to give me a ride to my Divisional Headquarters. We did not know where they were and I landed in the wrong place, but finally with the assistance of another car I made my way to Beaufort. There I found our Division had established themselves in huts and dugouts at the back of an ancient château. With great difficulty I made my way over to General Thacker's mess and asked for some dinner.

During the meal, the General sent off his A.D.C. on a message, and he soon returned with no less a person than the A.D.M.S., who, to my dismay, proceeded to feel my pulse and put a clinical thermometer in my mouth. My temperature being $103\frac{1}{2}$, he ordered me at once to go off to a rest camp, under threat of all sorts of penalties if I did not. I lay on the floor of his office till three in the morning, when an ambulance arrived and took me off to some place in a field, where they were collecting casualties. From thence I was despatched to the large asylum at Amiens which was operated by an Imperial C.C.S. The major who examined me ordered me to go to the Base by the next train, as they had no time to attend to cases of influenza. For a while I was left on the stretcher in a ward among wounded heroes. I felt myself out of place, but could do nothing to mend matters. Two sisters came over to me, and apparently took great interest in me till one of them looked at the tag which was pinned on my shoulder. With a look of disgust she turned and said to her companion, "He isn't wounded at all, he has only got the 'flu'". At once they lost all interest in me, and went off leaving me to my fate. Stung by this humiliation, I called two orderlies and asked them to carry me out into the garden and hide me under the bushes. This they did, and there I found many friends who had been wounded lying about the place. My batman had come with me and had brought my kit, so a box of good cigars which I handed round was most acceptable to the poor chaps who were waiting to be sent off. By a stroke of good luck, an accident on the railway prevented my being evacuated that evening. I knew that if they once got me down to the Base my war days would be over.

On the following morning, feeling better, I got up, shaved, put on my best tunic, and, with a cigar in my mouth, wandered into the reception room, where I found the major who had ordered me off on the previous day. Puffing the smoke in front of my face to conceal my paleness, I asked him when he was going to send me down to the Base. He looked a little surprised at finding me recovered, and then said, "Well, Padré, I think I will let you go back to your lines after all." It was a great relief to me. The chaplain of the hospital very kindly took me in charge and allowed me to spend the night in his room. The next day I got a ride in a Canadian ambulance and made my way back to Beaufort. There, to my horror, I found that the Division, thinking they had got rid of me for good, had appointed another padré in my place. Through the glass door of my room, I could see him giving instructions to the chaplain of the artillery. I felt like Enoch Arden, but I had not Enoch's unselfishness so, throwing the door wide open, I strode into the room, and to the ill-concealed consternation of both my friends who had looked upon me in a military sense as dead, informed them that I had come back to take over my duties. Of course, everyone said they were glad to see me, except General Thacker, who remarked dryly that my return had upset all the cherished plans of well-ordered minds. The A.D.M.S. had told them that he had thought I was in for an attack of pneumonia. It was really a very amusing situation, but I was determined to avoid the Base, especially now that we felt the great and glorious end of our long campaign was coming nearer every day.

CHAPTER XXXI.

WE RETURN TO ARRAS

August, 1918

ON Friday the 16th of August our Division left Beaufort and moved back to billets at Le Quesnel. Here there was a good sized château which was at once used for office purposes. The General and his staff made their billets in a deep cave which was entered from the road. It was of considerable extent, lit by electric light, and rooms opened out on both sides of the central passage. I had one assigned to me, but as I did not feel well enough to stand the dampness I gave it to the clerks of the A.D.M.S., and made my home with the veterinary officer in the cellar of the school-house which stood beside the church. The latter, which had been used by the Germans as a C.C.S., was a modern building and of good proportions. The spire had been used as an observation-post. One or two shells had hit the building and the interior, though still intact, was in great disorder. The altar ornaments, vestments, and prayer books were thrown about in confusion. The school-house where I was lodged must have been also the Curé's residence. A good-sized room downstairs served as a chapel for my Sunday services. The cellar, where the A. D. V. S. and I slept was quite comfortable, though by no means shell-proof. As the only alternative abode was the cave, he and I, deciding we would rather die of a shell than of rheumatism, chose the cellar. The Corps ambulances were all together in a valley not far away, and in trenches to the east, near the cemetery where the 8th Battalion officers and men had been buried, there were some reserves of the 3rd Brigade.

Things were quiet now in the front line, so I determined to make a trip to Albert to see my son's grave. It was a long and dusty journey and the roads were rough. We passed back through the district over which we had advanced, and saw everywhere gruesome traces of the fighting. When we came to Albert, however, we found it was still in the possession of the enemy. The Americans were holding the line, and an American sentry stopped us at a barrier in the road and said that no motor-cycles were allowed to go any further in that direction. It was strange to hear the American accent again, and I told the lad that we were Canadians. "Well", he said, with a drawl, "that's good enough for me." We shook hands and had a short talk about the peaceful continent that lay across the ocean. There was nothing for us to do then but to return.

On the following Sunday, the Germans having evacuated Albert a day and a half before, I once more paid a visit to the old town. I left my side-car on the outskirts of the place and was taken by Mr. Bean, the Australian War Correspondent, into his car. He was going up to take some photographs. The day was intensely hot, and the dust of the now ruined town was literally ankle-deep and so finely powdered that it splattered when one walked as though it had been water. I saw the ruins of the school-house which our ambulances had used, and noticed that the image of the Virgin had been knocked down from the tower of the Cathedral. I passed the house where our Headquarters had been. The building was still standing but the front wall had gone, leaving the interior exposed. I made my way up the Bapaume road to Tara Hill, and there to my great delight I found the little cemetery still intact. Shells had fallen in it and some of the crosses had been broken, but the place had been wonderfully preserved. A battery on one side of it had just ceased firing and was to advance on the following day. While I was putting up some of the crosses that had fallen, Mr. Bean came up in his car and kindly took a photograph of my son's grave. He also took a photograph of the large Australian cross which stands at one corner of the cemetery. Tara Hill had been for six months between the German front and reserve lines, and I never expected that any trace of the cemetery would have been found. I shall probably never see the place again, but it stands out in my memory now as clear and distinct as though once more I stood above the dusty road and saw before me the rows of little crosses, and behind them the waste land battered by war and burnt beneath the hot August sun. Over that very ground my son and I had ridden together, and within a stone's throw from it two years before we had said good-bye to one another for the last time.

Our Division had now come out of the line and were hurrying north. On August 26th Lyons and I started off in the car, and after a tedious and dusty journey, enlivened by several break-downs,

19

arrived in Arras very late at night and found a billet with the Engineers in the Place de la Croix. Once more our men were scattered about the old city and its environs as if we had never left it. Our Battle Headquarters were in the forward area and rear Headquarters in a large house in Rue du Pasteur. It was a picturesque abode. The building itself was modern, but it was erected on what had been an old Augustinian Monastery of the 11th century. Underneath the house there was a large vaulted hall with pillars in it which reminded one of the cloisters of Westminister Abbey. It was below the level of the ground and was lit by narrow windows opening on the street. It was a most interesting place and had been decorated with heraldic designs painted on canvas shields by a British Division that had once made its headquarters there. We used the hall as our mess and from it passages led to several vault-like chambers and to cellars at the back, one of which was my bedroom. A flight of steps led down to stone chambers below these and then down a long sloping passage to a broken wall which barred the entrance into the mysterious caves beneath the city. The exhalations which came up to my bedroom from these subterranean passages were not as fresh or wholesome as one could have wished, but, as it was a choice between foul air and running the chance of being shelled, I naturally chose the former.

We moved into this billet in the evening, and early the following morning I was lying awake, thinking of all the strange places I had lived in during the war, when close by I heard a fearful crash. I waited for a moment, and then, hearing the sound of voices calling for help, I rushed up in my pyjamas and found that a huge shell had struck a house three doors away, crushing it in and killing and wounding some of our Headquarters staff. Though Arras was then continually being shelled, some of the inhabitants remained. Opposite our house was a convent, and in cellars below the ground several nuns lived all through the war. They absolutely refused to leave their home in spite of the fact that the upper part of the building had been ruined by shells. Our nearness to the railway station, which was a favourite target for the German guns, made our home always a precarious one.

One day the Paymaster was going into our Headquarters, when a shell burst in the Square and some fragments landed in our street taking off the fingers of his right hand. I was away at the time, but when I returned in the evening the signallers showed me a lonely forefinger resting on a window sill. They had reverently preserved it, as it was the finger which used to count out five-franc notes to them when they were going on leave.

Our Corps dressing-station was in the big Asylum in Arras. The nuns still occupied part of the building. The Mother Superior was a fine old lady, intensely loyal to France and very kind to all of us. When the Germans occupied Arras in the beginning of the war, the Crown Prince paid an official visit to the Asylum, and, when leaving, congratulated the Mother Superior on her management of the institution. She took his praises with becoming dignity, but when he held out his hand to her she excused herself from taking it and put hers behind her back.

The dressing-station was excellently run and the system carried out was perfect. The wounded were brought in, attended to, and sent off to the C. C. S. with the least possible delay. The dead were buried in the large military cemetery near the Dainville road where rest the bodies of many noble comrades, both British and Canadian. A ward was set apart for wounded Germans and it was looked after by their own doctors and orderlies.

Meanwhile our Division was preparing for the great attack upon the Drocourt-Quéant line. The 2nd Division were in the trenches and had taken Monchy. We were to relieve them and push on to the Canal du Nord and, if possible, beyond it. Movements were now very rapid. All the staff were kept intensely busy. The old days of St. Jans Cappel and Ploegsteert, with their quiet country life, seemed very far away. This was real war, and we were advancing daily. We heard too of the victories of the French and Americans to the South. It was glorious to think that after the bitter experience of the previous March the tables had been turned, and we had got the initiative once more. Our Battle Headquarters, where the General and his staff were, lay beyond Neuville Vitasse. They were in a deep, wide trench, on each side of which were dugouts and little huts well sandbagged. Over the top was spread a quantity of camouflage netting, so that the place was invisible to German aeroplanes. The country round about was cut up by trenches, and in many of these our battalions were stationed. All the villages in the neighbourhood were hopeless ruins. I tried to get a billet in the forward area, as Arras was so far back, but every available place was crowded and it was so difficult to get up rations that nobody was anxious to have me.

CHAPTER XXXII.

The Smashing of the Drocourt-Queant Line

September 2nd, 1918.

ON Saturday, August 31st, I paid a visit to our Battle Headquarters, and the General asked me to have a Celebration of the Holy Communion there the next morning at eight. I knew that the attack was almost due, so I prepared for it and took my iron rations with me. We had the Communion Service in a tent at the General's Headquarters. There were only three present, but the General was one of them. I had breakfast in a quaint little hut in the side of the trench, and then started off to the forward area. The great stretch of country was burnt dry by the summer heat and the roads were broken up and dusty. I was taken by car to the Headquarters of the 2nd Brigade which were in a trench, and from thence I started on foot to Cherisy. Here the 8th Battalion were quartered, the 5th being in the line. Zero hour, I was told, was early the next morning. The 2nd and 3rd Brigades were to make the attack. The 5th Battalion was to have advanced that day and taken possession of a certain trench which was to be the jumping off line on the following morning. I heard that they had had a hard time. They had driven out the Germans, but had been seriously counter-attacked and had lost a large number of men. I determined therefore to go out and take them some cigarettes and biscuits which the Y. M. C. A. generously provided. I started off in the afternoon to go to the front line, wherever it might be. I went down the road from Cherisy past the chalk-pit, where we had a little cemetery, and then turning into the fields on the left walked in the direction in which I was told the 5th Battalion lay. It was a long, hot journey, and as I had not quite recovered from my attack of influenza I found it very fatiguing. On all sides I saw gruesome traces of the recent fighting. I came across the body of a young artillery officer of the 2nd Division, but, as all his papers had been taken away, I could not discover his name. My way passed through the remains of what had been an enemy camp. There were a number of well-built huts there, containing much German war-material, but they had been damaged by our shells. The Germans had evidently been obliged to get out of the place as quickly as possible. I was just leaving the camp when I met several of our men bringing up a number of prisoners. While we were talking, some shells fell, and we all had to dive into two trenches. The Huns took one; we Canadians took the other. We had no desire, in case a shell landed in our midst to have our bits mingled with those of the Germans. When the "straffing" was over, the others went back, and I continued my way to the front. It must have been about six or seven o'clock when I arrived at the 5th Battalion Headquarters, which were in a deep German dugout. The Colonel was absent at a conference, so the Adjutant was in command. I told him that I had come provided with cigarettes and other comforts for the men, and asked him to give me a runner to take me to the front line. He absolutely refused to do anything of the kind, as he told me he did not know where it was himself. The situation was most obscure. Our men had attacked and had been driven back and then they had attacked again, but he thought they were now in shell holes and would be hard to find. In fact, he was most anxious about the condition of affairs and was hoping the Colonel would soon return. I asked him if he would like me to spend the night there. He said he would, so I determined to settle down and wait for an opportunity of getting up to the men.

I went over to a trench a little way off, passing two dead Germans as I did so, and saw the little white flag with the red cross on it which showed that a dugout there was used as the regimental aid post. I went down into the place, which had two openings, and found the M.O. and his staff and a number of machine-gunners. Being Sunday, I told them that I would have service for them. We all sat on the floor of the long dugout. Two or three candles gave us all the light we had, and the cigarettes which I had brought with me were soon turned into smoke. In the meantime a young stretcher-bearer, unknown to me, made a cup of tea and brought that and some buttered toast for my supper. When I had finished and we were just going to begin the service, a voice suddenly shouted down the steps in excited tones. "We've all got to retreat; the Germans are coming." At once a corporal shouted up to him, "Shut up, none of that talk out here." Of course, I had not said a word to any of the men about the condition of our front line, but remembering what the Adjutant had told me about it, I thought now that there might be some reason for the alarm. As I have said on a former occasion, I had a great objection to being bombed in a dugout, so I said to the men, "Well, boys, perhaps we had better take it seriously and go up and see what the matter is." We climbed up to the trench, and there on looking over the parapet we saw an exciting scene. It was not yet dark, and in the twilight we could see objects at a certain distance, but it was just light enough and dark enough to confuse one's vision. Along the line to the right of our front trenches, rockets and S. O. S. signals were going up, showing that the Germans were attacking. Our reserve battalions were far back at Cherisy, and our artillery had not yet come up. At any rate, somewhere in the glimmering darkness in front of us the Germans were advancing. They actually did get between us and our front line. The machine-gunners at once went to their posts, and the M. O. wanted orders as to what he and his staff were to do. I went back down the trenches past the dead Germans to Battalion Headquarters, and asked the Adjutant what orders he had for the M. O. He said we were all to congregate at Headquarters; so I went back and gave the message. I remember looking over the waste of ground and wondering if I could see the Germans. For a time it was really very exciting, especially for me, because I did not know exactly what I should do if the Germans came. I could not fight, nor could I run away, and to fold one's arms and be taken captive seemed too idiotic. All the time I kept saying to myself, "I am an old fool to be out here." Still, we got as much fun out of the situation as we could, and, to our intense relief, the arrival of some of our shells and the sudden appearance of a Highland Battalion of the 4th Division on our left, frightened the Germans and they retired, leaving us to settle down once more in our trench home.

On the return of the Colonel, we learned that, on account of the heavy losses which the 5th Battalion had suffered that day, the 7th Battalion would attack on the following morning. Later on in the evening, I saw some machine-gunners coming up, who told us that they had left some wounded and a dead man in a trench near the road. I determined to go back and see them. The trench was very crowded, and as it was dark it was hard to find one's way. I nearly stepped on a man who appeared to be sleeping, leaning against the parapet. I said to one of the men, "Is this a sleeping hero?" "No, Sir," he replied, "It's a Hun stiff." When I got down to the road, I met two men and we hunted for the place where the wounded had been left, but found they had been carried off to Cherisy. So I started back again for Battalion Headquarters, and as numbers of men were going forward I had no difficulty in finding it.

The dug-out was now absolutely crowded. Every available space, including the steps down from the opening, was filled with men. I managed to secure a little shelf in the small hours of the morning, and had two or three hours sleep. The atmosphere was so thick that I think we were all overcome by it and sank into profound slumber. At last, one of the men suddenly woke up and said to me, "It's ten minutes to five, Sir." The barrage was going to start at five. As far as I could see, everyone in the dug-out but ourselves, was sound asleep. I climbed up the steps, waking the men on them and telling them that the barrage would start in ten minutes. The sentries in the trench said that the 7th Battalion had gone forward during the night with a number of 4th Division men. The morning air was sweet and fresh after that of the dug-out, but was rather chilly. A beautiful dawn was beginning, and only a few of the larger stars were visible. The constellation of Orion could be seen distinctly against the grey-blue of the sky. At five o'clock the barrage started, and there was the usual glorious roar of the opening attack. Very quickly the Germans replied, and shells fell so unpleasantly near, that once again we crowded into the dugout. After a hasty breakfast of bacon and tea the battalions moved off, and I made my way to the front. I saw an officer of the 7th Battalion being carried to the M. O.'s dug-out. He was not badly hit, and told me he was just back from leave and had been married only a fortnight ago. I shook hands with him and congratulated him on being able to get back to Blighty and have a wife to look after him. He was being carried by some Germans and had two of our bearers with him. I went down into a communication trench and the next instant a shell burst. I did not know then that anybody had been hit by it, but I learned afterwards that the officer, the stretcher-bearers and the Germans had all been killed.

I made my way to a mud road, where to my infinite delight I saw large numbers of German prisoners being marched back. By the corner of a wood the 8th Battalion were waiting their turn to advance. To the left was the hill called The Crow's Nest, which our 3rd Brigade had taken that day. I crossed the Hendecourt-Dury road, which had trees on both sides of it, and then meeting the 2nd Battalion went forward with them. There were some deep trenches and dug-outs on the way, which our units at once appropriated and which became the headquarters of two of our Brigades. Our artillery had also come up and their chaplain was with them. The C. O. of the 7th Battalion was having breakfast in the corner of a field, and feeling very happy over the result of the morning's work. Far off we could see the wood of Cagnicourt, and beyond that in the distance we could see other woods. I went off in the direction of Cagnicourt and came to some German huts, where there was a collection of military supplies. Among them was a large anti-tank rifle. As it had begun to rain, I was very glad to find some German water proof sheets which I put over my shoulders as I was eating my bully-beef. Cagnicourt lay in a valley to the right and, when I got there, I found a battery of artillery had just arrived and were taking up their positions by a road which led on to Villers-Cagnicourt. We were all in high spirits over our fresh achievement. In some dug-outs on the way, I found the headquarters of the 13th and 14th Battalions, and learned of the very gallant deed of the Rev. E. E. Graham, the Methodist chaplain attached to the 13th Battalion. He had carried out, under the barrage, five wounded men of the 2nd Division, who had been left in No Man's Land. He was recommended for the Victoria Cross, but unfortunately, for some reason or other, only got the D. S. O. In a trench near Villers-Cagnicourt I found the 4th Battalion, who told me that they thought our advance was checked. I sat talking to them for some time, but was so tired that I absolutely could not keep awake. The men were much amused to see me falling asleep in the midst of a conversation. I managed, however, to pull myself together, and went over to the main Cherisy road, on the side of which one of our ambulances had taken up its position and was being attended by one of our military chaplains. I was feeling so seedy by this time that I got a seat by the side of the driver on a horse ambulance, and made my way back to Cherisy. The road was narrow and crowded with traffic, and had been broken in places by shells. Quite a number of bodies were lying by the wayside. I arrived back at my billet in Arras in the evening feeling very tired. At the Corps dressing station that night I saw large numbers of our men brought in, among them the C. O. of the 2nd Battalion, who had especially distinguished himself that day, but was very badly wounded.

SMASHING THE DROCOURT-QUEANT LINE

In spite of the fact that we had not been able to go as far as we had intended, another glorious victory was to our credit, and we had broken the far-famed Drocourt-Queant line with its wire entanglements which the Germans had thought to be impregnable. Two days afterwards, on September 4th, our Division was taken out of the line and sent back for rest and reorganization.

CHAPTER XXXIII

PREPARING FOR THE FINAL BLOW.

September, 1918.

OUR Divisional Headquarters were now established in the delightful old château at Warlus. In Nisson huts near-by, were the machine-gun battalion and the signallers, and, as I had one end of a Nisson hut all to myself, I was very comfortable. The three infantry brigades were quartered in the villages round about. The engineers and artillery were still at the front. As usual our men soon cleaned themselves up and settled down to ordinary life, as if they had never been through a battle in their lives. The weather was very pleasant, and we were all glad at the prospect of a little quiet after the strenuous month through which we had passed. Our concert party at once opened up one of the large huts as a theatre, and night after night their performances were witnessed by crowded and enthusiastic audiences. Just across a field towards Bernaville the 15th Battalion was quartered in a long line of huts and in the village itself were the 14th and 16th Battalions. I was therefore quite near the men of my old 3rd Brigade. The 16th Battalion concert party gave a fine performance there one evening, which was attended by some Canadian Sisters who came up from one of our C. C. S's. The play was called, "A Little Bit of Shamrock," and was composed by members of the concert party. It was exceedingly pretty and very clever, and evoked thunders of applause. The Colonel was called upon for a speech, and, although his words were few, the rousing cheers he got from his men told him what they thought of their commanding officer, who soon afterwards was to be awarded the Victoria Cross. As one sat there in the midst of the men and thought of what they had gone through, and how the flames in the fiery furnace of war had left their cheery souls unscathed, one's heart was filled with an admiration for them which will never die.

On looking over my diary during those delightful days while we were waiting to make the great attack, I see records of many journeys to our various battalions and artillery brigades. Wanquetin, Wailly, Dainville, Bernaville, Hautes Avesnes—what mem-

PREPARING FOR THE FINAL BLOW

ories these names recall! I would rattle over the dusty roads in my side-car and pull up at Battalion Headquarters and get an invitation to dinner. On such occasions I used to visit the cooks first and ask them if they had enough food on hand for me in case the officers invited me to dine with them, and in case they didn't, if they (the cooks) would feed me later on in the kitchen. When the invitation had been given, I used to go back to the cooks and say, "It's all right, boys, you won't be bothered with my society, the officers have asked me to dinner." In the evening, before I rode off, I used to go round to the men's billets, or to the Y. M. C. A. tent, if there was one, and have a talk with the men on the war outlook or any other topic that was perplexing them at the time. Often I was followed to my car by some man who had deeper matters to discuss, or perhaps some worry about things at home, and who wanted to unburden himself to a chaplain. On the way back, when darkness had fallen and my feeble headlight warned us against speeding. I would meet or overtake men and have a talk, or tell them to mount up on the box at the back of the car and I would give them a ride. The rows of tall trees along the road would stand out black against the starlit sky, and in the evening air the sweet smells of nature would fill us with delight. We felt too, that nearer and nearer the hour of the great victory was approaching. Who amongst us would be spared to see it? How would it be brought about? What great and fierce battle would lay the Germans low? The supreme idea in the mind was consecration to a sublime sacrifice, which dwarfed into insignificance all previous events in life. We had our fun, we had our jokes, we met our friends, we saw battalions go on a route march, we watched men play their games in the fields; but to me it seemed that a new and mysterious light that was born of heaven hid behind the sunshine, and cast a glory upon men and even nature. To dine at the rude board table with the young officers of one of the companies of a battalion, perhaps in a bare hut, on the floor of which lay the lads' beds, was something sacred and sacramental. Their apologies for the plainness of the repast were to me extremely pathetic. Was there a table in the whole world at which it was a greater honour to sit? Where could one find a nobler, knightlier body of young men?

In the garden round the Château at Warlus were many winding paths, where old trees gave a delightful shade. Here at odd moments one could get away for a time into the leafy solitude and think quietly and wonder. Although we were in rest there was of course no remission of warlike activity and preparation. We knew that the next thing that lay before us was the crossing of the Canal du Nord and the push to Cambrai. That was a deed which would not only tax our strength and courage, but depended for its success upon the care and diligence of our preparation.

On the two Sundays that we were at Warlus I had splendid church parades with the Machine-Gun Battalion. Part of their billets were in huts beside the road to Dainville. In one of them one night I found some Imperial officers who were in charge of the wireless telegraph station. They told me some interesting facts about their work. The night was divided into different periods when the communiques of the various countries would be sent out. These, of course, were for all the world to read. The most wonderful thing they told me, however, was that they could pick up the code messages sent from the German Admiralty Headquarters at Kiel to their submarines under the sea. Of course not knowing the code, our officers could not translate these despatches.

I received a great blow at this time, for my friend Lyons, who acted as the chauffeur of my side-car, was sent off to the 3rd Division to replace one of the despatch riders whom they had lost in the attack. Our own signallers could not give me another man. As I could not run the car myself, a sudden move might compel me to leave it behind. Someone, too, might appropriate it, for the honesty of the army was, as I knew from experience, a grace on which one could not place much reliance. The only person to whom I could apply was my good and kind friend, the builder of my churches and huts, Colonel Macphail, our C.R.E. He was always my refuge in distress. He looked upon the building of churches at the front as an act of such piety that it would guarantee to him at any time the certain admission into heaven. He attributed his piety to the claim which his clan made to be the descendants of St. Paul. Apparently in Gaelic, Macphail means "the son of Paul." The Colonel was always fond of insisting upon his high lineage. He came to see me once when I was ill at Bruay, and after stating the historical claims of his ancestors, asked me if I had not observed some traits in his character which were like those of St. Paul. I told him that the only resemblance to the Apostle which I had discovered in him was that his bodily presence was weak and his speech contemptible. In spite of those unkind thrusts, however, the colonel manifested the Apostle's quality of forgiveness, and was always ready to try and make me comfortable. I wrote to him now and asked if he could send me a driver for my car. He did not fail me. A few days afterwards, a young sapper appeared, saluted most properly, and told me that he had been ordered by the C. R. E. to report to me for duty as chauffeur. I was so delighted that I at once despatched the following letter to my friend:-

"Dear Colonel Macphail,
  If I had but a tail
    I would wag it this morning with joy,
At your having provided
My car that's one-sided
  With a good and intelligent boy.

May your blessings from heaven
  Abound in this war,
And be seven times seven
  More than ever before."

The possession of a new driver for my car enabled me to pay a last visit to Le Cauroy, where I had left some of my possessions on our trip to Amiens. I found the Curé in high good humor over the way the war was going. The outlook was very different now from what it had been when I was there before. I also visited Arras and the forward area, where I dined one night in a tent with Major Price, who was then in command of my original battalion, the 14th. The men were billeted in trenches and as usual were making the best of things. It was strange to look back to the early days of the war and talk about old times. As I returned in the twilight and gazed far away over the waste land towards the bank of low clouds in the eastern sky, my heart grew sick at the thought of all which those fine young men might have to endure before the crowning victory came. The thought of the near presence of the Angel of Death was always coming up in the mind, changing and transfiguring into something nobler and better our earthly converse.

In the war, the Bible statement, "We have here no continuing city," was certainly true. Our happy life in Warlus and its neighbourhood came to an end. On Friday, September 20th, the Division moved to Achicourt near Arras. I took the opportunity to visit some friends in the 3rd Division who were taking our places. Among them was "Charlie" Stewart, of the P. P. C. L. I. I had taught him as a boy at school when I was curate of St. John's, Montreal. We talked over old times, and the great changes that had taken place in Canada and the world since we were young. He was killed not long afterwards before Cambrai. I went on through Dainville, where I met the 42nd Battalion, and reached Achicourt in the evening. My billet was in a very dirty room over a little shop. One corner of the house had been hit by a shell, and a great store of possessions belonging to the people was piled up on one side of my room. We knew we were not going to be there long, so we did not worry about making ourselves comfortable. I had a view out of my window of green fields and a peaceful country, but the town itself had been badly knocked about.

On Sunday morning, I got the use of a small Protestant church which stood by a stream in the middle of the town. It was a quaint place, and, instead of an altar, against the east wall there was a high pulpit entered by steps on both sides. When I stood up in it I felt like a jack-in-the-box. I had a queer feeling that I was getting to the end of things, and a note in my prayer-book, with the place and date, gives evidence of this. We had not many communicants, but that was the last Celebration of Holy Communion that I held in France. On the following Sunday I was to leave the war for good. I remember walking away from the church that day with my sergeant and talking over the different places where we had held services. Now we were on the eve of great events, and the old war days had gone forever. After the service, I started off in my side-car on a missionary journey to the battalions that had now gone forward. I went off up the road to the ruined town of Beaurains. Here I found the Headquarters of the 16th Battalion in the cellar of a broken house. The officers' mess was a little shack by the roadside, and among those present was the second-in-command, Major Bell-Irving, who had crossed with me on the "Andania." Alas, this was the last time I was to see him. He was killed in the battle of Cambrai.

After lunch I continued up the long pavé road which leads to Croisilles. On the way I saw the 8th Battalion in an open field. Near them were a number of Imperial officers and men of the

British Division which was on our right. We made our way through Bullecourt to Hendecourt, near which in trenches were the battalions of the 1st Brigade, and there too Colonel Macphail had his headquarters. There was a great concentration of men in this area, and the roads were crowded with lorries and limbers as well as troops. I stayed that night with the engineers, as the weather looked threatening. The sky grew black and rain began to fall. When one stood in the open and looked all round at the inky darkness everywhere, with the rain pelting down, and knew that our men had to carry on as usual, one realized the bitterness of the cup which they had to drink to the very dregs. Rain and darkness all round them, hardly a moment's respite from some irksome task, the ache in the heart for home and the loved ones there, the iron discipline of the war-machine of which they formed a part, the chance of wounds and that mysterious crisis called death— these were the elements which made up the blurred vision in their souls.

The next morning the weather had cleared, and I went on towards Cagnicourt. On the journey I was delayed by a lorry which had gone into the ditch and completely blocked the road. Here in a field the 1st Field Ambulance had established themselves. Later on I managed to get to Cagnicourt and found my son's battery in the cellars of the Château. They were getting their guns forward by night in preparation for the attack. They gave me a very pressing invitation to sleep there and I accepted it. We had a pleasant evening, listening to some remarkably good violin records on the gramophone. Good music at such times had a special charm about it. It reminded one of the old days of concerts and entertainments, but, at the same time, as in the background of a dream, one seemed to hear beneath the melodies the tramp of mighty battalions marching forward into battle, and the struggles of strong men in the fierce contests of war.

On the following day I went on to the quarry which was to be our Battle Headquarters near Inchy Station, from which the 2nd Division were moving. I had a view of the smiling country over which we were to charge. Between us and that promised land lay the Canal, the crossing of which was necessarily a matter of great anxiety. It was late at night before I got back to my home at Achicourt, where I had my last war dinner with my friend General Thacker, who, with his staff, was up to his eyes in work. The next day was taken up with arranging for the disposition of our chaplains during the engagement, and about six o'clock I told Ross to saddle Dandy, and on the dear old horse, who was fresh and lively as ever, I galloped off into the fields. The sun had set and the fresh air of the evening was like a draught of champagne. Dandy seemed to enjoy the ride as much as I did, and cleared some trenches in good style. For nearly three years and a half we had been companions. He had always been full of life and very willing, the envy of those who knew a good horse when they saw him. When I returned in the twilight and gave him back to Ross, I said, "You know, Ross, I am going into this battle and may lose my leg in it, and so I wanted to have my last ride on dear old Dandy." It was my last ride on him, and he was never ridden by anyone again. After I was wounded, he was kept at Headquarters until, in order to avoid his being sold with other horses to the Belgians, our kind A. D. V. S. ordered him to be shot. He was one of the best friends I had in the war, and I am glad he entered the horses' heaven as a soldier, without the humiliation of a purgatory in some civilian drudgery.

That night some bombs were dropped near the station at Arras on units of the 3rd Division, which passed through Achicourt in the afternoon, causing many casualties, and we felt that the Germans knew another attack was at hand. It was the last night I had a billet in France. On the next morning we moved forward to some trenches on the way to Inchy, and I parted from Headquarters there. This was really the most primitive home that the Division had ever had. We had in fact no home at all. We found our stuff dumped out in a field, and had to hunt for our possessions in the general pile. A few tents were pitched and the clerks got to work. In a wide trench little shacks were being run up, and I was to be quartered in the same hut as the field cashier, which was thus to be a kind of union temple for the service of God and the service of Mammon. I looked down into the clay pit and saw the men working at my home, but I knew that I should probably not occupy it. I determined to go forward to our Battle Headquarters, prepared for a missionary journey, and find out when the attack was going to be made. I put into my pack some bully-beef, hard-tack, tinned milk and other forms of nourishment, as well as a razor, a towel and various toilet necessaries. On the other side of the road, the signallers had their horse-lines, and our transports were near-by. I got my side-car and, bidding good-bye to my friends, left for Inchy. We passed down the road to Quéant, where we saw the wounded in the field ambulance, and from there started off through Pronville to Inchy Station. The roads as usual were crowded, and the dust from passing lorries was very unpleasant. We were going through the valley by Inchy Copse when we suddenly heard a loud crash behind us which made my driver stop. I asked him what he was about, and said, "That was one of our guns, there is nothing to be alarmed at." "Guns!" he said, "I know the sound of a shell when I hear it. You may like shells but I don't. I'm going back." I said, "You go ahead, if I had a revolver with me, I would shoot you for desertion from the front line. That was only one of our guns." He looked round and said, "You call that a gun? Look there." I turned and sure enough, about a hundred feet away in the middle of the road was the smoke of an exploded shell. "Well," I said, "you had better go on or there will be another one pretty soon, and it may get us." With extraordinary speed we hurried to our destination, where I left the car, taking my pack with me. I told the driver, much to his relief, that he could go home, and that when I wanted the car again I would send for it.

The quarry was, as I have said, our Battle Headquarters, and here in the deep dugouts which I had visited previously I found our staff hard at work. They told me that this was "Y" day, and that zero hour when the barrage would start was at 5.20 the next morning. At that hour we were to cross the Canal and then press on into the country beyond. We had a two battalion front. The 4th and 14th Battalions were to make the attack, and be followed up by the other battalions in the 1st and 3rd Brigades. When these had reached their objective the 2nd Brigade was to "leap frog" them and push on to Haynecourt and beyond. I was glad that I had come provided for the expedition, and bidding good-bye to General Thacker, whose parting injunction was not to do anything foolish, I got out of the quarry and made my way down the hill towards Inchy. A railway bridge which crossed the road near me was a constant mark for German shells, and it was well to avoid it. An officer met me and asked where I was going. I said, "I don't know, but I think the Spirit is leading me to the old 14th Battalion in Buissy Switch Trench." He told me the direction to take, which was to cross the road and follow the line of railway. The tins of milk and bully-beef cut into my back so I stopped by a culvert and taking off my pack and tunic, sat on the ground and cooled off. There was no sign of Buissy Switch anywhere, but I got up and went on. The evening was closing in by this time, and, as I am never good at seeing in the dark, it began to be difficult to keep from tripping over things. At last the road brought me to a trench in which I found the 14th Battalion. They were getting ready to move off at midnight and wait in the wood by the edge of the Canal until the barrage opened. It made one proud to be with those young men that evening and think what they were called upon to do. What difficulties they would encounter in the Canal they did not know. They said they might have to swim. We hoped, however, that there was not much water, as the canal was still unfinished.

I said good-bye to them and wished them all good-luck. Crossing the road I entered another trench, where I found the 13th Battalion, and beyond them came to the 1st Battalion. By this time, it was dark and rainy, and the ground was very slippery. I had to feel my way along the trench. A company of the 4th Battalion who were to be in the first wave of the attack, passed on their way forward to take up their position for the following morning. Probably never in the war had we experienced a moment of deeper anxiety. The men would have to climb down one side of the canal, rush across it, and climb up the other. It seemed inevitable that the slaughter would be frightful. At home in the cities of Canada things were going on as usual. Profiteers were heaping up their piles of gold. Politicians were carrying on the government, or working in opposition, in the interests of their parties, while here, in mud and rain, weary and drenched to the skin, young Canadians were waiting to go through the valley of the shadow of death in order that Canada might live.

CHAPTER XXXIV

The Crossing of the Canal Du Nord.

September 27th, 1918.

WHEN I got to the sunken road above Inchy I found that No. 1 Company of the Machine-Gun Battalion had a little sandbag house there, and were waiting for the attack. I went in and the young officers and men made me at home at once. I divested myself of my pack, coat and steel helmet, and determined to settle down for the night. Suddenly a shell burst in the road, and I went out to see if anyone was hit. Two or three men were wounded but not severely. We got them in and the young O. C. of the company bound up their wounds and sent them off. There was a row of these sandbag huts against the bank, and at one end of them was the entrance to a dugout in which the 1st Battalion and the General of the 1st Brigade had made their headquarters. I went down the steep steps into a long dark passage, lit here and there by the light which came from the rooms on either side. The whole place was crowded with men and the atmosphere was more than usually thick. I made my way down to the end where there was a pump which had been put there by the Germans. Here the men were filling their water-bottles, and I got a fresh supply for mine. Not far from the pump a few steps led down into a room where I found the C. O. and a number of the officers of the 1st Battalion. It was about two a.m., and they were having a breakfast of tea and bacon and invited me to join them. After the meal was finished, the Colonel, who was lying on a rough bed, said to me, "Sit down, Canon, and give us some of your nature poems to take our minds off this beastly business." It was very seldom that I was invited to recite my own poems, so such an opportunity could not be lost. I sat down on the steps and repeated a poem which I wrote among the Laurentian mountains, in the happy days before we ever thought of war. It is called, "The Unnamed Lake."

> "It sleeps among the thousand hills
> Where no man ever trod,
> And only nature's music fills
> The silences of God.

Great mountains tower above its shore,
    Green rushes fringe its brim,
And o'er its breast for evermore
    The wanton breezes skim.

Dark clouds that intercept the sun
    Go there in Spring to weep,
And there, when Autumn days are done,
    White mists lie down to sleep.

Sunrise and sunset crown with gold
    The peaks of ageless stone,
Where winds have thundered from of old
    And storms have set their throne.

No echoes of the world afar
    Disturb it night or day,
But sun and shadow, moon and star
    Pass and repass for aye.

'Twas in the grey of early dawn,
    When first the lake we spied,
And fragments of a cloud were drawn
    Half down the mountain side.

Along the shore a heron flew,
    And from a speck on high,
That hovered in the deepening blue,
    We heard the fish-hawk's cry.

Among the cloud-capt solitudes,
    No sound the silence broke,
Save when, in whispers down the woods,
    The guardian mountains spoke.

Through tangled brush and dewy brake,
    Returning whence we came,
We passed in silence, and the lake
    We left without a name."

There is not much in the poem, but, like a gramaphone record, it carried our minds away into another world. For myself, who remembered the scenery that surrounded me when I wrote it and who now, in that filthy hole, looked at the faces of young men who in two or three hours were to brave death in one of the biggest tasks that had been laid upon us, the words stirred up all sorts of conflicting emotions. The recitation seemed to be so well received that I ventured on another—in fact several more—and then I noticed a curious thing. It was the preternatural silence of my audience. Generally speaking, when I recited my poems, one of the officers would suddenly remember he had to dictate a letter, or a despatch rider would come in with orders. Now, no one stirred. I paused in the middle of a poem and looked round to see what was the matter, and there to my astonishment, I found that everyone, except the young Intelligence Officer, was sound asleep. It was the best thing that could have happened and I secretly consoled myself with the reflection that the one who was unable to sleep was the officer who specialized in intelligence. We both laughed quietly, and then I whispered to him, "We had better go and find some place where we, too, can get a little rest." He climbed over the prostrate forms and followed me down the passage to a little excavation where the Germans had started to make a new passage. We lay down side by side on the wooden floor, and I was just beginning to succumb to the soothing influences of my own poetry, when I thought I felt little things crawling over my face. It was too much for me. I got up and said, "I think I am getting crummy, so I'm going off." I looked in on the General and the Brigade Major, and then climbed up the steps and went to the machine-gun hut.

The night was now well advanced so it was time to shave and get ready for zero hour. A little after five we had some breakfast, and about a quarter past I went up to the top of the bank above the road and waited for the barrage. At 5.20 the savage roar burst forth. It was a stupendous attack. Field guns, heavy guns, and siege batteries sent forth their fury, and machine-guns poured millions of rounds into the country beyond the Canal. So many things were flying about and landing near us, that we went back under cover till the first burst of the storm should subside. At that moment I knew our men were crossing the huge ditch, and I prayed that God would give them victory. When the barrage had lifted I started down towards the Canal, passing through a field on my way where I found, lying about, dead and wounded men. Four or five were in a straight line, one behind another, where a German machine-gun must have caught them as they advanced. A young officer of the 2nd Battalion was dying from wounds. Two or three decorations on his breast told his past record in the war. While I was attending to the sufferers, a sergeant came up to me from the direction of the Canal and asked the way to the dressing station. He had a frightful wound in his face. A bit of a shell had dug into his cheek, carrying off his nose. He did not know at the time how badly he had been hit. I asked him if he wanted me to walk back with him, but he said he was all right as the dressing station was not far off. I often wondered what became of him, and I never heard till the following year when a man came up to me in the military hospital at St. Anne's, with a new nose growing comfortably on his face and his cheek marked with a scar that was not unsightly. "The last time I met you, Sir," he said, "was near the Canal du Nord when you showed me the way to the dressing station." I was indeed glad to find him alive and well, and to see what surgical science had done to restore his beauty.

I went on to the Canal, and found that at that point it was quite dry. I climbed down to the bottom of it in which men were walking and the sappers were at work. Some ladders enabled me to get up on the other side and I had the joy of feeling that the Canadians had crossed the great Canal du Nord. Our battalions were now moving up and I joined them, avoiding a part of a field which the men told me was under the fire of a machine-gun from the mill in Marquion. The country was open and green. The day was fine, and once more we experienced the satisfaction of taking possession of the enemy's territory. Before us the ground rose in a gradual slope, and we did not know what might meet us when we arrived at the top, but it was delightful to go with the men feeling that every step was a gain. When we got to the top of the rise, we had a splendid view of the country beyond. Before us, in the distance running from right to left, lay the straight Arras-Cambrai road with its rows of tall trees. Where we stood, there were a number of deserted German trenches. Here the M. O. of the 3rd Battalion opened up an aid post, and the chaplain went about looking for the wounded. Our men went on down into the valley and got into some forward trenches. I stayed on the hill looking at the wonderful scene through my German glasses. On the left in a quarry beside the village of Marquion, I saw two Germans manning a machine-gun. Our 3rd Brigade had taken the place, and some Highlanders were walking on the edge of the quarry just above the Huns, of whose presence they were unaware. I saw the enemy suddenly hide themselves, having noticed the approach of the Highlanders, but when the latter had passed the two Boches reappeared and went on firing as before. It was not long before the German artillery turned their guns on our hill and I told some men of the 2nd Brigade, who were now coming forward, to take cover in the trench or go in extended order. I had hardly uttered the words when a shell burst, killing one man and wounding in the thigh the one to whom I was talking. I went over to him and found that no artery had been cut, and the chaplain of the 3rd Battalion got him carried off. Down in the valley our advance had evidently been checked for a time. While I was trying to see what the trouble was, a young officer, called Cope, of the 8th Battalion came up to me. He was a splendid young fellow, and looked so fresh and clean. He had lost a brother in the Battalion in the early part of the war, I said, "How old are you, Cope?" He replied, "I am twenty." I said, "What a glorious thing it is to be out here at twenty." "Yes," he said, looking towards the valley, "it is a glorious thing to be out here at twenty, but I should like to know what is holding them up." He had hardly spoken when there was a sharp crack of a machine-gun bullet and he dropped at my side. The bullet had pierced his steel helmet and entered his brain. He never recovered consciousness, and died on the way to the aid post.

The 2nd Brigade was now moving forward, so I went down the hill past a dugout which had been used as a German dressing station. There I secured a bottle of morphine tablets, and spoke to our wounded waiting to be carried off. Just before I reached the Arras-Cambrai road, I came to the trench where the C. O. of the 3rd Battalion had established himself. The chaplain and I were talking when an officer of the 2nd Battalion came back with a bad wound in the throat. He could not speak, but made signs that he wanted to write a message. We got him some paper and he wrote, "The situation on our right is very bad." The 4th Division were on our right, and they had been tied up in Bourlon Wood. So now our advancing 2nd Brigade had their right flank in the air. As a matter of fact their left flank was also exposed, because the British Division there had also been checked in their advance. I crossed the road into the field, where I found the 5th and 10th Battalions resting for a moment before going on to their objective. In front of us, looking very peaceful among its trees, was the village of Haynecourt which the 5th Battalion had to take. The 10th Battalion was to pass it on the left and go still further forward. We all started off, and as we were nearing the village I looked over to the fields on the right, and there, to my dismay, I saw in the distance numbers of little figures in grey which I knew must be Germans. I pointed them out to a sergeant, but he said he thought they were French troops who were in the line with us. The 5th Battalion went through Haynecourt and found the village absolutely deserted and the houses stripped of everything that might be of any value. Their C. O. made his headquarters in a trench to the north of the village, and the 10th disappeared going forward to the Douai-Cambrai road.

It was now quite late in the afternoon. The sun was setting, and I feared that if I did not go back in time I might find myself stuck out there for the night without any food or cover. I thought it was wise therefore to go to Deligny's Mill, where I understood the machine-gunners were established. In the road at the entrance of Haynecourt, I found a young German wounded in the foot and very sorry for himself. I think he was asking me to carry him, but I saw he could walk and so showed him the direction in which to make his way back to our aid posts. I was just going back over the fields when I met a company of our light trench mortar batteries. The men halted for a rest and sat down by the road, and an officer came and said to me, "Come and cheer up the men, Canon, they have dragged two guns eight kilometres in the dust and heat and they are all fed up." I went over to them, and, luckily having a tin of fifty cigarettes in my pocket, managed to make them go round. I asked the O. C. if he would like me to spend the night with them. He said he would, so I determined not to go back. Some of the men asked me if I knew where they could get water. I told them they might get some in the village, so off we started. It makes a curious feeling go through one to enter a place which has just been evacuated by the enemy. In the evening light, the little brick village looked quite ghostly with its silent streets and empty houses. We turned into a large farmyard, at the end of which we saw a well with a pump. One of the men went down into the cellar of the house hunting for souvenirs, and soon returned with a German who had been hiding there. We were just about to fill our water-bottles, when I suggested that perhaps the well had been poisoned. I asked the German, "Gutt wasser?" "Ja, ja," Then I said, "Gutt drinken?" "Nein, nein," he replied, shaking his head. "Well, Sir," the men said, "we are going to drink it anyway." "But if the well is poisoned," I replied, "it won't do you much good." "How can you find out?" they said. A brilliant idea flashed upon me. "I tell you what, boys," I said, "we will make the German drink it himself and see the effect." The men roared with laughter, and we filled a bottle with the suspected liquid and made the unfortunate prisoner drink every drop of it. When he had finished, we waited for a few minutes (like the people who watched St. Paul on the

Island of Melita after he had shaken off the viper into the fire) to see if he would swell up or die, but as nothing of that kind happened we all began to fill our water-bottles. Just as the last man was about to fill his, a big shell landed in the garden next to us, and he, catching up his empty bottle, ran off saying, "I'm not thirsty any longer, I don't want any water."

After their rest and refreshment, the company went over to a sunken road on the east side of the village. It was now getting very chilly and the daylight was dying rapidly. From the ground above the road one could see in the distance the spires of Cambrai, and in some fields to the southeast of us, with my glasses I could distinctly see numbers of little grey figures going into trenches, apparently with the idea of getting round to the south of our village on our exposed flank. I met a young officer of the machine-gun battalion, and lending him my glasses pointed out where the Germans were massing. He got the men of his section and took up a forward position along a ditch which ran at right angles to the sunken road. Here too were some of the companies of the 5th Battalion. They had hardly got into position when the Germans shelled the road we had been on, most unmercifully. I took refuge with a number of the men of the 5th Battalion in a garden, beside a brick building which had been used by the German troops as a wash-house and which was particularly malodorous. Two or three shells dropped in the orchard, breaking the trees, and we had to keep down on the ground while the shelling lasted. I could not help thinking of the warning the 2nd Battalion officer had given us about the situation on our right. It did seem pretty bad, because, until the arrival of the 7th and 8th Battalions, our right flank was exposed, and the enemy might have gone round to the southeast of the village and attacked us in the rear. When things settled down, I went back up the sunken road, and, as I did so, thought I saw some men going into a gateway in the main street of the village. I made my way to the open trenches where the Colonel of the 5th Battalion had his headquarters, and I determined to spend the night there, so they kindly provided me with a German overcoat. I was just settling down to sleep when a runner came up and reported that some men were wounded and were asking the way to the dressing station. Someone said they thought the M.O. had made his headquarters in the village. Then I remembered having seen some men enter a gateway in the street as I passed, so two of us started off to find out if this was the regimental aid post. The night was absolutely black, and my companion and I had to feel our way along the street not knowing who or what we might bump into, and expecting every moment that the Germans would begin to shell the place as soon as they thought we had had time to find billets there. At last to our great relief, we came to a large gateway in a brick wall and found some of our men, who told us that the M.O. had made his dressing station in the cellar of a building to the right. We went down into it and came upon a place well lighted with candles, where the devoted M.O. and his staff were looking after a number of men on stretchers.

The Germans were determined that we should not have a quiet night and very soon, as we had expected, they began to shell the village. The dressing station was in a building which they themselves had used for the same purpose, so they knew its location, and shells began to fall in the yard. We got all the men we could down to the cellar; but still there were some stretcher cases which had to be left in the rooms upstairs. It was hard to convince them that there was no danger. However the "straffing" stopped in time, and I went down to the end of the cellar and slept in a big cane-seated chair which the Germans had left behind them. In the morning I went back again to our men in the line. The 10th Battalion had established themselves partly in a ditch along the Cambrai road not far from Epinoy, and partly in outposts behind the German wire. The country was undulating, and in places afforded an extensive view of the forward area. German machine-gun emplacements were in all directions, and our men suffered very severely. I was in an outpost with one of the companies when I saw in the distance one of our men crawling on his hands and knees up to a German machine-gun emplacement. The helmets of the enemy could be distinctly seen above the parapet. It was very exciting watching the plucky fellow approach the place of danger with the intention of bombing it. Unfortunately just as he had reached the side of the trench the Germans must have become aware of his presence, for they opened fire, and he had to crawl back again as fast as he could.

Though many wounded were brought in, we knew that some were still lying out on the other side of the wire in full view of the enemy. As soon as it was dark enough, a bearer party, which I accompanied, started off to try and collect these men. With my cane I managed to lead the party through a gap in the wire. I came to a poor fellow who had been lying there since the previous night with a smashed arm and leg. He was in great pain, but the men got him in safely, and the next time I saw him was in a Toronto hospital where he was walking about with a wooden leg, and his arm in a sling. I went down to an outpost where I saw some men. We could only talk in whispers, as we knew the Germans were close at hand. They told me they were one of the companies of the 10th Battalion. I asked, "Where are your officers?" They said, "They are all gone." "Who is in command?" They replied, "A Lance-Corporal." I rejoined the bearers and we had great difficulty in getting back, as we could not find the gap in the wire, which seemed to go in all directions.

The 10th Battalion was relieved that night by the 8th, the C.O. of which made his headquarters with the C.O. of the 5th Battalion in a large dug-out by the sunken road. There, late at night, I shared a bunk with a young machine-gun officer and had a few hours of somewhat disturbed sleep. The next morning, Sunday, September the 29th, the fourth anniversary of our sailing from Quebec, our men were having a hard time. The German defence at Cambrai was most determined, and they had a large quantity of artillery in the neighbourhood. I went back to the road and into the trench beyond the wire and found a lot of men there. The parapet was so low that the men had dug what they called, "Funk holes" in the clay, where they put as much of their bodies as they could. Sitting in a bend of the trench where I got a good view of the men, I had a service for them, and, as it was that festival, I read out the epistle for St. Michael and All Angel's Day, and spoke of the guardianship of men which God had committed to the Heavenly Hosts. Going down the trench later on, I came to a place from which I could see, with my glasses, a German machine-gun emplacement and its crew. I went back and asked for a sniper. A man who said he was one came up to me and I showed him the enemy and then directed his fire. I could see from little puffs of dust where his bullets were landing. He was a good shot and I think must have done some damage, for all of a sudden the machine-gun opened fire on us and we had to dive into the trench pretty quickly. I told him that I thought we had better give up the game as they had the advantage over us. To snipe at the enemy seemed to be a curious way to spend a Sunday afternoon, but it was a temptation too hard to resist. I crawled back through the trench to the road, and there finding a man who had just lost his hand, directed him to the aid post near Battalion Headquarters. I accompanied him part of the way and had reached the edge of the sunken road, when a major of the Engineers came up to me and said, "I have got a better pair of German glasses than you have." It was an interesting challenge, so we stood there on a little rise looking at the spires of Cambrai and comparing the strength of the lenses. Very distinctly we saw the town, looking peaceful and attractive. Suddenly there was a tremendous crash in front of us, a lot of earth was blown into our faces, and we both fell down. My eyes were full of dirt but I managed to get up again. I had been wounded in both legs, and from one I saw blood streaming down through my puttees. My right foot had been hit and the artery in the calf of my leg was cut. I fell down again with a feeling of exasperation that I had been knocked out of the war. The poor major was lying on the ground with one leg smashed. The same shell had wounded in the chest the young machine-gun officer who had shared his bunk with me the night before. I believe an Imperial officer also was hit in the abdomen and that he died. The chaplain of the 10th Battalion who happened to be standing in the sunken road, got some men together quickly and came to our help. I found myself being carried off in a German sheet by four prisoners. They had forgotten to give me my glasses, and were very much amused when I called for them, but I got them and have them now. The major not only lost his leg but lost his glasses as well. The enemy had evidently been watching us from some observation post in Cambrai, for they followed us up with another shell on the other side of the road, which caused the bearers to drop me quickly. The chaplain walked beside me till we came to the aid post where there were some stretchers. I was placed on one and carried into the dressing station at Haynecourt. They had been having a hard time that day, for the village was heavily shelled. One of their men had been killed and several wounded. I felt a great pain in my heart which made it hard to breathe, so when I was brought into the dressing station I said, "Boys, I am going to call for my first and last tot of rum." I was immensely teased about this later on by my friends, who knew I was a teetotaller. They said I had drunk up all the men's rum issue. A General wrote to me later on to say he had been terribly shocked to hear I was wounded, but that it was nothing in comparison with the shock he felt when he heard that I had taken to drinking rum. Everyone in the dressing station was as usual most kind. The bitter thought to me was that I was going to be separated from the old 1st Division. The nightmare that had haunted me for so long had at last come true, and I was going to leave the men before the war was over. For four years they had been my beloved companions and my constant care. I had been led by the example of their noble courage and their unhesitating performance of the most arduous duties, in the face of danger and death, to a grander conception of manhood, and a longing to follow them, if God would give me grace to do so, in their path of utter self-sacrifice. I had been with them continuously in their joys and sorrows, and it did not seem to be possible that I could now go and desert them in that bitter fight. When the doctors had finished binding up my wounds, I was carried off immediately to an ambulance in the road, and placed in it with four others, one of whom was dying. It was a long journey of four hours and a half to No. 1 C.C.S. at Agnez-les-Duisans, and we had to stop at Quéant on the way. Our journey lay through the area over which we had just made the great advance. Strange thoughts and memories ran through my mind. Faces of men that had gone and incidents that I had forgotten came back to me with great vividness. Should I ever again see the splendid battalions and the glad and eager lives pressing on continuously to Victory? Partly from shell holes, and partly from the wear of heavy traffic, the road was very bumpy. The man above me was in terrible agony, and every fresh jolt made him groan. The light of the autumn afternoon was wearing away rapidly. Through the open door at the end of the ambulance, as we sped onward, I could see the brown colourless stretch of country fade in the twilight, and then vanish into complete darkness, and I knew that the great adventure of my life among the most glorious men that the world has ever produced was over.

CHAPTER XXXV.

VICTORY.

November 11th, 1918.

THEY took me to the X-ray room and then to the operating-tent that night, and sent me off on the following afternoon to the Base with a parting injunction that I should be well advised to have my foot taken off; which, thank God, was not found necessary. From the C.C.S. at Camiers, two days later I was sent to London to the Endsleigh Palace Hospital near Euston Station, where I arrived with another wounded officer at 2.30 A.M. I was put in a little room on the seventh storey, and there through long nights I thought of our men still at the front and wondered how the war was going. The horror of great darkness fell upon me. The hideous sights and sounds of war, the heart-rending sorrows, the burden of agony, the pale dead faces and blood-stained bodies lying on muddy wastes, all these came before me as I lay awake counting the slow hours and listening to the hoarse tooting of lorries rattling through the dark streets below. That concourse of ghosts from the sub-conscious mind was too hideous to contemplate and yet one could not escape them. The days went by and intimations at last reached us that the German power was crumbling. Swiftly and surely the Divine Judge was wreaking vengeance upon the nation that, by its over-weaning ambition, had drenched the world in blood.

On November 11th at eleven in the morning the bells of London rang out their joyous peals, for the armistice had been signed and the war was over. There was wild rejoicing in the city and the crowds went crazy with delight. But it seemed to me that behind the ringing of those peals of joy there was the tolling of spectral bells for those who would return no more. The monstrous futility of war as a test of national greatness, the wound in the world's heart, the empty homes, those were the thoughts which in me over-mastered all feelings of rejoicing.

On Sunday morning, the 4th of May, 1919, on the Empress of Britain, after an absence of four years and seven months, I returned to Quebec. On board were the 16th Battalion with whom I had sailed away in 1914, the 8th Battalion, the Machine Gun Battalion,

318

the 3rd Field Ambulance and some of the Engineers. Like those awaking from a dream, we saw once more the old rock city standing out in the great river. There was the landing and the greeting of loving friends on the wharf within a stone's throw from the place whence we had sailed away. While I was shaking hands with my friends, an officer told me I had to inspect the Guard of Honour which the kind O.C. of the vessel had furnished. I did not know how to do this properly but I walked through the rows of stalwart, bronzed men and looked into their faces which were fixed and immovable. Each man was an original, and every unit in the old 1st Division was represented. For four years and seven months, they had been away from home, fighting for liberty and civilization. Many of them wore decorations; many had been wounded. No General returning victor from a war could have had a finer Guard of Honour.

The troops had to wait on board the ship till the train was ready. All along the decks of the great vessel, crowded against the railings in long lines of khaki, were two thousand seven hundred men. Their bright faces were ruddy in the keen morning air. On their young shoulders the burden of Empire had rested. By their willing sacrifice Canada had been saved. It made a great lump come in my throat to look at them and think of what they had gone through.

I went back to the gangway for a last farewell. In one way I knew it must be a last farewell, for though some of us will meet again as individuals it will be under altered conditions. Never again but in dreams will one see the great battalions marching on the battle-ploughed roads of France and Flanders. Never again will one see them pouring single file into the muddy front trenches. All that is over. Along the coasts of the Atlantic and Pacific, among our cities, by the shores of lakes and rivers and in the vast expanse of prairies and mountain passes the warrior hosts have melted away. But there on the vessel that day the fighting men had come home in all their strength and comradeship. I stood on the gangway full of conflicting emotions.

The men called out "Speech," "Speech," as they used often to do, half in jest and half in earnest, when we met in concert tents and estaminets in France.

I told them what they had done for Canada and what Canada owed them and how proud I was to have been with them. I asked them to continue to play the game out here as they had played it in

France. Then, telling them to remove their caps, as this was our last church parade, I pronounced the Benediction, said, "Good-bye, boys", and turned homewards.

INDEX

A

Abbeville, 160, 161.
Abeele, 132, 134.
Achicourt, 302, 303, 304.
Aeroplane, first ride in, 261, 264.
Agnez-les-Duisans, 317.
Albert, 136, 140, 146, 147, 148, 154, 158, 179, 288, 289.
"Alberta," 149, 174, 178, 205, 231, 243, 244, 245, 249, 252.
Alberta Dragoons, 93, 115.
Alderson, Gen. 89, 98, 108, 109, 111.
Ambulance drivers, 130.
Americans, 240, 242, 288.
American declaration of war, 165.
Amesbury, 32.
Amiens, 135, 186, 271, 273.
"Andania," 24, 25, 27, 302.
Anzin, 165, 166, 249.
Anzin-St. Eloi. rd., 164.
Archbishop of York, 190.
Argyle & Sutherland Highlanders, 82.
Arleux, 170, 177, 253.
Armagh Wood, 131, 133.
Armentieres, 38, 41, 98, 181.
Armistice, 318.
Army, 1st, 205.
  " 5th, 242.
  " Hqrs., 211.
  " " 2nd, 134.
  " Service Corps, 50, 99.
  " Mind, the, 222.
Arras, 150, 235, 246, 247, 251, 270, 290, 296, 301, 304.
Arras-Bethune rd., 164, 171, 173, 174, 176.
Arras-Cambrai, 310, 311.
Arriane Dump, 164, 175, 176, 178.
Artillery, Canadian, 285.
  " Monument, 239.
Attention to detail, effect of, 209.
Aubigny, 154.
August 4th, 271.

Australians, 122.
Australian Tunnellers, 201.
Averdoignt, 258, 259.
Avonmouth, 35.

B

Bac St. Maur, 42.
Bailleul, 38, 76, 98, 109, 112, 113, 114.
Bailleul-sur-Berthouit, 170.
Bailly-sur-Lys, 43, 46.
Bapaume, 136, 137.
Baptism at the Front, a, 122.
Barlin, 161, 162, 206, 207, 230.
Barrage, 168, 172, 198, 276, 309.
Base, 267.
Battalion, British, 165.
  " Guards, 79.
  " Headqrs., 249, 250, 251, 252, 269, 276, 280, 281, 294, 295,
  " Machine Gun, 258, 298, 300, 307, 313, 318.
  " of Engineers, 3rd, 272.
  " Pioneer, 199.
  " 1st, 109, 181, 246, 306, 307.
  " 2nd, 181, 207, 278, 296, 309, 311.
  " 3rd., 125, 149, 181, 285, 311.
  " 4th., 181, 296, 305, 306.
  " 5th., 181, 242, 275, 277, 282, 284, 292, 294, 311, 313.
  " 5th., Headqrs., 293.
  " 7th., 181, 203, 235, 236, 282, 294, 295, 296, 313.
  " 8th., 159, 181, 235, 236, 282, 283, 288, 292, 295, 302, 311, 313, 314, 318.
  " 10th., 61, 181, 270, 280, 311, 312, 314, 315, 316.

21

Battalion, 13th., 52, 80, 118, 120, 181, 277, 296, 306.
" 14th., 23, 24, 27, 54, 58, 61, 111, 118, 125, 159, 160, 181, 246, 282, 295, 298, 301, 305, 306.
" 15th., 37, 38, 39, 42, 55, 118, 181, 274, 298.
" 16th., 37, 42, 57, 60, 72, 82, 106, 118, 119, 120, 125, 152, 164, 181, 246, 272, 273, 274, 275, 277, 279, 298, 302, 318.
" 22nd., 282.
" 24th., 282.
" 42nd., 302.
" 87th., 147, 148, 157, 178.
Battery, my son's, 303.
" Siege, 193.
" " 7th., 166, 198, 199.
" " 11th., 154, 155.
Battle Headqrs., 136, 176, 272, 273, 290, 291, 292, 303, 304, 305.
Bean, C. W. E. Mr., 289.
Beaufort, 282, 286, 288.
Beaurains, 303.
Bedford House, 126, 132.
Bed of Chairs, 79.
Bell-Irving, Major, 302.
Berles, 260, 261, 264.
Bernaville, 147, 298.
Bethune, 88, 89, 90, 159, 190, 230, 234.
Bishop du Pencier, 234.
" of London, 48.
Bishop's College men, 114.
Blind Organist, 89.
Borden, Sir Robert, 22, 72, 102, 266.
Boulogne, 240, 267.
Bourlon Wood, 311.
Boves, 272, 273.
Bracquemont, 151, 191, 192, 197, 235, 240.
Bray Hill, 167.
Brielen, 75.
Brigade, 206.
" Artillery, 171, 245, 260.
" " 1st., Hqrs., 199.
" " 2nd., " 199.
" " 3rd., " 177.

Brigade, Artillery, 3rd., 36, 53, 75, 76, 77, 87, 97, 103, 168, 181.
" Cavalry, 82, 98, 103.
" Headqrs., 93, 156, 201.
" Infantry, 65, 98.
" " 3rd., Headqrs., 107, 118.
" Machine Gun, 207.
" Motor Machine Gun, 130.
" Schools, 208.
" 1st., 128, 179, 234, 246, 279, 280, 285, 303, 305, 307.
" 2nd., 80, 181, 205, 234, 242, 255, 257, 279, 280, 282, 292, 305, 310, 311.
" 2nd., Hqrs., 235.
" 3rd., 31, 43, 75, 76, 77, 93, 97, 98, 242, 246, 292, 295, 298, 305. 310.
British Artillery, 106.
" Cavalry, 46.
" Tribute, 169.
Bruay, 159, 161, 178, 179, 180, 181, 203, 204, 205, 206, 232, 234, 235, 300.
Brutenell, Col., 130.
Buissy Switch Trench, 305.
Bulford Camp, 95, 96.
Bullecourt, 303.
Bully-Beef Wood, 269.
Bully-Grenay, 192, 193, 194, 208.
Byng, Gen., 132.

C

"C" Mess, 99, 149, 217, 231, 243, 245.
C. C. S., 267, 270, 286, 291, 317, 318.
" British, 128, 129.
Caestre, 38, 49.
Cagnicourt, 296, 303.
Caix, 279, /280, 281.
Calais, 227.
Camblain L'Abbe, 149, 151, 152, 158, 159, 238.
Cambligneul, 203.
Cambrai, 302, 315.
Camiers, 318.
Cam Valley, 249.

INDEX

Canadian Cavalry, Hqrs., 160.
" Corps, 72, 108, 132, 149, 150, 178, 189, 190, 220, 240, 265, 270, 271, 272, 274.
" Corps Headqrs., 109, 132, 150, 238, 260, 270.
" Cyclist Corps, 142.
" Light Horse, 93.
" Prisoners of War Fund, 109.
" Sisters, 254.
" War Records Office, 184.
Canal du Nord, 291, 305.
Canaples, 135, 137, 147, 161.
Canteen, 138.
Cassel, 49, 50, 52, 134.
Caves, 246.
Cemetery, 152, 158, 176, 180, 291.
" Canadian, 56, 136, 138.
" at Ecoivres, 174.
" Military, 214.
" near Thélus, 156.
Centre Way, 155.
Chalk Pit, 199.
Chamounix, 186.
Chaplain, American, 270.
" British, 111.
" General, 34.
" Junior, 194.
" Praise of, 116.
" Rest Home, 190.
" Roman Catholic, 184.
" Senior, 98, 173, 181, 190, 203, 207, 231.
" Senior of Australian Div., 138.
" Senior Roman Catholic, 34, 76.
" 1st. Army, 205.
" Service Headqrs., 135.
Chateau d'Acq., 183, 184, 185, 189, 251.
" de la Haie, 178, 181, 230, 242, 243.
" Longeau, 272.
" of Le Cauroy, 147.
" of Ranchicourt, 150.
Cheerfulness of Men, 255.

Cheery word, effect of, 67.
Cherisy, 292, 294, 295, 296.
Chinese Labour Companies, 192.
Christmas, 32, 118, 159, 233.
Church Parade, 18, 21, 22, 38, 320.
" Service, 315.
" under Chestnut Tree, 256.
Cité St. Pierre, 238.
"City of Chester," 36.
Clayton, 230.
Clino, 259, 260, 267.
Comradeship, effect of, 78.
Concert Party, 180, 192, 203, 231, 242, 243, 254, 261, 298.
" " 1st Divisional, 159.
Concerts, 153.
Confirmation Service, 109.
Congreve, General, 40.
Connaught, Duke & Duchess, 22, 266.
Consecration the Supreme Idea, 299.
Contalmaison, 137.
Cope, 311.
Convalescent Camp, 133.
Coupigny, 181.
Courcelette, 115, 138, 140, 142, 144, 145, 155, 157, 179.
Court-o-Pyp, 96, 97.
Croisilles, 302.
"Crown & Anchor," 264.
Crow's Nest, The, 295.
Crucifix Corner, 235.
" Dump, 193.
Crucifixes, 105.
Crucifixion of Canadian Soldier, 76.
Currie, Gen., 80, 109, 112, 222, 239, 242, 260.

D

Dainville, 291, 298, 300, 302.
"Daily Mail," 187, 191.
"Dandy." 90, 91, 95, 103, 107, 108, 110, 113, 122, 128, 134, 165, 180, 253, 256, 265, 304.
Day of Young Men, the, 182.
Death Valley, 138, 156, 157, 179.
Deligny's Mill, 312.
Desertion, procedure for death penalty, 211.

Desertion, death penalty inflicted, 214.

Dish washing in the trenches, 236.

Divion, 234.

Division, 106, 122, 132, 162, 177, 192, 199, 203, 207, 209, 216, 220, 226, 227, 228, 242, 251, 253, 260, 265, 268, 280, 287, 288, 289, 291.

" 1st., 33, 46, 93, 108, 130, 149, 172, 178, 194, 264, 266, 274, 317, 319.

" 2nd., 108, 138, 175, 281, 291, 296, 303.

" 3rd., 129, 274, 300, 302, 304.

" 4th., 146, 154, 158, 231, 232, 242, 294, 295, 311.

" Guards, 123, 132.

" Scots, 250.

Divisional Area, 2nd., 282.

" 1st. Wing, 267, 268.

" Headqrs., 123, 134, 135, 147, 159, 173, 183, 191, 213, 230, 256, 271.

" Headqrs., 1st. Can., 264, 286.

" Rest Camp, 132.

" Sports, 261.

" Train, 133, 208, 209.

Dominion Day, 189.

" " Sports, 266.

Douai, 249.

Douai-Cambrai, 312.

Double-Crassier, 194.

Douve, 118.

Dregs of the Cup, 303.

Dressing Station, 140, 142, 144, 177, 200, 201, 227, 235, 284, 285, 291, 296, 309, 314, 316.

Drocourt-Quéant Line, 291, 297.

Duffy, 62, 73.

Durham Light Infantry, 39.

Duty as a guide, 250.

" " runner, 250.

E

Easter Day, 48, 123, 245.

" " 1916, 128.

Ecoivres, 162, 166, 167, 172, 232, 252.

Edinburgh, 240.

"Empress of Britain," 318.

Endsleigh Palace Hospital, 318.

Engineer Companies, 245.

English Channel, 28.

Epinoy, 314.

Estaires, 46, 48, 49.

Etrun, 247, 248, 251, 268, 270.

Estrée-Cauchie, 204.

Evins-les-Bains, 187.

F

Fampoux, 249, 250, 263.

Farbus, 177.

Festubert, 80, 82, 89.

Feuchy, 249, 250, 263, 269.

Field Ambulance, 1st., 303.

" " 2nd., 68, 69, 70, 74.

" " 3rd., 37, 133, 319.

" Co. Engineers, 3rd., 135.

Fight in a Church Service, 102.

Fletre, 38, 122.

Fleurbaix, 43.

Florence, 223, 226.

"Florizel," 26.

Foch, Marshal, 254, 255.

"Follies, The," 123.

Fort Glatz, 193, 199, 235.

Fosseaux, 245, 247.

"Four Winds, The," 152, 154.

France, Patriotism of, 188.

Fresnicourt, 185, 190.

Fresnoy, 177, 178, 233.

Frevent, 253, 254.

Frohen Le Grand, 147.

G

Gas Attack, 240, 241.

Gas Poisoning, 201.

Gas Shells, 269.

Gaspe Basin, 26.

Gasquet, Cardinal, 222.

General Hospital, No. 2, 35, 36, 37, 80, 97.

Gentelles Wood, 272, 273, 279.

INDEX

German Aeroplane, 111.
" Dugouts, 136.
" Prisoners, 65, 80, 82, 142, 144, 200, 278, 283, 284, 295, 312, 316.
" Spy, 83, 89, 96, 108.
" Thoroughness, 66.
Ghurkas, 79.
Glasgow Highlanders, 81.
Good Friday, 48, 165, 245.
Gouldberg Copse, 227.
Gouy-Servins, 231.
Graham, Rev. E. E., 296.
Graves, Unrecorded, 158.
Great Memories of the War, 117.
Grenade School, 132, 133.
Grenay, 235.
Groves, Vaughan, 234, 235.
Gwynne, Bishop, 99, 100, 135.

H

Haig, Gen., 78, 79.
Hallicourt, 180.
Hangard Wood, 277.
Harter, Major, M.C., 40.
Hatchet Wood, 282.
Hautes Avesnes, 298.
Haynecourt, 305, 311, 312, 316.
Headquarters, 112, 122, 178, 206, 211, 267, 268.
Hell Fire Corner, 69.
Hendecourt, 303.
Hendecourt Dury, 295.
Hill 60—54, 55, 124.
Hill 63—91, 101, 106, 113, 117, 118.
Hill 70—197, 198, 202, 203, 205, 207, 208, 233, 235, 240.
"Hole in the Wall, The," 195.
Holy Communion 21, 27, 32, 40, 49, 66, 71, 77, 95, 96, 101, 119, 120, 132, 143, 146, 147, 150, 160, 163, 164, 166, 176, 190, 211, 232, 243, 245, 246, 292, 302.
Honor to a Belgian Maid, 111.
Hooge, 124.
Hooggraaf, 123, 128, 134.
Horne, Gen., 172, 176, 181, 205.

Hornoy, 271, 272.
Houdain, 180, 181.
Houplines, 39.
Hughes, Gen., 15, 17, 21, 22, 53, 102, 103.
Hugo Trench, 235.

I

Ignacourt, 280.
Inchy Station, 303, 304, 305.
Indian Troops, 74.
" Village, 80.
Ironside, Col., 148.
Italian, 1st. Div., 218.
" 3rd Army, 221.
Izel-les-Hameaux, 261, 262, 264.

J

Joffre, Gen., 72.
Johnson, Johnny, 261, 264.
Jutland, 129, 130.

K

Khaki University, 267.
King, The, 32, 72, 134.
"King Edward's Horse," 112.
Kitchener, Earl, 102, 103, 129.
Kort Dreuve, 101.

L

La Boisselle, 137.
Labyrinth, 173.
Lacouture, 79.
La Creche, 94.
Lake of Geneva, 187.
Lamb, Col., 219, 221, 223.
Lark Hill, 31.
La Targette Rd., 183.
Laventie, 45.
Le Brebis, 192, 235.
Le Cauroy, 253, 254, 261, 270, 271, 301.
Lectures on Leave Trip to Rome, 257, 258.
Leicesters, 45.
Lens, 197, 202, 235, 241, 263.
Lens-Arras, 176, 185, 207.

Lens-Bethune Rd., 200.
Les Tilleuls, 239.
Le Touret, 80, 82.
Liencourt, 271.
Liéven, 208, 240, 262, 263.
Loison, 267, 268.
London, 91, 93, 240, 318.
Loos, 109, 110, 192, 193, 197, 201, 207, 235, 240.
Loos Crassier, 200.
Lord's Prayer, 71, 142.
Lyons, 259, 260, 273, 289, 300.

M

MacDonald, Murdoch, 44, 52, 53, 54, 67, 68, 75, 81, 87, 94, 95.
Macdonell, Gen., 82, 189.
Macphail, Col., 300, 303.
Maison Blanche, 164, 169.
Mametz, 146.
Maple Copse, 133.
Maroc, 192, 193, 194, 195, 196, 197, 198, 199, 200, 201, 235.
Maroeil, 249.
Marquion, 310.
Marseilles, 216.
Mazingarbe, 192, 235.
Memorial Service for Hill 70 Attack, 206.
Memories of the War, 132.
Mercer, Gen., 128, 129.
Merville, 46.
Messines, 101.
Military Prison, 123.
Ministering to German Prisoners, 278.
Miraumont, 139, 157.
Moment Before Attack, 276.
Mons, 260.
Mont des Cats, 112, 128, 129.
Montreuil, 267.
Mont St. Eloi, 149, 150.
Morgue, 124.
Mount Kemmel, 112.
Murray, Major, 112.

N

Nazebrouck, 37.

Neuve Chapelle, 45.
Neuve Eglise Rd., 95, 96.
Neuville St. Vaast, 169.
Neuville Vitasse, 291.
New Year, 160, 233.
Nieppe, 98, 99, 108, 109, 112.
"Nine Elms," 174.
Noeux les Mines, 191.
"No Man's Land," 120, 126, 149, 207, 249, 269.

O

Observation Balloons, 181, 182.
    "   Post, 280.
Ohlain, 152, 205.
Ouderdom, 74.

P

Paris, 186, 187, 227.
Parish Visiting, 20, 192, 235, 267, 269.
Passchendale 220, 227, 228, 229, 230, 233.
Patricia, Princess, 22.
Petit Moncque Farm, 103, 107, 118.
"Philo," 91, 94, 95, 104, 134, 149.
"Pineapples," 236, 237, 238.
Pisa, 217, 226.
Place St. Croix, 251.
Ploegsteert, 38, 91, 94, 100, 102, 103, 110, 113, 118.
Plymouth, 28.
Poems: "The Unnamed Lake," 307; "Requiescant," 75.
Pope, The, 220.
Poperinghe, 123, 128, 132, 207, 227, 230.
Poppies, 261.
Pozieres, 137, 138, 142, 144, 155.
Price, Major, 301.
Pronville, 305.
Pudding Lane, 249.
    "   Trench, 249, 269.
Puzzling Question, A, 163.
Pys., 139, 157.

INDEX

Q

Quatre Vents, 203.
Quéant, 305, 317.
Quebec, 318.
Queen's Own Westminsters, 41.
Quesnel, 288.

R

Railway Dugouts, 124, 126, 130, 131, 132.
" Triangle, 270.
Ranchicourt, 152, 193.
Ravine, 133.
Recitation of Poem Under Difficulties, 195.
Record Attack, A, 172.
Record-beating Advance, 280.
Refugees, 69.
Regina Trench, 138, 148, 156, 157, 158, 180.
Religion of Men at Front, 116, 134.
Rest Camp, 185, 190.
Riviera, 217.
Robecq, 78, 230.
Roberts, Lord, 32.
Robertson, Sir Wm., 220.
Roclincourt, 176.
Roellencourt, 147, 148, 149.
Romarin, 94, 111.
Rome, 216, 217.
Rome, March Through the Streets, 218.
Rosières, 280, 282.
Ross, Pte., 95, 104, 112, 114, 154, 254, 304.
Rouville, 246.
Rouvroy, 285.
Royal Canadian Regiment, 189.
Royal Horse Artillery, 281.
Royal Rifles, 8th, 15, 16.
Rubempre, 135, 136, 137.
Ruitz, 180, 181.

S

Sad stories, 139, 141.
Sains-en-Gohelle, 235.

Salient, 122, 128, 130, 132, 230, 270.
Salisbury Plain, 30, 34.
Sanctuary Wood, 125, 133.
Sappers, 78.
Sausage Valley, 137.
Scarpe, 165, 247, 250, 251, 269.
Scarpe Valley, 249.
Second Army School, 190.
Seely, Gen., 98, 111.
Shells, 17 inch, 57.
Shell Trap Farm, 65.
"Shock Troops," 255.
"Silent Toast, The," 174.
"Sky Pilot," 181.
Smith-Dorrien, Gen., 38, 52, 53.
Somme, 134, 137, 179.
Sons, My, 46, 146, 147, 148, 165, 176, 178, 190, 230, 262, 267, 289.
Son's Grave, 157, 158, 180, 288.
Souchez, 231.
Spy Fever, 196.
Squadron, 13th, 261.
St. Aubin, 249.
St. Eloi Rd., 167, 249.
St. Feuchien, 272, 273.
St. George's Church, 123, 175, 176, 189.
" " " No. 2, 184.
" " " No. 3, 232.
" " Rectory, 184, 233.
St. Jans Cappel, 112, 113, 114, 122.
St. Jean, 61, 67.
St. Julien, 54, 61.
St. Lawrence, 26.
St. Nazaire, 36.
St. Nicholas, 249.
St. Omer, 99, 100, 134, 135, 190.
St. Pol Rd., 147, 160, 161, 258, 259, 261, 267.
St. Sauveur Cave, 246.
St. Sylvestre, 50.
St. Venant, 230.
Steenje, 77, 78, 93.
Steenvoorde, 54, 134.
Stewart, Charles, 302.
Stonehenge, 32.
Strand, 151.

Strathcona Horse, 107.
Strazeele, 37.
Stretcher Bearers, 145.
Sunday Program, 132.
Swan Chateau, 127.

T

Talbot House, 123, 230.
Talbot, Neville, 123.
"Tanks," 140, 274, 277, 282.
Tara Hill, 136, 137, 147, 154, 158, 180, 289.
Telegraph Hill, 246.
Tent Hospitals, Canadian, 208.
Terdeghem, 52, 53.
Thacker, Gen., 134, 192, 260, 272, 287, 303, 305.
Thélus, 170.
"The Times," 180.
Tilloy, 269.
Tilques, 135.
Tincques, 264, 266.
Training for Final Attack, 255.
Tully, 160.
Turcos, 63, 72.
Turin, 226.

U

"Unbroken Line, The," 7.

V

Valcartier, 16, 17, 19, 24.
"   Departure, 23.
Vandervyver, M., 54, 60, 67, 68.
Venezelos, M., 221.

Verbranden Molen, 126.
Verdrel, 259.
Victory Year, 234.
Villers au Bois, 183, 189.
Villers-Cagnicourt, 296.
Villers-Chatel, 205, 256, 257, 263.
Vimy Ridge, 150, 151, 162, 164, 167, 169, 178, 181, 233, 239, 263.
Vlamertinghe, 59, 68, 69, 70, 72, 73, 130, 132, 227.

W

Wailly, 298.
Wanquetin, 298.
Warlus, 245, 247, 299, 300, 301.
Warvilliers, 282, 284, 286.
Westhof Farm, 98.
Wieltje, 54, 55, 61, 62.
Willerval, 170, 177.
Wingles, 193.
Wippenhock, 130.
Wisques, 190.
Wounded, 316.
Wreath on Victor Emmanuel Statue, 221.
Wulverghem, 106, 115.

Y

Y.M.C.A., 30, 138, 155, 166, 203, 204, 208, 267, 292, 298.
Ypres, 49, 50, 54, 55, 124, 128, 130, 132, 227, 230.
Yser Canal, 54, 55.

Z

Zillebeke Bund, 125.
Zulus, 192, 193.

Warwick Bros. & Rutter, Limited
Printers and Bookbinders
Toronto